African Histories and Modernities

This book series serves as a scholarly forum on African contributions to and negotiations of diverse modernities over time and space, with a particular emphasis on historical developments. Specifically, it aims to refute the hegemonic conception of a singular modernity, Western in origin, spreading out to encompass the globe over the last several decades. Indeed, rather than reinforcing conceptual boundaries or parameters, the series instead looks to receive and respond to changing perspectives on an important but inherently nebulous idea, deliberately creating a space in which multiple modernities can interact, overlap, and conflict. While privileging works that emphasize historical change over time, the series will also feature scholarship that blurs the lines between the historical and the contemporary, recognizing the ways in which our changing understandings of modernity in the present have the capacity to affect the way we think about African and global histories.

More information about this series at
http://www.springer.com/series/14758

George Klay Kieh, Jr.
Editor

Contemporary Issues in African Society

Historical Analysis and Perspective

palgrave
macmillan

Editor
George Klay Kieh, Jr.
University of West Georgia
Carrollton, GA, USA

African Histories and Modernities
ISBN 978-3-319-49771-6 ISBN 978-3-319-49772-3 (eBook)
https://doi.org/10.1007/978-3-319-49772-3

Library of Congress Control Number: 2017950713

Cover credit: Wsfurlan/Getty Images

Printed on acid-free paper

This Palgrave Macmillan imprint is published by Springer Nature
The registered company is Springer International Publishing AG
The registered company address is: Gewerbestrasse 11, 6330 Cham, Switzerland

Preface

Like other regions of the world, there are some major frontier issues facing Africa as we enter the latter half of the second decade of the twenty-first century. Among these major issues are: the troubling practice of some African states abdicating the responsibility for their citizens' material well-being to non-governmental organizations (NGOs), and the resulting contestation for power between the state and NGOs, democratization, the growing influence of Evangelical Christian churches, civil conflicts and the efforts to resolve them, and Africa's international relations. Collectively, these issues have serious ramifications for stability and human-centered development and democracy, especially, the linkages between political democracy and human well-being. As the evidence shows, since the 1990s, the African Continent has made laudable strides in terms of political democracy, but has faltered in terms of addressing the material conditions of the majority of their citizens. Importantly, the failure of the state has led to the erosion of state legitimacy and in some cases—Liberia, Sierra Leone, Guinea Bissau, the Democratic Republic of the Congo, Cote d'Ivoire and Mali—the resulting collapse of the state has reached its terminal phase; implosion and violence in the form of civil wars and other types of militarism.

Against this backdrop, this book seeks to examine some of the major frontier issues that are currently facing the African Continent. The central purpose is to problematize them, and proffer some suggestions for addressing them. This is because the role of scholarship is not simply to catalog the African Continent's challenges with the twin processes of state-building and nation-building, but to suggest some concrete ways in which these lacunas can be addressed.

I would like to thank the many organizations and individuals who made invaluable contributions to the research and writing of the book, as well as the African Studies and Research Forum (ASRF) which organized the research project that led to the writing of the chapters that constitute this book. Also, I would like to thank the contributors to this volume for conducting the research, writing their respective chapters and submitting them to thorough review.

Carrollton, USA

George Klay Kieh, Jr.

Acknowledgements

Thanks and appreciation are extended to two journals for granting permission to use copyright materials. *Peace and Conflict Studies* granted permission to use materials from the article by George Klay Kieh, Jr., "An Anatomy of Conflict Resolution in Africa's Civil Conflicts", Volume 17, Number 2, 2010, pp. 277–306, in Chap. 7 on Conflict Resolution in this book.

The *Africa Journal on Conflict Resolution* gave permission to use materials from the article by Kelechi Kalu, "Resolving African crises: Leadership Role for African States and the African Union in Darfur," Volume 9, Number 1, 2009, pp. 9–39.

Contents

Editor and Contributors

About the Editor

George Klay Kieh, Jr. is Professor of Political Science at the University of West Georgia. Prior to that, he served as Dean of the College of Arts and Sciences at the University of West Georgia; Dean of International Affairs and Professor of Political Science and African and African American Studies at Grand Valley State University, Michigan and Chair of the Department of Political Science; and Professor of Political Science and International Studies at Morehouse College, Georgia. His research interests are in the areas of security studies, American foreign policy, the state, democratization and democracy, development studies, political economy, regional and global institutions.

Contributors

Theodora O. Ayot is Professor of History at North Park University, Chicago, Illinois. She has taught previously at Kenyatta University, Nairobi, Kenya; State University of New York; College at Fredonia, New York; as a visiting Professor at the University of Jonkoping, College of Health Sciences, Jonkoping, Sweden; and at Tecnologico de Monterrey, Chihuahua Campus, Chihuahua, Mexico, Tecnologico de Monterrey, Aguascalientes Campus. She is also the Director of the Daniel Katete

Orwa Foundation for Humanity, and a Board Member of the Soul Source Foundation and Operation My People.

Earl Conteh-Morgan is Professor of Government and International Studies, and Director of Graduate Studies, University of South Florida. His research interests include international conflict, the military and American foreign policy; all areas in which he has been published quite extensively.

Kelechi A. Kalu is Vice Provost for International Affairs at the University of California at Riverside. Prior to that, he served as Associate Provost for Global Strategies and International Affairs at The Ohio State University; Director of the Center for African Studies at Ohio State University; Professor of African American & African Studies, and Faculty affiliate at the Mershon Center for International Security Studies at The Ohio State University; a Mellon Research Fellow in the Department of Government, Connecticut College, New London, Connecticut; Professor of Political Science at the University of Northern Colorado, Greeley; and Adjunct Professor of African Politics and Political Economy at the Joseph Korbel School of International Studies, University of Denver. He has also served as a consultant to the World Bank on Public Sector Governance, and to the Asian Development Bank on Managing Sustainable Development in Resource-Rich Countries. He specializes in international politics, conflict & conflict resolution and Third World development studies with an emphasis on Africa and has been widely published. He is a recipient of grants from The Ford Foundation, The Mershon Center for International Security Studies, and The Korea Foundation.

Johnson W. Makoba is Associate Professor of Sociology at the University of Nevada, Reno, where he has been teaching since 1990. He has served twice as Chair of the Department of Sociology. His research interests are organizations and bureaucracies, alternative African development strategies, and other Third World development issues. He is the author of two books on development in Africa, and has also published several book chapters and articles in the International Journal of Sociology of Law, Austrian Journal of Development Studies, Journal of Third World Studies, African Development, and other scholarly journals. His most recent book is *The Triple Partnership as an Alternative Approach—The Case of Uganda*.

Jack Mangala is Associate Professor of Political Science and African Studies at Grand Valley State University, Michigan. Prior to that, he served as the Director of the African and African American Studies Program, and the Director of the Area Studies. His scholarly interests center on the nexus between international law and human security, and on Africa's international relations, with a particular emphasis on its EU and US dimensions. His publications include: *Africa and the New World Era: From Humanitarianism to a Strategic View*, Palgrave, 2010, *New Security Threats and Crises in Africa: Regional and International Perspectives*, Palgrave, 2010, and *Africa and the European Union: A Strategic Partnership*, Palgrave, 2012.

Samuel Zalanga is a Professor of Sociology at Bethel University, Minnesota. He has served as an Associate Editor for Africa for the *Journal of Third World Studies*. He is very passionate in the struggle for social justice and the creation of a more just and egalitarian society at the global, national and community levels. His most recent publications are two book chapters on *"Christianity in Africa: Pentecostalism and Sociocultural Change in the Context of Neoliberal Globalization,"* and *"Economic Development and Cultural Change in Islamic Context: The Malaysian Experience."*

List of Tables

CHAPTER 1

Introduction: Framing the African Condition

George Klay Kieh, Jr.

Introduction

The vagaries of colonialism—the suppression of political rights, mass abject poverty and social malaise, among others—provided the major causes that galvanized Africans from across the broad ethnic, class, gender, ideological, regional and religious divide into organizing various anti-colonial movements. In other words, the pedigree of colonialism was uniformly unacceptable to Africans to the extent that they were prepared to set aside their various differences, and join forces in struggling against it. Amid the anti-colonial struggles, Africans entertained the hope that the end of colonialism would usher in a new dispensation in which their cultural, economic, political, religious and social rights, among others, would be respected and promoted by the emergent post-colonial state. Hence, when the wave of independence began to sweep across the African Continent in the 1950s, the collective hope of Africans for a

G.K. Kieh, Jr. (✉)
University of West Georgia, Carrollton, Georgia

G.K. Kieh, Jr. (ed.), *Contemporary Issues in African Society*,
African Histories and Modernities,
https://doi.org/10.1007/978-3-319-49772-3_1

democratic and prosperous future reached fever pitch. Ramsay (1993: 3) captured the tenor of the exuberance at independence:

> The times were electric. In country after country, the flags of Britain, Belgium, and France were replaced by the banners of the new states, whose leaders offered idealistic promises to remake the continent and the world. Hopes were high, and the most ambitious goals [seemed] obtainable. Even non-Africans spoke of the resource-rich continent as being on the verge of a development take-off. Some of the old, racist myths about Africa were [at] last being questioned.

Regrettably, while Africans were singing the requiem for the demise of colonialism and demonstrating exuberance over the prospects of a new beginning for the continent, the reality began to set in that the post-colonial era would not be fundamentally different from its progenitor. The overarching evidence was that the first generation of African leaders—with few exceptions (Kwame Nkrumah (Ghana), Julius Nyerere (Tanzania), Modibo Keita (Mali), and Seewoosagur Ramgoolam (Mauritius)—failed to provide the requisite leadership for the dismantling, rethinking and democratic reconstitution of the "Berlinist state", which had been bequeathed to the continent by the colonialists (Kieh 2007, 2014). Clearly, the state is important because it sets the parameters within which all societal activities occur. Hence, a state that is of the wrong type cannot shepherd the process of constructing a human-centered democratic and developed society. In other words, the "Berlinist state" was intrinsically anti-people, anti-democracy and anti-development. Hence, it was incapable of serving as the foundation on which human-centered development could be promoted, and holistic democracy (one that transcends the political realm, and includes the cultural, economic, environmental, religious, and social as well) could be championed.

Consequently, over the past six decades, the African peoples' hopes for a democratic and prosperous continent has been betrayed by the subsequent generations of African leaders, with few exceptions (Longman 1998). Rather than focus on the needs of the African peoples, every regime in every African state, with few exceptions, has made the primitive accumulation of wealth through the instrumentality of the state its preoccupation. Accordingly, the state in Africa has become akin to a buffet service in which the members of the faction or fraction of the ruling class that has control over state power at a particular historical juncture and their relations "eat all the can eat" (Kieh 2009: 10).

One of the major resulting effects was the serious deterioration of the material conditions of ordinary Africans in the 1980s—the pervasiveness of mass abject poverty, high unemployment, food insecurity, etc. This led to the characterization of the decade of the 1980s as "Africa's lost decade" (Meredith 2010).

Against this background, this chapter has several purposes. First, it will examine some of the major dimensions of the African condition, especially the challenges that need to be addressed in order for human-centered democracy and development to take place on the continent. Second, the chapter lays out the purposes of the book. Third, the theoretical framework that provides the analytical compass for the book is articulated. Fourth, the chapter provides a summary of the key points of the various constituent chapters of the book.

Dimensions of the African Condition

Background

As has been discussed, Africa has faced multiple cultural, economic, environmental, gender, political, regional, religious, security and social problems over the past six decades of the post-colonial or post-independence era. However, it is not possible to discuss all of these problems in either a single chapter or a volume. Accordingly, only some of the dimensions—ethnicity, religion, democratization, civil conflicts, conflict resolution, non-governmental organizations, and international cooperation with the European Union (EU) and the rest of the "Global South"—which are reflections of the topics that are covered in the various chapters, will be examined.

The Dimensions

Ethnicity is the most demonized social identity in the study of African societies. This is reflected in two major ways. Some scholars and practitioners portray ethnicity in Africa in a manner that suggests that it is inherently bad (Reynolds 1985; Angstrom 2000). The other way is that ethnicity is blamed by some scholars and practitioners as well as the principal culprit for virtually every dimension of the multifaceted crises of underdevelopment that has bedeviled the African Continent since the post-colonial era (Lian and Oneal 1997; Adesina et al. 1999). For example, the ethno-communal paradigm, the dominant perspective on the root causes of civil conflicts and the resulting wars in the continent, identifies ethnicity as the major causal factor (Horowitz 2000; Sriskandarajah 2005; Denny and Walter 2014). This has led Mkandawire (2012: 107–108) to observe, “In some essentialist (and often poorly veiled racist) accounts, it is suggested there is something fundamentally wrong with African cultures—and that senseless violence is an undisavowable excrescence of that culture.” So, the question is what is distinctively wrong with ethnicity in Africa that makes it the cardinal source of the continent’s problems? Is ethnicity in Asia, Europe and the Americas of a different type that makes it inherently different? In the case of Europe, how do we explain the implosion of ethnic conflicts and the resulting wars with the associated deaths, injuries and destruction that rocked the Balkans region, especially the former Yugoslavia, in the 1990s? Did these wars also mean that ethnicity in Europe, like in Africa, is intrinsically conflictual? Or were these ethnic conflicts aberrations?

Undoubtedly, ethnicity, in the post-colonial era, has contributed to civil conflicts and other problems in various states in Africa. However, on the other hand, ethnicity has also made major contributions to both nation-building (the efforts to create nations out of the various ethnic groups) and state-building on the continent (the efforts to construct the governance multiplex and its associated values, institutions, rules and processes). So, there is the need for a balanced approach to the examination of the role of ethnicity in African society. Such an approach must begin with the historicization of the ethnicity-state-building nexus.

During the pre-colonial era, ethnicity was the central pillar of the various indigenous polities that adorned the African landscape (Deng 1997; Martin 2012). As Deng (1997: 1) notes,

> Traditionally, African societies and even states functioned through an elaborate system based on the family, the lineage, the clan, the tribe, and ultimately confederation of groups with ethnic, cultural, and linguistic characteristics in common. These were the units of social, economic, and political organizations and intercommunal relations.

This meant that ethnicity was both the overarching tapestry of traditional African societies, and a positive force for cultural, economic, political and social development. And this was reflected in the major contributions that were made by several African polities in these areas. For example, in the political domain, traditional African states made invaluable contributions to the development of the rule of law and "checks and balances," among others. In Pharaonic Egypt, for example, the rule of law was reflected in the fact that the law applied to all citizens and foreigners, irrespective of gender, class, and other forms of identities (Martin, 2012).

However, colonialism aborted the process of indigenous development in Africa, as well as transformed ethnicity and intra- and inter-ethnic relations. One major way was the division of ethnic groups into various sections (Deng 1997). The other was the spreading of various ethnic groups over several colonies (Deng 1997). In both cases, there was "little or no regard for [the various ethnic groups'] common characteristics or distinctive attributes" (Deng 1997: 1). The reason for the transformation was to subordinate ethnicity to the imperatives of the colonial project, including its core pillar of external domination. The resulting effects were the loss of sovereignty by the various ethnic groups, and the establishment of the "Berlinist state as the pivot of the colonial governance architecture" (Kieh 2008: 3). To make matters worse, the hitherto sovereign and autonomous ethnically-based African polities were subjugated by the colonialists and placed under the control of "outsider[s], foreigner[s]" (Deng 1997: 1).

Importantly, the various colonial powers used ethnicity in various negative ways in order to achieve their goals of political domination and economic exploitation. For example, the colonial powers constructed the mythology of so-called "superior" and "subordinate" ethnic groups. In Rwanda, for instance, Belgian colonialism designated the Tutsis as the so-called "superior" ethnic group and the Hutus as the "subordinate one" (Mamdani 2001). The rationale for the Tutsis status was their so-called European ancestry (Mamdani 2001). Accordingly, the Belgian colonialists privileged the Tutsis by, among other things, giving them access to education and mid-level positions in the colonial bureaucracy. This laid the foundation for the polarization that developed between the Tutsis and the Hutus, culminating in the 1994 genocide, in which almost one million people were killed by *genocidaires* under the auspices of the Interhamwe, a Hutu-based militia.

At independence, the colonizers continued the twin processes of dividing and combining ethnic groups as the centerpiece of the process of the construction of the post-colonial state. Since then, following the footsteps of the colonialists, the first and subsequent generations of African leaders in some of the states have continued to use ethnicity as an instrument of "divide and rule." For example, those Osaghae (2006: 6) aptly refers to as "ethnic gladiators," have used ethnicity as an instrument for personal economic and political gains in the name of serving the broader interests of the ethnic groups. In other cases, the bureaucratic wings of the local ruling class have privileged some ethnic groups, while marginalizing others. And this has found its most profound expression in the skewed distribution of societal resources, as well as patronage (Berman 1998).

Consequently, the lack of ethnic pluralism and peaceful coexistence has been one of the major pathologies of the neocolonial state in Africa. That is, the managers of the neocolonial state failed to formulate and implement pro-people policies that would have, *inter alia*, promoted social justice, equality, fairness in the distribution of state resources, political pluralism and tolerance. A major resultant effect was the occurrence of civil wars in various countries. For example, the failure of the neocolonial Nigerian state to promote human-centered democracy and development and their associated values of fairness, justice, equity, equality, pluralism and tolerance led to, among other things, ethno-regional marginalization. In turn, this was one of the major precipitants of the Nigerian civil war of 1967. The conflict pitted the Igbo ethnic group and the eastern region against the Nigerian government. The Igbos and the other easterners alleged that they had been marginalized by the Nigerian government in the political and other spheres. Hence, they had made the determination that secession was the best solution to the resolution of the conflict. However, the Nigerian government rejected both the claims and the drive for secession. Thus, unable to reach a peaceful resolution, war broke out. Similarly, in the civil wars in the Sudan, Senegal, Somalia, Djibouti, Rwanda and the Democratic Republic of the Congo, among others, ethno-communal conflicts constituted major dimensions of the root causes.

One of the major emergent issues in the religious sphere on the African continent has been the proliferation of charismatic churches in the past two decades. These churches are grounded in the genre of the Pentecostal tradition. Several factors have accounted for this development. A major one is the argument that a traditional Christian sect such as Catholicism lacks dynamism—the phenomenon Asamoah-Gyadu (2014: 1) refers to as "cerebral Christianity." Second, there is the postulate that traditional Christianity lacks the experiential aspects of faith (Asamoah-Gyadu 2014). Another factor is based on the claim that "charismatic Christianity" fills the void concerning the importance of instant healing and deliverance as part of the pantheon of "signs and wonders." As well, there is the imperative of the "prosperity gospel" factor. That is, "charismatic Christianity" is pivoted on the notion of encouraging its adherents to believe that all will be well, including the acquisition of personal wealth. In other words, "charismatic Christianity" portrays the religion in idyllic terms.

Clearly, the theology of "charismatic Christianity" is resonating well with many Africans, most of whom are living precariously on the margins of various African states. And this is evidenced by abject mass poverty and deprivation, unemployment, food insecurity and social malaise, among others. The power of gospel of the "charismatic" Christian churches is reflected in, for example, the burgeoning increase in the number of adherents. In Nigeria, for instance, the Deeper Life Ministry in Lagos claims attendance of about 120,000 people (Knight 2013). The Living Faith Church in Lagos also asserts that its attendance is around 50,000 (Knight 2013). In the southern region of the African Continent, the Rhema Bible Church North located in Johannesburg, South Africa, claims attendance of more than 45,000 (Knight 2013). In East Africa, the Jesus Celebration Center in Mombasa, Kenya notes an attendance of 15,000 (Knight 2013).

Undoubtedly, the charismatic Christian churches have become major players in several major spheres in various African states. In the area of education, for example, various charismatic Christian churches have established schools, including universities, in Nigeria and other African countries. While these institutions are providing academic training for thousands of young people, this is always major sources of revenue for these churches. Especially, since the costs of these charismatic-church based schools are prohibitively expensive, only the children of the members of the local upper classes in these various African states can afford to send their children to these institutions.

In the economic sphere, several of the charismatic Christian churches have major businesses, including convention centers and hotels, which rival those owned by both local and foreign-based capitalists. Importantly, these businesses also serve as major sources of revenues for these churches. In addition, these businesses employ several of the local folk, especially the members of these churches. Overall, these businesses have positioned these churches as major players in various African states' economies.

Politically, these charismatic churches serve two major functions. A key one is legitimation. Given their large memberships, the leaders of these churches are heavily sought after by presidents, cabinet ministers and other government officials to endorse their performances. In addition, their massive youth following makes them attractive to politicians for electoral purposes (Asamoah-Gyadu 2014). For example, Pastor T.B. Joshua, the General Overseer of The Synagogue Church of All Nations (SCOAN), a Nigerian-based emerging international charismatic Christian ministry, has become the coveted friend of presidents, and other government officials in Nigeria, Ghana and in other West African states.

The other major function is that of the providers of "supernatural powers" (Asamoah-Gyadu 2014). It is widely believed both among politicians and the masses of the people that the leaders of these charismatic churches possess "supernatural powers." Thus they are sought with missionary zeal by politicians for access to these so-called powers with the belief that these "supernatural powers" will serve as a protective shield around politicians to ensure that they have a long and uninterrupted tenure of office. Seizing on this "golden opportunity" to amass personal wealth and to acquire other material possessions such as private jets, the leaders of these charismatic churches have successfully marketed the mythology of their so-called "supernatural powers" to vulnerable and gullible politicians, including corrupt and authoritarian leaders (Asamoah-Gyadu 2014).

The struggle for people-centered holistic democracy (the combination of political and other rights and freedoms, including economic and social ones) in Africa has spanned three major cycles: the "first wave," (1885–1960s), the "second wave," (1960s–1990), and the "third wave" (the current cycle) (1990–present). Each wave was shaped by major domestic and external forces and factors. Some of these forces and factors were, and are inimical to the establishment of human-centered democracy in Africa, while others are struggling for such transformation.

The "first wave" had as its central thrust ridding the various African societies of European colonialism, which was imposed upon hitherto sovereign and independent African polities, as the result of the notorious Berlin Conference of 1884–1885. The conclave of European imperialist powers witnessed the carving up of African territories for the overarching purpose of exploiting them for their natural and other resources. The results were the labyrinthine of cultural, economic, political, religious and social vagaries, including the demonization of African cultures and the resulting imposition of Euro-Western ones; economic marginalization and exploitation; the suppression of political rights and civil liberties such as the right to participate in the political process, as well as the freedoms of assembly, association, press and speech; the vilification of traditional African religions as barbaric and heathenistic; and the willful neglect of the educational, health and related needs of the colonized Africans.

Exasperated by the adverse effects of colonialism, the colonized Africans organized various nationalist movements with anti-colonialism as its pivot. Using their anti-colonial anchor, these movements were able to mobilize Africans from across the ethnic, regional, gender, professional, religious and class divides. Importantly, these anti-colonial movements employed various methods to wage their struggles. Some used the armed struggle as the instrumentarium, these included movements in Algeria, Angola, Cape Verde, Guinea-Bissau, Mozambique and Zimbabwe. On the other hand, others, the majority, employed non-violent methods such as protests, demonstrations, strikes and petition drives. Yet, others used a combination of violent and non-violent methods.

Cumulatively, the various anti-colonial struggles that were waged on the African continent along with other factors, such as the devastating impact of World War Two on the economies of the European colonial powers, led to the collapse of colonialism and the resulting process of decolonization, and then political independence. That is, the various European colonial powers were overwhelmed by the combined cost of these anti-colonial struggles and the Second World War, as well as the demands from their citizens for them to address pressing domestic economic and social issues. In addition, the United States, which emerged as the new leader of the global capitalist bloc, pressured the European colonial powers to dismantle their respective colonial empires. Clearly, the American intervention was dictated by the U.S.' desire to deal directly with African societies. In other words, as an emergent "superpower," the U.S. saw the African Continent as a prime region for the pursuance of its economic, political and strategic interests. But, this could not have been done in the context of colonialism, especially the practice of absolute control of African colonies by the various colonial powers.

Significantly, the decolonization process was attended, by and large, by hastily organized elections based on the governmental models of the various colonial powers. For example, the British imposed their parliamentary model on their colonies such as Nigeria, while France forced its mixed model (the combination of the parliamentary and presidential models) on its colonies, like Senegal. One of the central issues was that the various African societies had no understanding of the operations of these models of government. Hence, they were destined to fail. In addition, in the majority of the cases, the departing colonial powers handpicked Africa's "first generation of leaders." Essentially, these new leaders were compradors, who had been socialized in the ways of the various colonial powers, and were thus subservient to these imperialist powers' interests. However, Portugal refused to give up its colonies in Angola, Cape Verde, Guinea Bissau and Mozambique, until 1975.

Africans greeted the end of European colonialism with great relief and expectation for the construction of human-centered democratic and developed states. However, just a few years later the horrendous performance of most of the continent's post-colonial first generation regimes brought Africans to the realization that the colonial state was still intact, howbeit, with fellow Africans as the rulers. This was because the first generation regimes, with few exceptions, continued the colonial policies of political repression, the manipulation of ethno-communal identities, and the neglect of basic human needs, among others. Thus, the post-independence era became more of a "struggle for survival" (Ramsay 1993: 3).

Disappointed by this outcome, various pro-democracy movements emerged throughout the continent with the primary goal of waging struggles against these emergent authoritarian regimes that had simultaneously failed to promote the material well-being of the majority of Africans. Amid the "tugs and pulls" between the pro-democracy forces and the continent's various authoritarian regimes, putschits and other militarists hijacked the democratic struggles by staging military coups, and instigating rebellions that eventually led to civil wars (Japhet 1978; Mwakikagile 2001; Kandeh 2004; Kieh 2002, 2004; Keller 2014). For example, in the 1960s, there were 23 successful military coups on the continent (Kieh 2004, 2008). Also during the same period, civil wars broke out in the countries like Sudan, Senegal, Nigeria and Chad. Coup-making and war-making continued throughout the decades of the 1970s and 1980s. Similarly, the support received by some of the continent's various authoritarian regimes from the United States and its allies and the Soviet Union and its allies undermined the success of the various pro-democracy struggles as well.

The dawn of the decade of the 1990s witnessed an upsurge in pro-democratic activities throughout the continent (Bratton and Van de Walle 1997; Nzongola-Ntalaja 1998; Kieh 2008). This led Africa News (1992: 1) to proclaim, "Africa is experiencing a revolution as profound as the wave of independence that began to sweep through the continent three decades ago." This development was caused by several major factors. A major one was the collapse of the Soviet Union and Stalinist socialism in Central and Eastern Europe, and the resulting end of the Cold War. Importantly, this development adversely affected some of the continent's authoritarian regimes that were client states of the Soviet Union and its allies. Similarly, with the end of the Cold War, the United States and its allies also determined that some of their client regimes on the continent were also disposable. In turn, these client African regimes lost their supply of the "economic, political and military oxygen" that enabled them to rule. Another factor was the success of the various pro-democracy movements in Central and Eastern Europe in forcing the removal of various Stalinist regimes from power, and the resulting setting into motion the process of democratization.

Interestingly, the "third wave" on the African Continent has focused primarily on the attainment of liberal democracy and its attendant battery of political rights and civil liberties. This means that very little attention has been paid to the centrality of the material well-being of the majority of Africans. This is quite unfortunate, because the clamor for democracy on the continent was caused by the ardent desire of the majority of Africans to democratically reconstitute the postcolonial African state, so that it could adequately address their cultural, economic, environmental, political, security and social needs. To make matters worse, the suzerains of the world capitalist system—the United States, its allies and the international economic institutions (the International Monetary Fund and the World Bank)—have imposed on African states a neoliberal development strategy that has led to the deterioration of human material well-being throughout the continent (Harrison 2005; Mensah 2008; Harrison 2010).

So, after more than two decades, what is the current state of democratization on the African continent? In order to address this important question, two major sets of variables are examined: political democratization (political rights and civil liberties), and socioeconomic democratization (human development or well-being). Based on the data from Freedom House for 2016 on political democratization, 10 African states were politically democratic. In terms of the regional break-down, this consists of 1 country each in Central Africa and North Africa, none in East Africa, 4 in West Africa and 4 in Southern Africa (see Table 1.1). Twenty two countries were authoritarian; of these, 9 are in Central Africa, 6 in East Africa, 3 in North Africa, and 2 each in West Africa and Southern Africa. The remaining 22 states were hybrid (with elements of political democracy and authoritarianism): none in Central Africa one in North Africa, 5 in East Africa six in Southern Africa, and 10 in West Africa.

In terms of socioeconomic democratization(human material well-being), according to the data from the United Nations Development Program's Human Development Report, in 2015, no African state attained the 'very high' category of socioeconomic democratization (see Table 1.2). Five states attained a 'high' level of socioeconomic democratization, including Algeria and Libya, which were both classified as authoritarian states, and the Seychelles that was categorized as a hybrid state. This is a reflection of the fact that a high level of political democratization does not automatically lead to a high level of socioeconomic democratization. In other words, politically democratic states can have high, medium or low levels of socioeconomic democracy, as the cases of democratic states (politically) such as Botswana, South Africa, Cape Verde, Namibia and Ghana show (see Table 1.2). All of the aforementioned democracies had a 'medium' level of socioeconomic democratization. Fourteen states were classified as attaining 'medium' level of socioeconomic democratization, while the overwhelming majority of 35 states attained only a 'low' level of socioeconomic democratization (see Table 1.2 for the regional distribution).

Since the post-independence era, the African continent has been plagued with various types of civil conflicts. For example, as has been discussed, the *coup d'état* has been one of the major enduring forms of civil conflicts on the continent. Beginning in 1952, with the Free Officers-led military coup in Egypt, the phenomenon spread like an epidemic throughout the continent with the exception of Southern Africa (Japhet 1978; Mwakikagile 2001; Kieh 2002, 2004; Kandeh 2004; Collier and Hoeffler 2005). Clearly, the multidimensional crises—cultural, economic, political, security and social—of the neocolonial African state provided the causes of the phenomenon. But the various military regimes

Table 1.1 The State of Political Democratization in Africa, 2016

Democratic States	
State	Region
Benin	West
Botswana	Southern
Cape Verde	West
Ghana	West
Mauritius	Southern
Namibia	Southern
Sao Tome and Principe	Central
Senegal	West
South Africa	Southern
Tunisia	North
Authoritarian States	
State	Region
Algeria	North
Angola	Southern
Burundi	Central
Cameroon	Central
Central African Republic	Central
Chad	Central
Democratic Republic of the Congo	Central
Djibouti	East
Egypt	North
Equatorial Guinea	Central
Eritrea	East
Ethiopia	East
Gabon	Central
Gambia	West
Libya	North
Mauritania	West
Rwanda	Central
Somalia	East
South Sudan	East
Sudan	East
Swaziland	Southern
Hybrid States	
State	Region
Burkina Faso	West
Comoros	East
Congo	Central
Cote d'Ivoire	West
Guinea	West
Guinea-Bissau	West
Kenya	East
Lesotho	Southern

(continued)

Table 1.1 (continued)

State	Region
Liberia	West
Madagascar	East
Malawi	Southern
Mali	West
Morocco	North
Mozambique	Southern
Niger	West
Nigeria	West
Seychelles	Southern
Sierra Leone	West
Tanzania	East
Togo	West
Uganda	East
Zambia	Southern
Zimbabwe	Southern

Source Compiled from Freedom House, Freedom in the World, 2016, (Washington DC: Freedom House, 2017)

Table 1.2 The State of Socioeconomic Democratization (Human Well-Being) in Africa, 2014

Very High Level of Socioeconomic Democratization	
State	Region
No country	
High Level of Socioeconomic Democratization	
State	Region
Libya	North
Mauritius	Southern
Seychelles	Southern
Tunisia	North
Algeria	North
Medium Level of Socioeconomic Democratization	
State	Region
Botswana	Southern
Egypt	North
Gabon	Central
South Africa	Southern
Cape Verde	West
Namibia	Southern
Morocco	North
Ghana	West
Congo	Central
Zambia	Southern
Sao Tome and Principe	Central

(continued)

Table 1.2 (continued)

State	Region
Equatorial Guinea	Central
Angola	Southern Africa
Cameroon	Central Africa
Low Level of Socioeconomic Democratization	
State	Region
Kenya	East
Swaziland	Southern
Angola	Southern
Rwanda	Central
Cameroon	Central
Nigeria	West
Madagascar	East
Zimbabwe	Southern
Comoros	East
Tanzania	East
Mauritania	West
Lesotho	Southern
Senegal	West
Uganda	East
Benin	West
South Sudan	East
Sudan	East
Togo	West
Djibouti	East
Cote d'Ivoire	West
Gambia	West
Ethiopia	East
Malawi	Southern
Liberia	West
Mali	West
Guinea-Bissau	West
Mozambique	Southern
Guinea	West
Burundi	Central
Burkina Faso	West
Eritrea	East
Sierra Leone	West
Chad	Central
Central African Republic	Central
Democratic Republic of Congo	Central
Niger	West

Source Compiled from United Nations Development Program, Human Development Report, (New York: Oxford University Press, 2016) that came to power after these coups, by and large, failed to perform better than their civilian predecessors (Agbese 2004; Brooker 2013; Houngnikpo 2013). Furthermore, in some cases, the military regimes disengaged from politics as rulers, and were replaced by civilian regimes. That is, the military regimes presided over the process of returning the affected countries to civilian rule, and then transferred power to the newly elected civilian leaders, for example, Nigeria in 1979 and 1999. But, in other cases, the military regimes consolidated their rule through a process of civilianization—the military rulers simply replaced their uniforms with civilian regalia. Zaire (now the Democratic Republic of the Congo), Benin, Burkina Faso and Niger provide excellent cases. Yet, in other cases, the military re-intervened in the political process and seized power: Ghana, Congo, the Central African Republic and Nigeria are noteworthy examples.

Civil wars constitute another major dimension of civil conflicts on the continent. Like military coups, civil wars were, and remain the by-products of the failure of the neocolonial state in Africa to address the cultural, economic, political, security and social needs of the majority of Africans. The resulting crisis of legitimacy and the erosion of mass support have made the various affected countries ripe for implosion. For example, in the case of the Sudan, the country degenerated into civil war months after it declared its independence from the United Kingdom in 1956. This was followed by civil wars in Senegal and Nigeria in the 1960s; Chad, Angola, Ethiopia and Mozambique, among others, witnessed the eruption of civil war in the 1970s; Somalia and Liberia, among others, were gripped by civil war in the 1980s; while in the 1990s, Rwanda, Burundi, Sierra Leone, Guinea Bissau and the Democratic Republic of Congo, as well as several other African states were ravaged by internecine war, and in the first decade and half of the twenty-first century, Somalia, the Democratic Republic of the Congo, Mali, and the newly independent state of South Sudan joined the list of civil war-affected countries on the continent.

In addition, terrorism is the other important dimension of the civil conflict grid. Although, it is not a new phenomenon in Africa or elsewhere in the world, it has become the frontier global security issue ever since Al Qaeda carried out its terrorist attacks against the American homeland on September 11, 2001(Kieh and Kalu 2012). Particularly, the emergent focus is on private terrorist groups like Al Qaeda and its various affiliates such as Al Qaeda in the Islamic Maghreb (AQIM),

Al-Shabaab and Boko Haram. There is no doubt that these groups have carried out horrendous terrorists attacks against various African states, and American interests on the continent. However, the current discourse on terrorism woefully neglects state-sponsored terrorism: the inflicting of physical violence on citizens by various authoritarian states in Africa. For example, an authoritarian state such as Equatorial Guinea has subjected its citizens to various acts of terror (Human Rights Watch 2015). In short, there are two major dimensions of terrorism in Africa: privately-sponsored terrorism by groups such as Boko Haram and the Islamic State of Iraq and Syria (ISIL), and state-sponsored terrorism by various authoritarian regimes on the continent. Clearly, attention needs to be given to both genres of terrorism, especially the domestic and global forces and factors that contribute to creating the conditions that lead to them.

Various methods have been employed by the African Union (AU), African regional organizations such as the Economic Community of West African States (ECOWAS), and the Southern African Development Community (SACC), the United Nations, the International Criminal Court (ICC), various African states, the European Union (EU), and the United States to resolve the various civil conflicts on the continent. In the case of military coups, the African Union has developed an anti-coup regime that is ostensibly designed to discourage the military from intervening in politics, and imposing itself as the ruler. The centerpiece of the regime is not to recognize governments that come to power through coups. For example, the anti-coup regime was applied, when the military staged a coup in Togo in 2005, and installed Faure Gnassingbé, as the country's new president (Levitt 2008), and in Mali in 2012 (Arieff 2013).

In the area of civil wars, the African Union, African regional organizations such as ECOWAS, and the United Nations have employed two major methods: peacekeeping and peacemaking. The former is designed to create an enabling environment, such as the implementation of a ceasefire, so that peaceful means can be sought to end a civil war. The latter consists of an array of methods, including mediation, which is intended to peacefully end a civil war. Both methods have succeeded in ending various civil wars, but without addressing the underlying causes of these wars. Even the various post-conflict peace-building projects that have been developed as ancillaries have not fully addressed the root causes of the continent's various civil wars.

In addition, as part of post-conflict peace-building, the International Criminal Court has emerged as the dominant global actor for meting out retributive justice against the perpetrators of war crimes and crimes against humanity during civil wars. However, the ICC's role in transitional justice in post-civil war African states has suffered from two major problems. A major one is that the ICC is quite selective in choosing conflict-affected African states. For example, the ICC has yet to help bring to justice the alleged perpetrators of various heinous crimes committed during the second Liberian civil war (1999–2003). On the other hand, the ICC issued indictment against the alleged perpetrators of war crimes and crimes against humanity in the mini-civil war that followed Kenya's contentious presidential election in 2007 (Lynch and Zgonec-Rozej 2013). The other shortcoming is that ICC's indictment process is often politicized. For example, after the second Ivorian civil war in 2010, the ICC only indicted former President Laurent Gbagbo, but not the current President Alassane Ouattara. The truth of the matter is that both leaders' militias committed war crimes during the civil war (Human Rights 2011). Hence, both men should have been indicted.

Alternatively, effective conflict resolution in Africa will require the democratic reconstitution of the neocolonial African state. This is because civil conflicts on the African Continent are primarily caused by the pathologies of the neocolonial state, including the suppression of political rights and civil liberties, the skewed distribution of wealth and income, and the resulting class inequities and inequalities, injustice, social malaise, and the lack of ethnic and religious pluralism.

The democratic reconstitution process would then produce a new state construct that is anchored on the promotion of human-centered development and democracy with "social citizenship" (Marshall 1950) as its pivot. This is the only type of social formation that could provide an enabling environment for the prevention, containment and resolution of conflicts.

The last two decades have witnessed the phenomenal increase in the number of development-oriented non-governmental organizations (NGOs) on the African continent. Essentially, there are two major types of development-oriented NGOs operating on the continent: domestic (local) and metropolitan-based (United States, Europe, etc.) ones. Both domestic and external NGOs are operating in virtually every area of the development sector of African society—agriculture, education, healthcare, etc.

Several major factors gave rise to these NGOs. One key one is the unwillingness and/or the lack of the capacity of various African states to address basic human needs such as education, healthcare and food security. Thus, these NGOs have tried to fill the vacuum. Another major reason is that NGO work can be personally and economically profitable for some of the founders and leaders. That is, given the fact that governments, groups and individuals in the "global north" are often willing to contribute to development causes in Africa as a demonstration of their compassion, NGOs have available sources of funding. So, in the case of some NGOs, their leaders also have the opportunity to enrich themselves from these donations. This is particularly the case for most domestic development-oriented NGOs on the African Continent. Furthermore, an appreciable number of domestic NGOs are donor-driven; that is, they were organized in response to the interests of externally-based donors, and the resulting linking of funding.

Undoubtedly, some NGOs are engaged in meaningful development activities on the continent that are helping to address some of the basic needs of Africans, against the background of neglect by the government. However, some of these organizations are basically what Tandon (1996: 293) calls "functional NGOs." That is, as he argues,

> these NGOs do not sit back and reflect on what they are doing, and how their particular activity is related to the broader issues related to state, society and development in the present international conjecture. [Instead, these] mainly purely functional NGOs act as mere palliatives to reduce the effects of the deteriorating social conditions in Africa. (Tandon 1995: 3)

International cooperation is an important aspect of the African condition. Basically, it has assumed three major forms. The first is regional cooperation anchored by the African Union (AU), which covers the broad gamut of cultural, economic, environmental, political, security and social issues. The AU, which succeeded the Organization of African Union (OAU) in 2002, is structurally patterned after the European Union: it is based on a commission as the executive arm headed by a president. However, unlike Europe, Africa has not been integrated in terms of some of the policy areas that are the kernels of the cooperation. For example, unlike the EU, the AU has not been able to achieve a common external tariff structure, or the free movement of labor, capital and technology.

The second is sub-regional, and this is being led by various organizations such as ECOWAS (West Africa), SADCC (Southern Africa), the Maghreb Union (North Africa), the East African Community and the Inter-governmental Authority for Development for East Africa, and the dormant Central African Community. By and large, all of these organizations are primarily concerned with the fostering of socioeconomic cooperation. However, these organizations have taken cognizance of the fact that socioeconomic development occurs in a broader political context that is mediated by civil conflicts, among others. Accordingly, some of these organizations, such as ECOWAS, SADC and IGAD have developed security architectures for the ostensible purpose of addressing internal conflicts that might arise in their various member states. For example, ECOWAS has played a pivotal role in efforts to resolve civil wars in Liberia, Sierra Leone, Guinea Bissau, Cote d'Ivoire and Mali, through the use of various conflict resolution methods such as peacemaking, peacekeeping and peace enforcement.

The third concerns various cooperative activities with non-African organizations such as the Non-Aligned Movement, the Group of 77, and the European Union (EU). The Non-Aligned Movement (NAM) and the Group of 77 are "global south-based" organizations. The former is a political organization that is designed to enable the states in the "global south" to collectively exert their influence on international affairs. Originally, NAM was established in response to the bipolar international system that was created by the Cold War, and the resulting formation of two adversarial power blocs led by the United States and the former Soviet Union. NAM's intent was not to align with either of the two blocs, but rather to constitute a third one as a sort of "balancer." However, that goal was never realized, because each member state of NAM became aligned with either one of the power blocs. Since the end of the Cold War, NAM has been confronted with the challenge of rethinking its mission. As for the Group of 77, it is designed to provide a conduit through which states in the "global south" can influence global economic issues such as trade and aid. Born out of the "Global South's" major goal of pressing for the restructuring of the international economic order, the Group of 77 has had some modest successes, such as the Generalized System of Preferences (GSP), which was negotiated with the "global north." Under this arrangement, countries in the "global south," based on a "graduation provision," had access to the markets of states in the "global north." In terms of the EU, it has developed various cooperative relationships with African regional and subregional organizations, as well as individual states over the past three decades. For example, under the foundational Lome Agreement, the EU and African, Caribbean and Pacific states developed a cooperative framework for the promotion of trade relations. Since then, the EU and Africa have developed new cooperative arrangements that have, among other things, expanded the ambit of the original trade framework, and added political and security dimensions. One of the major issues that has emerged from EU-Africa cooperation is the impact of the asymmetries in economic, political and security power between the two on the dividends that are derived from the relationship.

The Purposes of the Book

The book has two major interrelated purposes. The first is to examine some of the major contemporary frontier issues that are generally shaping African societies. Although these issues are not new, their contemporary nature provides an interesting angle from which to analyze them. In other words, although the focus is on the contemporary dimension of each of these issues, the book, however, takes cognizance of the importance of putting them in historical perspective as a way of providing context.

The other purpose is not to simply map out these frontier issues, but to offer some suggestions for addressing them, so that both the African Continent and its constituent states can build stable societies in which human-centered democracy is promoted. This genre of democracy transcends the realm of political rights and civil liberties, their importance notwithstanding, and seeks to address the material well-being of citizens as well. This democratic trajectory was borne out of T. H. Marshall's (1950) pioneering work on "social citizenship"—the trilogy of political rights, civil rights and socioeconomic rights. The central argument is that in order to have both relevance and salience a democratic society must be anchored on these three major pillars. This is because none of these rights is individually sufficient to constitute the foundation of a democratic polity. For example, poor, uneducated and unhealthy citizens cannot exercise their political and civil rights in meaningful ways. In short, the book is policy relevant, in that it offers some ideas for reconstituting African societies, so that they can serve the interests of all Africans, rather than those of the small ruling classes and their relations.

The Theoretical Framework

Given its nature as a collection of essays contributed by scholars from divergent disciplinary and ideological backgrounds, the book therefore uses an eclectic theoretical framework. Essentially, the central postulates of the framework are twofold. First, the African condition is the by-product of the confluence of several cultural, economic, political, religious, security and social factors. Second, in order to improve the African condition, these multidimensional factors must be addressed. In order words, Africa's state-building and nation-building challenges are lodged in various underlying factors. Hence, it is imperative that all of these factors be addressed.

Importantly, both the diagnoses and solutions to the various dimensions of the African condition must not be formulaic. That is, these twin critical processes should not be based on the parroting of Western-based "African experts," who are citizens of the countries of the "global north". This tendency is reflected in some of the works on the African condition. Instead, these processes would require thorough and independent examination of the various dimensions of the African condition, based on an understanding of the forces and factors—both external and internal—that shape them.

The Organization of the Book

The book is divided into nine (9) chapters. In this chapter, George Klay Kieh, Jr. undertakes four major interrelated tasks. First, he provides the context for the book by surveying some of the major dimensions of the African condition. Second, he lays out the purposes of the volume. Third, he delineates the contours of the book's theoretical framework. Fourth, he summarizes the various chapters that constitute the volume.

Johnson Makoba examines the relationship between non-governmental organizations (NGOs) and the state in Africa in Chap. 2. The central argument of the chapter is that development-oriented NGOs are filling the needs gap that has been created as the result of the failure or neglect of African states to adequately provide basic services for the majority of their citizens. The failure is caused by three major sets of factors: (1) the structural adjustment programs that were imposed by the Bretton Woods institutions—the International Monetary Fund and the World Bank; (2) the strangulating effects of huge external debts; and (3) pervasive corruption in the political economies of African states. Similarly, he argues that, like the state in Africa, the "market" has also failed to provide for the basic needs of the majority of the citizens in these African states. In turn, this has led to the proliferation of development-oriented NGOs on the continent. Importantly, Makoba asserts that state-NGO relations in Africa are shaped by broader economic, political and social factors mediated by the compatibility of development objectives.

In Chap. 3, Samuel Zalanga probes the issue of the extent to which Pentecostal churches in Africa as civic associations contribute to the process of democratization on the continent. According to his findings, overall, Pentecostal churches have made, and continue to make negative contributions to the democratization process in Africa. This is because, according to Zalanga, the internal governance systems of the Pentecostal churches are, by and large, an anathema to democracy. For example, he argues that the Pentecostal ideology in Africa is anti-democratic. Also, the decision-making process that anchors governance is authoritarian. Another drawback is that there is a culture of a lack of accountability. Finally, open and frank discussions are not tolerated.

Earl Conteh-Morgan examines the enduring problem of militarism in Africa, and two of its major types: *coups d'état* and irregular warfare, in Chap. 4. In the case of coups, he traces their origins on the continent to the early post-independence era. In terms of their major causes, he identifies various societal and military-specific factors. In the case of the former, societal pathologies such as mass poverty and the violation of human rights provide an enabling environment for military intervention in politics. As for the latter, it entails various issues that are germane to the corporate interests of the military, such as salary and equipment. In the case of irregular warfare, Conteh-Morgan observes that they have become common occurrences on the African Continent, as evidenced by the outbreak of several in virtually every region of the continent. He attributes irregular warfare to several factors, including mass economic marginalization. He then suggests various ways for addressing militarism and its ancillaries on the continent, including the need to improve the economic conditions of the majority of Africans.

In Chap. 5, Theodora Ayot probes the roots and dynamics of ethnic conflicts in the Great Lakes Region of East Africa by focusing on three case studies: Kenya, the Democratic Republic of the Congo, and Rwanda. In the case of Kenya, she argues that the Moi regime was the chief architect of the instrumental use of ethnicity as a strategy for the maintenance of power. Using the 1992 Kenyan Presidential Election as an example, she asserts that President Moi used warriors from his ethnic group (the Kalenji) to target and visit harm on the members of other ethnic groups, who were supportive of democratic reforms. In the case of the Democratic Republic of the Congo, she blamed the Mobutu regime's anti-democratic proclivities for laying the foundation for the seemingly unending cycle of civil wars that has engulfed the country since 1997. Similarly, in the case of Rwanda, she posits that the Habyarimana regime, which learned from the "political playbook" of other autocratic regimes in the region, took steps to undermine the democratization process in the country. In turn, this helped set the stage for the genocide that occurred in the country in 1994.

Kelechi Kalu interrogates the role of the African Union (AU) in the genocidal conflict in Sudan's Darfur region in Chap. 6. He begins the chapter by mapping out the roots of the conflict. A major one is the marginalization of the Darfur region in the economic and political spheres of the Sudan. In turn, with all legal-constitutional options for redress blocked, some Darfuris opted to organize various armed groups for the ostensible purpose of fighting the Sudanese government. With regard to the role of the AU, he argued that the organization's intervention has been ineffective in terms of ending the conflict. He attributes this primarily to the fact that the organization is conflicted in light of the fact that some African governments are also visiting violence on their own people. Kalu then proffers some suggestions for helping to make the AU effective in helping to manage the conflict in Darfur, including the need for what he calls "robust peacemaking," effective peacekeeping, the imperative of labeling the conflict a genocidal civil war, and the need to impose travel bans and the freezing of the assets of the perpetrators of genocidal acts.

In Chap. 7, George Kieh examines the state of conflict resolution on the African Continent. He begins by summarizing the major models of conflict resolution that have been used to help terminate civil wars, and undertake post-conflict peace-building on the continent. He argues that while there has been some success in the termination of civil wars, the post-conflict peace-building projects in the continent's war-affected states has not addressed the underlying causes of the civil conflict and set these societies on the pathway to durable peace and human-centered democracy and development. Kieh places the blame for this shortcoming at the doorstep of the hegemonic liberal peace-building model that has been imposed by the suzerains of the global system led by the United States on post-conflict African states. Alternatively, he suggests that the precondition for addressing the conflict that underpins the continent's various civil wars is the democratic reconstitution of the state.

Jack Mangala probes the travails of the relations between Africa and the European Union (EU) in Chap. 8. He begins by historicizing the relationship, which is then followed by the examination of the various changes that have undergirded the relationship, including probing the forces and factors that have shaped and conditioned these developments. Then, using the current phase as the basis, he examines some of the major dimensions of the relationship spanning from governance to peace and security. He observes that the relationship has been mediated by fragmentation, the dominant-dominated context, the dynamics of the EU's quest for regional integration, and the broader "North-South" relationship, including the latter's clamor for the establishment of a just global political economy.

In Chap. 9, George Kieh concludes the volume with the mapping of some of the ways in which the African condition could be addressed. Using the democratic reconstitution of the state as the pivot, he argues that since the state in Africa is the arena of struggle, its portrait has a serious impact on the various activities that occur within an African country. Hence, a human-centered state that is anchored on real democracy that entails such things as popular empowerment, and the restructuring of power relations within the government, and the broader society and its various forces—class, gender, ethnic, region, and religion—would provide a firm foundation for tackling the various challenges that are confronting the continent.

Conclusion

The chapter has attempted to address several major issues that are collectively designed that provide the context for the book, and its constituent chapters. First, the chapter mapped out the key dimensions of the African condition that are the foci of the chapters in the book. Second, the major objectives of the book were discussed. Third, the contours of the mixed theoretical framework that serve as the analytical compass for the book were laid out. Fourth, the chapter summarized the constituent chapters by laying out their major arguments.

Finally, the overarching conclusion of the chapter is that the African condition cannot be addressed by either the imposition or importation of formulae that are concocted in the political and economic laboratories of the "Global North." Instead, this critical project would require a thorough analysis and understanding of each of the major dimensions of the African condition, beyond the theoretical prisms of the dominant paradigms in African Studies—neopatrimonialism, elite pathology, and ethno-communal antagonisms. Instead, the domestic and external forces and factors that are responsible for the continent's cultural, economic, political, religious, social and security challenges would need to be identified, based on empirics. This should then be followed by the design of the requisite modalities for addressing these challenges. Importantly, the foundational basis for the redesigning of contemporary African society must be provided by a democratic state that is human-centered.

References

Adesina, Alberto, Reza Baqir, and William Easterly. 1999. "Public Goods and Ethnic Divisions." *Quarterly Journal of Economics* 114 (4): 1243–1284.

Africa News. 1992. News Analysis: People Power 'Unstoppable.' December 23–31.

Agbese, Pita Ogaba. 2004. "Soldiers as Rulers. Military Performance in Africa." In *The Military and Politics in Africa*, ed. George Klay Kieh, Jr. and Pita Ogaba Agbese, 57–90. Aldershot, UK: Ashgate Publishing.

Angstrom, Jan. 2000. "The Sociology of Studies of Ethnic Conflict: Explaining the Causal Status of Development." *Civil Wars* 3 (3): 23–44.

Arieff, Alexis. 2013. *Crisis in Mali*. CRS Report for Congress. Washington D.C.: Congressional Research Service.

Asamoah-Gyadu, Kwabena. 2014. "African Pentecostal/Charismatic Christianity: An Overview." *Lausanne World Impulse* April: 1–3.

Berman, Bruce. 1998. "Ethnicity, Patronage and the African State: The Politics of Uncivil Nationalism." *African Affairs* 97 (388): 305–341.

Bratton, Michael, and Nicholas van de Walle. 1997. *Democratic Experiments in Africa*. New York: Cambridge University Press.

Brooker, Paul. 2013. *Non-Democratic Regimes*. New York: Palgrave.

Collier, Paul and Anke Hoeffler. 2005. *Coup Traps: Why does Africa have so many Coups d'état?* Paper. Department of Economics, Oxford University.

Denny, Elaine, and Barbara Walter. 2014. "Ethnicity and Civil War." *Journal of Peace Research* 51 (2): 199–212.

Deng, Francis. 1997. "Ethnicity: An African Predicament." *The Brookings Brief* Summer: 1–7.

Freedom House. 2017. *Freedom in the World*. Washington D.C.: Freedom House.

Harrison, Graham. 2005. "Economic Faith, Social Project, and a Misreading of African Society: The Travails of Neoliberalism in Africa." *Third World Quarterly* 21 (8): 1303–1320.

Harrison, Graham. 2010. *Neoliberal Africa*. London: Zed Books.

Horowitz, Donald. 2000. *Ethnic Groups in Conflict*. Berkeley, CA: University of California Press.

Houngnikpo, Mathurin. 2013. *Guarding the Guardians: Civil-Military Relations and Democratic Governance in Africa*. Aldershot, UK: Ashgate Publishing.

Human Rights Watch. 2011. World Report. New York: Human Rights Watch.

Human Rights Watch. 2015. *World Report 2015*. New York: Human Rights Watch.

Japhet, M. 1978. "Military Coups and Military Regimes in Africa." *Southern African Journal of Military Studies* 8 (4): 1–12.

Kandeh, Jimmy. 2004. *Coups from Below: Armed Subalterns and State Power in West Africa*. New York: Palgrave.

Keller, Edmond. 2014. *Identity, Citizenship and Political Conflict in Africa*. Bloomington, IN: Indiana University Press.

Kieh, George Klay. 2002. "Civil Conflicts in Africa: Patterns and Trends." In *Zones of Conflict in Africa: Theories and Cases*, ed. George Klay Kieh, Jr. and Ida Rousseau Mukenge, 35–50. Westport, CT: Praeger.

Kieh, George Klay. 2004. "Military Engagement in African Politics." In *The Military and Politics in Africa*, ed. George Klay Kieh, Jr. and Pita Ogaba Agbese, 3–22. Aldershot, UK: Ashgate Publishing.

Kieh, George Klay. 2007. "Introduction: The Terminally Ill Berlinist State in Africa." In *Beyond State Failure and Collapse: Making the State Relevant in Africa*, ed. George Klay Kieh, Jr, 3–22. Lanham, MD: Lexington Books.

Kieh, George Klay. 2008. *The First Liberian Civil War: The Crises of Underdevelopment*. New York: Peter Lang Publishing.

Kieh, George Klay. 2009. "The State and Political Instability in Africa." *Journal of Developing Societies* 25 (1): 1–25.

Kieh, George Klay and Kelechi Kalu (eds.). 2012. "Introduction: The Travails of the U.S.' War on Terror." In *West Africa and the U.S. War on Terror*, ed. George Klay Kieh, Jr. and Kelechi Kalu, 3–18. London: Routledge.

Kieh, George Klay. 2014. "False Starts and the Crises of Underdevelopment in Africa." In *The State in Africa: Beyond False Starts*, ed. Pita Ogaba Agbese and George Klay Kieh, Jr., 23–52. Ota, Nigeria: Third World Publishers.

Knight. Menno. 2013. *Charismatic Primer 12-Global Megachurches by Continent-Africa* October 8: 1–5.

Levitt, Jeremy. 2008. "Pro-democratic Intervention in Africa." In *Africa: Mapping New Boundaries in International Law*, ed. Jeremy Levitt, 103–148. New York: Bloomsbury Publishing.

Lian, Brad, and John Oneal. 1997. "Cultural Diversity and Economic Development: A Cross-National Study of 98 Countries, 1960–185." *Economic Development and Cultural Change* 46 (1): 61–77.

Longman, Timothy. 1998. "Chaos From Above." In *The African State at the End of the Twentieth Century*, ed. Leonardo Villalon and Phillip Huxtable, 75–91. Boulder, CO: Lynne Rienner Publishers.

Lynch, Gabrielle and Misa Zgonec-Rozej. 2013. The ICC Intervention in Kenya. Working Paper AFP/ILP 2013/01. London: Chatham House.

Mamdani, Mahmood. 2001. *When Victims Become Killers: Colonialism, Nativism, and the Genocide in Rwanda*. Princeton, NJ: Princeton University Press.

Marshall, T.H. 1950. *Social Citizenship, and Social Class and Other Essays*. Cambridge, UK: Cambridge University Press.

Martin, Guy. 2012. *African Political Thought*. New York: Palgrave.

Mensah, Joseph. 2008. *Neoliberalism and Globalization in Africa*. New York: Palgrave.

Meredith, Martin. 2010. *The Fate of Africa: From the Hopes of Freedom to the Heart of Despair: A History of Fifty Years of Independence*. New York: Public Affairs.

Mkandawire, Thandika. 2012. "The Terrible Toll of Post-Colonial Rebel Movements: Towards an Explanation of the Violence against the Peasantry." In *The Roots of African Conflicts: The Cases and Cost*, ed. Alfred Nhema and Paul Tiyambe Zeleza, 106–135. Athens, OH: Ohio University Press.

Mwakikagile, Godfrey. 2001. *Military Coups in West Africa since the Sixties*. Hauppauge: Nova Science Publishers.

Nzongola-Ntalaja, Georges. "The State and Democracy in Africa." In *The State and Democracy in Africa*, ed. George Nzongola-Ntalaja and Margaret Lee, 9–24. Trenton, NJ: Africa World Press.

Osaghae, Eghosa. 2006. *Ethnicity and the State in Africa*. Working Paper Series No. 7. Kyoto, Japan: Afrasian Center for Peace and Development.

Ramsay, Jeffress. 1993. "Introduction: Africa: The Struggle for Development." In *Global Studies: Africa*, ed. Jeffress Ramsay, 1–3. Guilford, CT: McGraw-Hill/Dushkin.

Reynolds, Lloyd. 1985. *Economic Growth in the Third World, 1850–1980*. New Haven, CT: Yale University Press.

Sriskandarajah, Dhananjayan. 2005. "Development, Inequality and Ethnic Accommodation: Clues from Malaysia, Mauritius and Trinidad and Tobago." *Oxford Development Studies* 33 (1): 63–79.

Tandon, Yash. 1995. Reclaiming Africa's Agenda: Good Governance and the Role of NGOs in the African Context. Paper presented at the Conference on Good Governance for Africa: Whose Governance? University of Limburg and ECDPM, November 23–24, Maastricht.

Tandon, Yash. 1996. "Reclaiming Africa's Agenda: Good Governance and the Role of NGOs in the African Context." *Australian Journal of International Affairs* 50 (3): 293–303.

United Nations Development Program. 2016. Human Development Report, 2015. New York: Oxford University Press.

CHAPTER 2

Non-Governmental Organizations and the African State

Johnson W. Makoba

Introduction

The rapid growth and expansion of NGOs worldwide attests to their growing critical role in the development process. At the international level, NGOs are perceived as vehicles for promoting democratization and economic growth in Third World countries. And within Third World countries, NGOs are involved in relief, rehabilitation, community development and sundry other activities that are aimed at complementing weak states and markets in the promotion of economic growth and provision of basic services to most people in these countries.

Increasingly, both international and indigenous development-oriented NGOs are making up for the failure or neglect of states and markets in countries in Africa and other Third World countries to deliver economic development. Because of pervasive government corruption and inefficiency in Africa, the international donor community prefers to channel development aid through developmental NGOs, thus avoiding or bypassing the African state. This raises the twin issues of the relevance of

J.W. Makoba (✉)
University of Nevada, Reno, NV, USA

G.K. Kieh, Jr. (ed.), *Contemporary Issues in African Society*, African Histories and Modernities,
https://doi.org/10.1007/978-3-319-49772-3_2

the African state in the development process and the nature of emergent NGO-state relations. The first issue has been discussed elsewhere,[1] while the second one is the concern of this chapter. The central question raised and discussed in this chapter is whether current and future NGO-state relations in Africa will be characterized by cooperation or confrontation.

The Failure of Economic Development in the Sub-Saharan Africa and NGO Growth

Background

In general, donor agencies are increasingly supporting NGOs in the provision of services to the poor in Third World countries where markets are inaccessible or weak and where governments lack capacity or resources to reach the poor. In most Third World countries, including African ones, both states and markets are weak or inadequate. In Africa, the persistence of the dual crises of weak states and nascent or inadequate markets pose a classic dilemma for proponents of either market-led or state-led economic development. The failure of both markets and governments in Africa to deliver economic development has contributed to the rapid growth and expansion of NGOs on the continent.

The Travails of Economic Development

Evidence accumulated over the past three decades shows "the inability of the African state to deliver on its development promise" (Ndegwa 1996: 15). In fact, the African state is now perceived as "the inhibitor of social, economic, and political development" (Ndegwa 1996: 15). The demise of the African state has inevitably given rise to the ascendancy of NGOs to fill the "development vacuum". The expansion of the NGO sector in Africa since the 1990s is most clearly reflected at the country level. For example, in Kenya, there are about 500 NGOs, while in Uganda there are an estimated 1000 registered foreign and indigenous NGOs. Similarly, other African countries have a large number of active NGOs including: "Zambia with 128, Tanzania with 130, Zimbabwe with 300, and Namibia with over 55" (Ndegwa 1996: 20). The growing role of NGOs in all sectors of development is an indication of the decreasing capacity of the African state to undertake meaningful development. Besides increases in NGO numbers, the amount of development resources they receive or handle for development purposes has grown over the years. It is estimated that "official aid to Kenyan NGOs amounts to about US$35 million a year, which is about 18% of all official aid received by Kenya annually [and]... in Uganda, NGOs disburse an estimated 25% of all official aid to Uganda" (Ndegwa 1996: 20).[2]

The weakening financial situation of Uganda and Kenya, like that of other African countries, is due to a combination of huge external debt, corruption and the effects of structural adjustment programs imposed by the International Monetary Fund (IMF). In particular, the structural adjustment programs have "strained the ability of the African states to provide services and has attracted more NGOs to cushion the adverse short-term effects of adjustment programs, such as by providing affordable healthcare services" (Ndegwa 1996: 2). Given the prevailing political and economic conditions in Uganda and Kenya, as well as elsewhere in Africa, the role and contribution of NGOs to the development process are expected to increase.

Donor agencies increasingly funnel development assistance through NGOs and other non-state institutions because states in sub-Saharan Africa are considered both inefficient and corrupt. As Dicklich observes, the "failure of the [African] state to provide basic services has led many official donors to use NGOs, rather than the local state, to provide services" (1998b: 6). In Uganda, for example, a succession of inefficient, violent and corrupt regimes since 1971 has contributed to the emergence of over 1000 indigenous NGOs to provide self-help solutions to the poor. Most "ordinary Ugandans have had to fend for themselves, relying on organizations outside of the state rather than on the state itself to provide basic necessities" (Dicklich 1998b: 22–23). In general, most service-oriented NGOs have "moved into service provision where the state has moved out" (Dicklich 1998b: 6). No doubt, NGOs have been necessary in Uganda and other African countries to fill the "developmental gaps" caused by weak post-independent states.

While African states have become increasingly weak, formal markets have steadily declined and in some cases they are nonexistent or have been replaced by informal or parallel markets. According to Callaghy, most African economies are faced with:

> declining or negative rates and stagnating or falling per capita income figures; balance of payments and debt problems (which have become more severe (since) the 1980s), requiring IMF and the World Bank programs with their attendant conditionality packages and consequences. Many (export) commodity prices remain low while most import prices remain high. In many countries, agricultural production is falling while aid levels stagnate. Health and nutrition levels are falling while informal or *magendo* economies (have) become more important as states weaken and formal markets decline. 'Socialist' states have performed poorly and 'capitalist' ones are not significantly better. Hopes for economic growth and development have shriveled on all sides. (1995: 201)

In Uganda and other African countries, authoritarian regimes "induced an 'exit' from the formal economy [as well as] a general avoidance of state institutions by a wide range of groups and occupations" (Dicklich 1998a: 145). Furthermore, economic restructuring due to structural adjustment programs and privatization contributed to the retreat of African states from their responsibilities of promoting economic development and providing "basic social services such as health care, education, sanitation and basic security,..." (Dicklich 1998a: 145). Given the weak private sector and the state withdrawal from the provision of basic economic necessities and social services, "many NGOs are being pressurized into dealing with poverty alleviation (not eradication), and the provision of basic social services..." (Dicklich 1998a: 149). Thus, NGOs increasingly fill in social and economic spaces created by weak markets or retreating states. As a result, "NGOs have been heralded as... new agents with the capacity and commitment to make up for the shortcomings of the state and market in reducing poverty" (Dicklich 1998b: 3).

Some critics of NGO participation in economic development contend that such involvement provides legitimacy and support to governments that have failed to deliver economic development or to provide basic social services to their citizens. Other critics charge that NGOs save "donors money and allow them to avoid addressing implementation difficulties, while also allowing them [the donors] to retain ultimate control over activities" (Van de Walle 1999: 346).

The absence of viable states or markets in most African countries has left NGOs as the most important alternative for promoting economic development (Makoba 2002). Thus, the failure or inability of both states and markets to meet the basic needs of the majority of the people in Africa and other Third World countries has given rise to the growing importance of the NGO sector in the development process (Vetter 1995: 2; Salamon 1994: 116). Such inability may have exposed the limitations of the state or private sector as major agents of promoting economic development in Africa or the Third World in general.

Some proponents of the state-market debate contend that rather than blaming either the government or market for Africa's poor economic performance, there is need to consider how both states and markets interact with internal and external factors to facilitate or hinder economic development on the continent (Mkandawire 2001; Luiz 2000). According to such a political economy approach, market failure in Africa may be partly due to the policy environment and partly due to the inability to achieve economies of scale (Mkandawire 2001: 294).

The politicization of the policy environment means that the political elite (leaders) rather than bureaucrats or technocrats tend to play an oversized role in making economic development decisions while relying on political considerations or assumptions. In addition, the African state or its institutions, often under the pressure of ethnic or political interests, is vulnerable to both corruption and patronage, which inevitably distort or undermine state development policy priorities. In contrast, there is sufficient evidence indicating that states with a high degree of administrative capacity concentrated in the executive branch of governments increases both the capacity and effectiveness of policy implementation (Makoba 2011: 8). A good example is the case of the postcolonial state in Botswana which, with a high degree of autonomy from popular interest groups and a strong institutional and administrative capacity, has continued to deliver democracy and a sustained economic growth since 1966 to the present.

Beyond the constrained political environments most African countries face, are the structural adjustment programs (SAPS) often imposed by the World Bank and the IMF. Very often the SAPS tend to marginalize and weaken the capacities of African states. In turn, such policies ensure that African states cannot provide the expected enabling institutional and regulatory environments necessary for the markets or private sectors to emerge and thrive on the continent.

Although market failure in sub-Saharan Africa is partly attributed to the lack of the necessary conditions and the regulatory environment to create and sustain viable or strong markets, market inability to achieve economies of scale is a major challenge. According to the World Bank, market failure in sub-Saharan Africa is partly due to "high transaction costs, risks, and [lack of] economies of scale" (World Development Report 2008: 12). Indeed, it is because of this challenge that the World Bank in the same report recommends strongly that "the [African] state has a role in market development providing core public goods, [and] improving the investment climate for the private sector..." (World Development Report 2008: 23).

This means that in the African context, states are not only expected to provide an enabling environment for the emergence of markets, but where necessary, the state must engage in the creation of markets. In particular, since most African countries have weak or underdeveloped markets, the state must first develop the private sector (Nkurayija 2011: 11). Hence, in order to bring about sustainable economic development in sub-Saharan Africa, it will require a strategic or pragmatic "combination of the activities of the market and the state" (Makoba 2011: 14).

NGO Growth and the Crisis of State Legitimacy in Sub-Saharan Africa

The Crisis of the State

As noted above, the failure of both states and markets in the Third World, including Africa, to meet the basic needs of the population has given rise to the growing importance of the NGO sector (Levy 1996: 1–3). Furthermore, the inability or unwillingness of either the African state or market to deliver expected economic development has exposed their inherent limitations as agents of development in sub-Saharan Africa. However, the stakes for state failure seem to be much higher than those for market failure. The most important explanation for this is that "the state as the guardian of national development [in African countries], has a moral and political obligation to initiate or accelerate development and promote equity throughout society" (Makoba 1996: 459). And as Nyangoro has correctly observed, "even the most repressive states in the [Third] World are theoretically committed to some socioeconomic agenda which makes state participation in the economy inevitable" (1992: 24). This suggests that the failure of the African state to deliver expected economic development is not only taken very seriously, but also threatens to undermine any residual legitimate authority the state may possess. It has been pointed out, for example, that as the African state is increasingly unable or unwilling to deliver economic development, "the issue of its authority and legitimacy [has begun] to loom large in the [context] of state-society relations" (Nyangoro 1989: 146–147).

In democratic countries, the legitimacy of the state depends on the consent of the governed, and the continued accountability of the administration to the electorate. In contrast, in African countries, where governments are predominantly authoritarian and unaccountable to the public, the legitimacy of the regime rests primarily on economic performance and maintaining political stability. After the achievement of political independence in most African countries, the social compact that had helped to mobilize the people in support of the nationalist leadership in the anti-colonial struggle came to an end. This occurred as civil society organizations such as trade unions, which had helped in the decolonization process, were either banned or co-opted under the one-party state. The concentration of power in the hands of a single political party or a military junta or dictatorship led to personal rule. Over time, personal rulers came to represent the law and the state. As a result, "the postcolonial [authoritarian] state floated above civil society much as the colonial state had" (Baregu 1994: 159). Furthermore, since the demand for national independence did not include a commitment by the nationalist leadership to democratic rule, the primary source of postcolonial regime legitimacy rested on economic performance and political stability as indicated earlier.

The postcolonial African state variously called "soft", "overloaded", "over-centralized", or "authoritarian" has failed to deliver economic development. No doubt, Africa's poor economic performance was affected by external factors such as huge foreign debt, poor terms of trade, the oil price shocks of the 1970s, and world recession of the 1980s. However, it is economic mismanagement and widespread corruption that has led to the severe economic crisis experienced from the mid-1980s to the present. Africa's economic decline made most African countries far more susceptible to outside pressure from the IMF and the World Bank and to internal opposition elements in the early 1990s. Thus, economic failure made the African state vulnerable to both outside intervention and to the internal erosion of its legitimacy. Indeed, I have argued elsewhere that Africa's economic crisis "critically eradicated [any residual] legitimacy of the authoritarian state and created the intellectual climate in which the democratic alternative [became] widely perceived as… the only viable solution to Africa's ills" (Makoba 1999: 63). According to Baregu, the legitimacy of the one-party state in Tanzania which rested on economic performance was seriously eroded due to the severe economic crisis that began in the 1980s and persisted through the early 1990s (Baregu 1994: 159).

Filling the Vacuum? NGOs and Development

There is no doubt that poor economic performance by the African state has eroded its legitimacy. However, the current retreat of the African state from active economic development followed by the donor community's promotion of the NGO sector as an alternative to state-led economic development threatens to further undermine state legitimacy. With the end of the Cold War, development assistance is no longer used primarily by the U.S. and its allies or Russia (successor to the former Soviet Union) to "buy" ideological allies. This implies that if aid is given at all nowadays, it is likely to go toward the promotion of genuine grassroots development (Craig and Mayo 1995: 10). In addition, the new thinking in development theory and practice views markets, private sector initiatives and especially NGOs as having the greatest potential for achieving economic growth and providing most services to most people including the poor, women and children. Under the new thinking, the role of the state or government is increasingly being reduced or rolled back. The "roll back of the state" in Third World countries including sub-Saharan African ones, partially manifests itself in the "reduction of state spending on social programs while promoting solutions based on the market forces or voluntary/NGO sectors and community based self-help" (Craig and Mayo 1995: 10). Because of the end of the Cold War and pressing financial needs in developed industrialized countries, official loans and grants from northern governments and multilateral lending agencies (such as the IMF and World Bank) have declined dramatically since the 1990s. As a result, the international donor community prefers to channel its scarce development aid through NGOs instead of governments that are perceived as both corrupt and inefficient. There has been increased donor funding through NGOs since the 1980s. According to Sandberg, "northern NGOs collectively now transfer to the South more than the World Bank does. Net grants to Africa from NGOs rose from $0.8 billion in 1982 to $1.4 billion in 1989, which was equal to more than half of all private financial follows to Africa in the same year". (cited in Craig and Mayo 1995: 21). Moreover, by the close of the decade of the 1980s, for example, about $1.5 billion of public funds were channeled to Africa through northern NGOs (Craig and Mayo 1995: 21). Southern indigenous NGOs are also increasingly being targeted by international donors as financial recipients of development assistance. As a result, African "NGOs often can secure more financial resources from both external and domestic sources to undertake a new development project than a local or national debt-ridden or authoritarian African government can [or will] secure" (Galjart 1995: 18–21). This, of course, threatens to render the state irrelevant in the development process. It also raises the central question of whether current and future NGO-state relations in Africa will be dominated by cooperation or confrontation.

NGO-state Relations in Sub-Saharan African Countries

The Frameworks

There are two broad perspectives on the NGO-state relations in Third World countries that may readily be applied to sub-Saharan Africa. The first perspective views the relationship between NGOs and the state as "essentially oppositional, antagonistic and conflictual" (http://www.bond.uk/wgroups/civils/report.html, 1997: 4). This notion is based on the assumption that civil society (including NGOs) serves as the means by which citizens' rights and interests are protected from the incursion of the state.

In contrast, the second perspective sees NGOs and the state as "mutually interdependent and complementary rather than as mutually antagonistic" (ibid.). This perspective regards the NGO and state sectors as complementary, since neither is fully autonomous nor fully self-sufficient. The perspectives are presented as if they were mutually exclusive.

Toward Synthesis

This chapter argues that the two perspectives of NGO-state interaction, when applied to Africa, are not mutually exclusive. The scope for NGO-state collaboration or confrontation in Africa, like elsewhere in the Third World, is determined "not only by the attitudes and ideas of individuals [who manage these] institutions, but also by broader political, social and economic factors" (Wellard and Copestake 1993: 5). At one end of the spectrum, NGOs operate largely within the official state policy framework. At the other end of the spectrum, they openly resist or confront government policy and seek to change it by mobilizing popular opinion, through advocacy or direct lobbying. It is important to understand why some NGOs cooperate with the state, while others resist and seek to change government policy (Ndegwa 1996: 109).

Both indigenous and international (or northern) NGOs involved in filling the gaps left by the state's withdrawal from the provision of social services or promotion of economic development through poverty reduction tend to view collaboration with the state positively. In particular, they consider collaboration with the state as providing an opportunity for improving their influence or leverage in order to achieve their stated objectives. On the other hand, collaborating government agencies view the relationship with NGOs as "a way of gaining access to NGO's local knowledge, expertise and external finance" (Wellard and Copestake 1993: 287). In most cases, NGO-state collaboration is based on compatible development goals or objectives. According to Wellard and Copestake, "constructive interaction is clearly impossible without some common purpose or shared goal" (1993: 300). But in situations where goals are not compatible, NGOs may be regulated and "coopted… by the regime which uses them for legitimacy building and social service gap-filling" (Dicklich 1998b: 19). Increased NGO-state collaboration depends on cordial relations with government and especially undertaking "grass roots, humanitarian, welfare or development activities that governments cannot or will not do" (Dicklich 1998b: 19).

In many sub-Saharan African countries, both local and international NGOs have taken a leading role not only in promoting economic growth and coordinating the delivery of services, but also by engaging in the production and distribution of technical information to various segments of the population. In Kenya, for example, the agro forestry research and development conducted jointly by the government and NGOs produces newsletters, magazines, community training workshops, educational kits for schools and radio programs aimed at making technical agricultural and environmental conservation information available and accessible to both the public and policymakers.

In addition to collaboration, NGOs may use lobbying or advocacy through their networks of members or set values derived from the wider (global) development movement, and may draw upon their professional and specialist knowledge to influence government policy such as on the environment and sustainable agricultural development. KENGO, a Kenyan NGO, aims to increase public awareness and debate on the (poor) state of the environment and to promote implementation of policy and practical means for its amelioration. To attain its objective, it has organized traveling workshops for scientists, community leaders, journalists and policymakers to meet farmers and visit places around the country.

The cooperative NGO-state relationship depends largely on the absence of major ideological or developmental differences between NGOs and the host African governments. Also, regular informal contacts between NGO leadership and the political or bureaucratic elite help to sustain the collaboration. And in most cases, mechanisms for coordination, regulation and resolution of disagreements between NGOs and host governments are set up to ease the interaction.

Close NGO identification and collaboration with the host government may undermine the NGO's objective of targeting the poor and other marginalized segments of the population. In addition, transaction costs involved in collaboration with government agencies can be exceedingly high. Critics claim that coordination meetings tend to be both time-consuming and unproductive (Wellard and Copestake 1993: 302). Coordination meetings with government representatives take too long to arrange, yet are frequently canceled or rearranged at short notice and time and effort spent building up rapport with key senior civil servants/ bureaucrats is wasted when they are transferred to other locations.

To make collaborative interactions meaningful to the NGO, two pathways are proposed (Wellard and Copestake 1993: 303). First, NGOs may accept government invitations to engage in collaborative efforts and, then afterwards, seek to negotiate more interactive involvement as government bureaucrats become more aware and trusting of NGO abilities and partnerships. Second, NGOs may concentrate upon preserving independent and successful work programs including developing local expertise and a base for constructive criticism of public policy and practice. NGOs can then decide either to remain and operate independently or to negotiate collaboration with host governments from a position of technical and financial strength. In the final analysis, NGO-state disagreements that are ideological or involve fundamental policy differences are likely to lead to confrontation rather than collaboration or permissive NGO autonomy.

NGO-state confrontation may arise from one or more of the following situations: (1) the NGO being too overtly political in its work (e.g., advocating human rights, democracy or environmental issues); (2)

NGO's success threatens bureaucratic interests; and (3) where the survival of NGOs themselves is threatened by government legislation. In the following analysis, each one of these situations is explored.

NGOs are generally viewed by politicians as being of marginal political and economic importance. However, in situations where their work is perceived as overtly political, they are taken very seriously by the political elite. In particular, NGOs involved in the advocacy of human rights, democracy or controversial environmental issues are viewed with suspicion and hostility by host African governments.

NGOs in Africa seek to contribute to the overall democratization process at two levels. First, NGOs seek to "pluralize" civil society by pursuing or encouraging actions that enable them to operate more independently of the host government. To this end, they may organize collectively, be assertive and pursue their own interests in the development process. In this way, NGOs help to "enlarge" and "safeguard" the political space that the post-independence African state has eroded over the past four decades.

Second, "NGOs contribute to the process of democratic development by empowering grassroots communities where they pursue their development activities" (Ndegwa 1996: 25). NGOs may serve as vehicles through which grassroots communities can channel, protect or articulate their interests. NGOs view the goal of empowering grassroots communities as "a crucial step toward social, economic, and political recovery in Africa" (Ndegwa 1996: 23). Grassroots empowerment by NGOs is not possible without "pluralizing" the civil society and ensuring that the African state accepts or tolerates other actors in the development process. However, African states with little legitimacy tend to be "highly suspicious of NGO activities, especially those that may be construed as political in any way" (Dicklich 1998b: 24). In most cases, the state allows NGOs to operate (or not to operate) on the basis of political consideration rather than the NGO's contribution to economic and social development. Overall, the parameters within which NGOs can promote "pluralization" or "empowerment" of clients in most Third World countries including African ones, are defined by the regime in power.

In Kenya in the 1980s, the Daniel arap Moi administration sought "to consolidate power and neutralize potential independent agents of agitation" (Ndegwa 1996: 25–26). The government's actions included dismantling several civic and political organizations and networks of patronage that had served Kenyatta's administration and had the potential to undermine Moi's power. From the 1980s until Moi's political party lost to the opposition in 2003, several organizations resisted attempts by the KANU government in Kenya to control them. The most notable ones included: the Law Society of Kenya, the National Council of Churches and the Green Belt Movement. The Green Belt Movement, a radical environmental organization led by the late Professor Wangari Maathia, a Nobel Peace Prize winner, and a cabinet minister in the Kibaki government, emerged as the most outspoken critic of the single-party regime in Kenya. Maathia's challenge to the single-party regime of former President Moi contributed to her "organization's abandonment of the self-restraint that was characteristic of NGOs…" (Ndegwa 1996: 28). As a result of state-NGO tensions in the late 1980s over human rights, democracy and environmental issues, the Kenya government responded in 1990 by passing the NGO Coordination Act designed to regulate and control NGO activities. Similarly in Uganda, the government created the NGO Registration Board to monitor and regulate NGOs and their activities throughout the country. In addition to monitoring NGO activities, the National Resistance Movement (NRM) Government in Uganda has tried to co-opt developmental NGOs into its national development strategy. As a result, critics contend that "NGOs are vehicles of NRM-inspired and led development. This distracts from the ability of NGOs,… to provide an alternative source of influence or accountability to the regime" (Dicklich 1998b: 25).

In Egypt, Dr. Saad Eddin Ibrahim, the founder and head of the Ibn Khaldun Center and prominent advocate of democracy and human rights, was convicted by a Cairo court on charges of defaming the country and he was sentenced to seven years in prison (The New York Times Editorials 2001: A22). Furthermore, his respected center on democracy and human rights education was closed by the Egyptian government. However, as a result of persistent international pressure on the Egyptian government, Dr. Ibrahim was released from prison and his sentence was commuted.

The second area of NGO-state confrontation is where NGO success threatens bureaucratic interests. As noted earlier, the legitimacy of many Third World countries, including those in Africa, is "based on their ability to deliver services" (Paul and Israel 1991: 73). And since the legitimacy of many states in the Third World still rests on performance or the ability to deliver services, "any NGO that delivers services more efficiently than government may be perceived as a political threat"

(Paul and Israel 1991: 73). According to Ndegwa "the growing presence and capacity of NGOs in all sectors of development and their 'overtaking' of [African] states in some instances due to the states' decreasing capacity have put the two on a sure collision course" (1996: 21). In such situations, successful NGOs are viewed by African countries as posing a direct challenge to the states' so-called "imperatives of sovereignty" which include; territorial integrity, security, autonomy, legitimacy and revenue collection. Because of this, "African governments have come to view NGOs as socioeconomic assets but also more warily as political challengers whose benevolence needs to be directed and coordinated in order not to undermine the state" (Ndegwa 1996: 22). In general, African governments are concerned about the growth and activities of NGOs for two political reasons. First, as NGOs constitute a vast network of resourceful organizations with international financial and technical support, they are growing more autonomous of the host governments.

Secondly, NGOs have the potential to reshape state-society relations, especially in the grassroots communities where they operate. For their part, NGOs have greatly challenged the state's monopoly over development—especially by penetrating remote areas that the state has been unable or unwilling to reach (such as northern Uganda or southern Sudan). The international donor community has continued to channel development aid through NGOs, thereby "bypassing" the state. As a result, Third World governments including African ones, view NGOs as competitors for scarce development aid. This has "led [such] governments to attempt to control NGOs and their resources in the name of preserving national sovereignty" (Ndegwa 1996: 22). As discussed earlier, the Moi government in Kenya responded to the NGO political challenges by enacting the NGO Coordination Act of 1990, which sought to monitor and control NGO activities. And in Uganda, the NRM Government created the NGO Registration Board under the Ministry of Internal Affairs (not planning or economic development ministries) to oversee NGO activities throughout the country.

The final area of NGO-state tension concerns government legislation that may threaten the survival of NGOs. Increasingly, "many governments in [sub-Saharan Africa] are moving towards some form of compulsory regulatory framework for the [NGO] sector, particularly for those [that] receive funds from abroad" (Wellard and Copestake 1993: 298). The state has often a wide repertoire of control strategies at its disposal. The state can monitor, coordinate, co-opt and if necessary, reorganize or ban NGOs from operating in the country. Although state power is overarching, NGOs can lobby, collaborate selectively, keep a low profile, disband or withdraw (if they are international NGOs). In general, "NGOs are likely to accept regulation and coordination if they are persuaded of the case for it, and fears that the state is attempting to dictate what they do can be assuaged" (Wellard and Copestake 1993: 300).

Previous studies on NGO-state tensions tend to stress state repression of NGOs and assume that NGOs merely submit to the repressive regime (Ndegwa 1996: 32). However, Ndegwa argues that "attempts to control NGOs have also presented opportunities to oppose the state at a time when resources and international good will are... in favor of non-state actions" (Ndegwa 1996: 32). In general, NGOs have reacted to authoritarian government control in three ways. First, they have tried to adjust and pursue amicable coexistence with authoritarian regimes. Secondly, they have opposed and agitated against repression. And, finally, they have lobbied or mobilized with international organizations and Western governments to force Third World states to loosen their control over the NGO sector.

The NGOs in Kenya, for example, were concerned about the scope and intent of the NGO Coordination Act of 1990. The NGO reaction which was initially informal and informational, quickly turned to collective mobilization and face-to-face lobbying with high-ranking Kenyan government officials. This strategy ultimately led to intense and sustained confrontations with the Moi government throughout the 1980s. But in 1992, the Moi government responded to NGO concerns about the legislation by revising it. Four major factors contributed to NGOs' success in Kenya. First, the availability of political opportunity to voice dissent and to pursue oppositional action without imprisonment. Second, the high level of NGO collective organization and combined human, technical and financial resources—in particular, the establishment of the NGO network and a powerful elected NGO Standing Committee gave NGOs a strong collective voice. Third, NGO alliance with international donor agencies: International donors consistently facilitated the NGO effort to fight the controlling legislation in various ways, including organizing discussion seminars and providing financial resources to enable the NGO Standing Committee to mobilize the stakeholders. Finally, NGO alliance with other oppositional forces in civil society was very important in challenging both the government and its policies such as the law controlling NGOs. In particular, the newly legalized opposition parties embraced the NGOs' cause as contributing to the broader goal of "pluralism" or democratization. In a nutshell, NGOs in Kenya were able to receive a less threatening controlling legislation because of their "enhanced leverage due to collective organization and resources, alliances with donors and oppositional forces and crucial access to the state as the result of the prevailing political opportunity" (Ndegwa 1996: 52). Thus, NGOs in Kenya were well organized, resourceful and conscious actors contributing to political reform and pluralism.

Conclusion

The collaborative and confrontational models of NGO-state relations in Africa are not mutually exclusive. Indeed, they should be perceived as being on a continuum or coexisting. It is argued that most NGO-state relations in Africa fall somewhere between collaboration and confrontation. For the most part, NGOs are "skeptical if not suspicious of state power, yet accepting of the government's necessary function" (Paul and Israel 1991: 30). In other words, NGOs in Africa are prepared to work with governments when opportunities arise that are consistent with their social mission, and to resist when governments impose their policies on NGOs.

Furthermore, governments vary in their ability or capacity to enforce NGO controlling legislation. As a result, "some governments that might like to constrain NGO activities simply lack the political and administrative strength to do so" (Paul and Israel 1991: 30). The simultaneous desire by the African state in seeking to control NGOs while at the same time reaping benefits that are offered by an autonomous NGO sector, is not inconsistent. African governments welcome NGOs as sources of resources, especially technical expertise and foreign aid, and provided their activities complement those of the government.

At the same time, governments strengthen mechanisms for the monitoring and control of the NGO sector to ensure their activities fit within the overall government policy framework. As a result, governments in Africa and other Third World countries tend to restrict NGO activity that is deemed too political, while co-opting or coordinating those whose activities are considered compatible with development objectives as stipulated in their national development or action plans. It is for this reason that critics assert that NGOs are essentially "service-providers and legitimacy providers" (Dicklich 1998b: 170). But in order for NGOs in

Africa and other Third World countries to transcend the role of "mere gap-filling" they will need to be more proactive, and empowerment-oriented when promoting both democracy and economic development. To successfully do so, NGOs need to develop a constructive relationship with host African governments and international donors that provides protection and the bulk of their financial resources, respectively.

Notes

1. See J. Wagona Makoba, "Nongovernmental Organizations (NGOs), Development and the Crisis of State Legitimacy in the Third World," unpublished paper, Fall 2003.
2. The 25% in Uganda represents the annual average expenditure by NGOs. During the particular fiscal years, NGO expenditures may be higher. For example, it is reported that during the 1992/1993 fiscal year, the expenditure of foreign and indigenous NGOs "was US$125 million,... almost equal to the expected World Bank contribution to the Rehabilitation and Development Plan for the same year" (Dicklich 1998a: 148).

References

Baregu, Mwesiga. 1994. The Rise and Fall of the One-Party State in Tanzania. In *Economic Change and Political Liberalization in Sub-Saharan Africa*, ed. Jennifer A. Widner, 158–181. Baltimore: The Johns Hopkins University Press.

Callaghy, Thomas M. 1995. State, Choice, and Context: Comparative Reflections on Reform and Intractability. In *Political Development and the New Realism in Sub-Saharan Africa*, ed. David E. Apter and Carl G. Rosberg, 184–219. Charlottesville and London: University Press of Virginia.

Craig, Gary, and Marjorie Mayo (eds.). 1995. *Community Empowerment and Development: A Reader in Participation and Development*. London: Zed Books.

Dicklich, Susan. 1998a. Indigenous NGOs and Political Participation. In *Developing Uganda*, ed. Holdger B. Hansen and Michael Tweedle, 145–158. Oxford: James Curry.

Dicklich Susan. 1998b. *The Elusive Promise of NGOs in Africa: Lessons from Uganda*. New York: St. Martin's Press.

Galjart, Benno. 1995. Counter Development: Possibilities and Constraints. In *Community Empowerment and Development: A Reader in Participation and Development*, ed. Gary Craig and Marjorie Mayo, 12–23. London: Zed Books.

http://www.bond.UK/wgnup/civils/report.html. 1997, pp. 1–14.

Levy, Daniel C. 1996. *Building in Third Sector*. Pittsburgh: University of Pittsburgh Press.

Luiz, John M. 2000. The Politics of State, Society and Economy. *International Journal of Social Economics* 27: 227–243.

Makoba, J. Wagona. 1996. Beyond the State-Market Debate: The Role of the State and Market in Third World Economic Development. *Austrian Journal of Development Studies* 12 (4): 447–461.

———. 1999. Rethinking Current Explanations of Political Changes in Sub-Saharan Africa. *Journal of Third World Studies* 14 (2): 61–73.

———. 2002. Nongovernmental Organizations (NGOs) and Third World Development: An Alternative Approach to Development. *Journal of Third World Studies* 19 (1): 53–63.

———. 2003. *Nongovernmental Organizations (NGOS), Development and the Crisis of State Legitimacy in the Third World.* Unpublished Paper.

———. 2011. *Rethinking Development Strategies in Africa.* Oxford, UK: Peter Lang.

Mkandawire, Thandika. 2001. Thinking About Developmental States in Africa. *Cambridge Journal of Economics* 25: 289–313.

Ndegwa, Stephen N. 1996. *The Two Faces of Civil Society: NGOs and Politics in Africa.* Westford, Connecticut: Kumarian Press.

Nkurayija, Jean dela Croix. 2011. *The Requirements of the African Continent's Development: Linking Peace, Governance, Economic Growth, and Global Interdependence.* A Paper, Berlin, Germany.

Nyang'oro, Julius E. 1989. *The State and Capitalist Development in Africa: Declining Political Economics.* New York: Praeger.

———. 1992. The Evolving Role of the African State Under Structural Adjustment. In *Beyond Structural Adjustment in Africa: The Political Economy of Sustainable and Democratic Development*, ed. Julius E. Nyang'oro, and Timothy M. Shaw, 11–27. New York: Praeger.

Paul, Samuel, and Arturo Israel (eds.). 1991. *Nongovernmental Organizations and the World Bank: Cooperation for Development.* Washington, DC: World Bank.

Salamon, Lester M. 1994. The Rise of the Nonprofit Sector. *Foreign Affairs* 73 (4): 109–122.

The New York Times. 2001. Editorials. May 26, p. A22.

Van de Walle, Nicolas. 1999. Aid's Crisis of Legitimacy: Current Proposals of Future Prospects. *African Affairs* 98: 337–352.

Vetter, Stephen G. 1995. The Business of Grassroots Development. *Grassroots Development* 19 (2): 2–11.

Wellard, Kate, and James G. Copestake (eds.). *Nongovernmental Organizations and the State in Africa.* New York: Routledge.

World Bank. 2008. *World Development Report. 2008.* Washington, DC: World Bank.

CHAPTER 3

Civil Society in Africa: Interrogating the Role of Pentecostal Christianity in Africa's Democratization and Development Processes

Samuel Zalanga

Introduction

Since the end of the Cold War, democratization has emerged as a central component of most development strategies, although the hegemonic dominance of neoliberalism has been characterized as a threat to the genuine process of democratization and development (Harvey 2005). Beyond this, a major challenge has been to identify the preconditions for the effective institutionalization of democracy. Numerous scholars have identified the existence of civil society associations as critical to the effective operation of democratic institutions and society, which in turn is critical for participatory development (Veltmeyer and O'Malley 2001; Howel and Pearce 2001).

S. Zalanga (✉)
Department of Sociology, Bethel University, Saint Paul, MN, USA

G.K. Kieh, Jr. (ed.), *Contemporary Issues in African Society*, African Histories and Modernities,
https://doi.org/10.1007/978-3-319-49772-3_3

This chapter is an attempt to examine the extent to which Pentecostal churches as civic society associations in sub-Saharan Africa contribute to the institutionalization of democracy as part of a broader project for promoting participatory development. The first part of the chapter discusses conceptual issues about the role of civil society and civil society organizations/associations in the literature in general and with particular reference to the role of civil society organizations and associations in Africa. The second part summarizes and analyzes empirical studies on the role of Pentecostal churches in the processes of democratization and development in sub-Saharan Africa. The third section of the chapter uses insights from the literature to interrogate the empirical studies summarized and analyzed on Pentecostal churches in sub-Saharan Africa. The concluding part attempts to ponder on why Pentecostal Christian revival in Africa is by and large taking place peacefully while a kind of Islamic revival on the continent uses violent means to achieve its goals.

The Role of Civil Society in Social, Political, and Economic Development: An Overview

Civil society has been defined in many ways, but generally it is assumed to be the institutional space between the state, the market and the family. In this social space, citizens organize themselves and pursue their interests presumably within the legitimate institutional framework of the society. Ideally, such civil society organizations and groups transgress horizontal and vertical differences among people and transcend kinship and patronage ties, by forming solidarity associations. Examples of such civil society associations are: non-governmental organizations (NGOs), trade unions, religious groups, community-based organizations, networks of activist groups, media agencies and professional associations. There are two dominant conceptions of civil society: the liberal conception and the radical or Gramscian one.

The liberal conception of civil society believes that civil society associations help in promoting good governance and disciplining the capitalist system by making it adopt social responsibility as an ethical commitment (Tocqueville 1969; Putnam 1993). This view of civil associations in capitalist society became very popular under neoliberal hegemony where the goal is to reduce the scope of state intervention in public affairs by creating more space for private corporations and civil society organizations (Friedman 1962).

The second conception of civil society is the radical one which sees civil society organizations as engaged in the contestation of power and alternative visions of a good society. In this respect, civil society organizations mobilize and organize to challenge the dominant paradigm of development which legitimizes the status quo, and in doing so the organizations provide an alternative vision of development (Wood and Murray 2007: 19–41). On this basis, it can be argued that the meaning of the term civil society is ambiguous and so one can only decipher what it is depending on the context in which it is used. In one respect, it is relevant and used as a mechanism for explaining the process of social and political change in a comparative sense. In some cases, it is just referred to as a description of real-life concrete situations of what is going with particular organizations in a society. In this case, it is an analytical tool. Lastly, civil society is sometimes conceptualized as a normative ideal in the sense that it is the best hope of a society to create a pathway to a more just and egalitarian society.

With regard to the contemporary development literature as it affects the developing world, development experts perceive civil society as a necessary ingredient in the promotion of greater democratization and bringing about market reforms through good governance (Quadir 2011: 289–292). In the 1990s, the World Bank and other development agencies, such as the United Kingdom's Department for International Development, were in consensus that the goal of good governance was not only to promote balanced growth but growth with equity by creating balance and equilibrium between the state, the market/private corporations, and civil society. The way to realize this is through the creation and strengthening of NGOs both within developing and developed countries. If this strategy is pursued very well, the hope is that the NGOs will promote good governance and increase the participation of citizens in the democratic and the development processes, while ensuring that neoliberal capitalism and globalization remain socially responsible and competitive for the benefit of society.

For some time, NGOs became erroneously synonymous with civil society even though the concept of civil society in the literature has a much broader meaning than that. Indeed, the emphasis on NGOs as the main engine of civil society led to greater development activities and to NGOs being provided funding to carry out their activities and increase their institutional capacity through training. Unfortunately, this approach to civil society has not necessarily always been successful given that some of the NGOs are more concerned about maintaining the status quo, whatever it is, or just being agents for the implementation of foreign donor programs in the host country, irrespective of the genuine relevance of the donor programs to the host country (Makumbe 1996: 305–317). Given this realization, it is fair to say that NGOs as such and their foreign sponsors became part of the development problem in many respects rather than the solution.

In view of the realization of the problems of NGOs as agents of national development, there emerged a new approach to civil society which focused more on promoting human rights, building more effective institutions or institutional capacity, and helping to facilitate citizen action. The point is not that foreign donor agencies and NGOs have had nothing positive to offer in terms of development, but often they tend to assume that development can be totally insulated from politics. The reality is that in some cases and situations, genuine development will require some civil society organizations to resist and challenge the vision of neoliberal globalization and orthodoxy, which is a highly political act (Jenkins 2001; Piketty 2014). Given this, it is fair to say that there are different types of civil society organizations, both foreign and local. Some foreign and local NGOs play a very active role in promoting people-oriented development by advocating on behalf of the poor and peasants (Kanji, Braga and Mitullah 2002).

Thus, it needs to be highlighted that at the global level there are two dominant ways to think of civil society: the neoliberal paradigm and the radical/Gramscian approach which is credited to Antonio Gramsci. The neoliberal approach to civil society sees the promotion of civil society and civil society organizations as part of a larger development strategy to diminish or decenter the state from playing an important role in development. In this respect, civil society organizations became part of a broader paradigm shift to depoliticize development and reduce it to a technical and technicist process. Civil society organizations became part of the process of diversifying the means for providing public services in addition to the state (if any), and private corporations (the market). They became part of the neoliberal virtuous circle of small government and dynamic private sector and civil society organizations. It is simplistically assumed that civil society organizations always play a positive role in society.

The Gramscian/radical approach to civil society with which this chapter identifies sees civil society and civil society organizations as a crucible for the contestation of power and diverse visions of society that are open-ended. Civil society in this case is a social space, outside the market and the state where people organize, contest and challenge ideological hegemony. In this case, we will find in civil society organizations that are calling for a paradigm shift from the existing hegemonic social order, while there are certain civil associations that are satisfied with the status quo and want to perpetuate what in reality is social violence by the strong against the weak, which manifests itself in numerous forms (Freire 2000). In this respect, we must recognize the term coined by Keane (1998), which he referred to as "uncivil society": a situation where civil society groups organize and mobilize others to promote ideas or vision of a society that excludes other people or denies the full humanity of others. The Gramscian view of civil society acknowledges the existence of civil associations that constitute part of what is called new social movements, which have played a very critical role in challenging and undermining dictatorial and authoritarian regimes in Eastern Europe, Asia, Latin America, the Middle East and Africa. The goal of such social movements is to bring about social transformation, rejuvenate and recreate the human spirit and shared sense of community.

In view of the foregoing analysis, the role of civil society and civil society organizations is an open-ended question, subject to empirical evaluation. Thus, one can only decipher the substantive role played by any civil society organization by critically evaluating the structure and process of the organization's mode of operation within a specific historical context, while embedding that within the intricate connection between the global and the local (Blaney and Pasha 1993). With this general background discussion, it is now appropriate to proceed to examine civil society in contemporary postcolonial African development and societal evolution.

Civil Society in Contemporary Postcolonial African Development

Given the limited space in this chapter, a detailed debate about civil society in Africa cannot be delved into—an issue that has been well-documented by Hutchful (1996). What the chapter intends to do here is to summarize the functions, history, challenges, constraints and opportunities associated with civil society in contemporary Africa. Building on the insights from Blaney and Pasha (1993), the chapter will pursue this agenda by focusing on the structure and process of civil society organizations and do so within their social and historical specificities, while entwining the global and the local. To begin with, Larry Diamond provides the following explanation to account for some of the critical roles played by civil society in Africa:

> Civil society performs many … crucial functions for democratic development and consolidation: limiting the power of the state more generally, and challenging its abuses of authority; monitoring human rights and strengthening the rule of law; monitoring elections and enhancing the overall quality and credibility of the democratic process; educating citizens about their rights and responsibilities, and building a culture of tolerance and civic engagement; incorporating marginal groups into the political process and enhancing the latter's responsiveness to societal interests and needs; providing alternative means, outside the state, for communities to raise their level of material development; opening and pluralizing the flows of information; and building a constituency for economic as well as political reform (Diamond 1997: 24).

Using Diamond's account of what role civil society performs in Africa in idealistic terms, it will be pertinent to later interrogate the role of Pentecostal churches as part of civil society, to see whether they measure up to this expectation or not.

It must be highlighted that given the unique historical trajectory of African and Western countries, the meaning, role and function of civil society in the two regions will not be the same (Hutchful 1996). In precolonial Africa, civil society and civil society organizations did not exist in the strict sense of the term, except for a few instances where there was wide political consultation before decisions were made. This notwithstanding, most leaders in precolonial Africa inherited their positions instead of campaigning for it as we know it in the modern sense (Makumbe 1996: 306–307). Just as African countries were evolving in the late nineteenth and early twentieth centuries, they were colonized by European nations. One unfortunate consequence of European colonization was that the colonial state did not allow civil society to be nurtured among Africans, let alone allow Africans to form civil society associations (Mamdani 1996). The colonial authorities were afraid that granting Africans permission to form civil society organizations would threaten their ability to maintain colonial hegemony. In effect, the colonial state excluded Africans from being active participants in the modern colonial government. In the postwar period, modern educated African elites and urban middle classes organized and formed social movements that challenged the hegemonic and authoritarian mode of governances of the colonial state which excluded Africans (Cooper 2001).

With the success of anti-colonial struggle, and the emergence of modern African elites as the ruling elites in charge of the modern postcolonial state, what has unfortunately happened in terms of civil society organizations is similar to what colonial rulers did and in some cases even worse (Chazan et al. 1999). In the pursuit of national unity and constituting a united front for the pursuit of national development, the postcolonial state elites turned their countries into one-party rule or military dictatorship (Assensoh and Alex-Assensoh 2002). They never allowed civil society associations to flourish unless such associations were either part of the state, subservient or dutifully compliant to the state. In this respect, the naturally presumed idea of civil society associations occupying the social space between the state and the market and outside the family in early postcolonial African societies becomes an empirical question that needs to be problematized. Any civil society group that took the radical positon of critiquing the government or contesting the government's vision of an ideal society, was classified as an enemy of the state with its leaders imprisoned, killed or exiled (Makumbe 1996: 307). What this means is that postcolonial African states in the period immediately after independence demobilized and depoliticized citizens, thereby allowing the government to enjoy a monopoly of power (Schmidt 2005). This reality has had a devastating impact on the accountability of state institutions, and the scrutiny of public policy formulation and implementation, and public expenditure. In some cases, it led to the emergence of insurgent and irredentist social movements, owing to the extreme feeling of alienation or the selective provision of public goods to cater to electoral interests and support of ruling elites, while ignoring the opposition elites and their supporters (Horowitz 2000). This situation did not change until after the collapse of the Berlin Wall in 1989, which led to the revival and rejuvenation of civil society groups in their fight for greater democratization of society (Bratton and van de Walle 1997).

The collapse of the Berlin Wall also led to a new emphasis in the 1990s by the World Bank on good governance, and the neoliberal agenda of decentering the state as an agent of national development by favoring privatization of state enterprises, private corporations and civil society groups to become an alternative method for the delivery of public goods (Todaro and Smith 2015: 569–576). While there is diversity in structure and process, one important point that stands out in terms of the role played by civil society groups in Africa—especially from the early 1990s after the fall of the Berlin Wall—is the fight against racist, tribal, authoritarian, dictatorial and oppressive regimes across Africa with a view to creating a more democratic, accountable state, and a racially and ethnically inclusive society (Makumbe 1996). Some examples along this line include: the struggle that led to the collapse of apartheid in South Africa and the liberation of its black population, and the role that the movement for multiparty democracy played in changing the mode of governance in Zambia (Makumbe 1996: 308–310). Others are the role of civil society groups in supporting Laurent Kabila to overthrow Mobutu Sese Seko of Zaire and the role of a conglomeration of trade unions in using strike action to exert pressure for greater democratization in Congo Brazzaville, Niger, Gabon, Guinea, Cameroon and Mauritania, all in the early 1990s (Makumbe 1996: 308–310).

When one pays attention to the structure, process, substance and goals of civil society groups and associations that flourished in Africa in the period after the collapse of the Berlin Wall and the inauguration of the Washington Consensus agenda, Africa's civil societies can veritably be characterized as crucibles for the contestation of power, class and social and material interests, reflecting the struggles in the larger society. Larry Diamond provides a succinct description and characterization of the substance of civil society associations in contemporary Africa, their processes of operation and visions, which are diverse in contemporary African societies, especially after the collapse of the Berlin Wall:

> The problem is that civil society does not only consist of …. Democracy building groups and functions. It is also an arena of conflict (and often very intense conflict) between organized interests of various kinds – economic, social, and ethnic. And civil society organizations in Africa too often are crippled by the same problems of poverty, corruption, nepotism, parochialism, opportunism, ethnicism, illiberalism, and willingness to be coopted that plague the society in general (Diamond 1997: 24–25).

Diamond's characterization of the substance of civil society associations across Africa highlights the serious challenges and constraints that the continent faces, which warrants the need for serious reflection and consideration if the future is supposed to be informed by an important role for civil society organizations. There are surely great potential opportunities but given its complexity the reality on the ground suggests the need for caution.

By way of summary, here are some weakness and challenges of civil society organizations or groups in contemporary postcolonial Africa as relates to their great potential for contributing to the transformation of African societies. First, the great majority of civil society groups in Africa lack the capacity for self-sustenance. Because they rely on outside financial support that is external to their organizations, this prevents them from becoming as truly autonomous—as one would ideally desire them to be (Makumbe 1996). Second, the great majority of civil society groups rely on direct state funding to survive. This means that they rely on the state as benefactor to create opportunities for them to generate money, without which they cannot function. Consequently, they become glorified appendages of the state (Makumbe 1996). Third, because of the lack of capacity to independently fund themselves, civil society groups in Africa do not have the freedom to independently choose the sphere of society in which they can operate. The state, as their benefactor, decides or channels them to certain spheres that are more affirming of the state than interrogating.

Fourth, a large number of civil society groups in Africa rely on external funding from donors overseas. Given that overseas donors have their own agenda, such civil society groups lose any autonomy that they have by becoming implementers of foreign donor programs and projects (Lewis 2011: 483–488). Fifth, as Diamond highlighted above, some civil society groups in their structure and process of operation are uncivil to the extent that they try to use the state and its resources to marginalize, dehumanize and exclude other social groups by diminishing the meaning of shared citizenship and the rights it confers on people, in addition to their fundamental human rights (Keane 1998). Sixth, a large number of civil society groups in Africa are, as Robert Michels (1962) argues in his theory of the iron law of oligarchy, very authoritarian, unaccountable and undemocratic in terms of the structure and process of their operation. If, in terms of the internal structure of such civil society organizations, there are no ideals of accountability, democracy, inclusiveness and participation of the rank and file, such organizations lack the moral and ethical grounds to be able to call on the state to be transformed in terms of its structure and functioning. In brief, such civil society organizations have nothing exemplary about them and cannot therefore challenge the state with credibility and legitimacy.

Seventh, to worsen the preceding observation, a large number of civil society groups and associations in Africa lack in-depth and sophisticated knowledge of how the machinery of the state functions, or how public policy decisions are made and implemented (Makumbe 1996). Given that for the sake of monopolizing power, the governments of many African countries try to keep tight control of details of public policy formulation and implementation, this makes it exceedingly difficult for civil society groups to use sophisticated knowledge and understanding to interrogate and critique state policy by offering reliable, more viable and efficient alternatives. Eighth, as I alluded to above, the state in many African countries controls the mass media as the main source of information, directly and indirectly. In terms of direct control, state ownership of the mass media is high in Africa and such media outlets simply sing the praises of the ruling elites and the state (Makumbe 1996). While there has been a burgeoning of private media ownership across Africa with increased political and economic liberalization, often the survival of many such media outlets in the marketplace depends on the goodwill of the state. And the state, indeed, does not hesitate to make the survival of any private media outlet untenable if the outlet is perceived as hostile to the state by reporting true but unflattering information about the ruling elites or state institutions.

Ninth, although in some cases people treat private business as part of civil society, often in Africa, such local or indigenous businesses cannot hold the state accountable because their survival is contingent on state projects such as contracts or favors, such as the granting of import licenses (Diamond 1997). Thus, such organizations cannot even donate money or support a civil society group or organization that is, for instance, pushing for reform that is legitimate, legal and desirable but perceived by the ruling elites as a threat to their monopoly of power. Indeed, most such businesses donate to the ruling party in order to ensure a favorable government policy or business climate. Finally, even though there are thriving foreign businesses such as multinational corporations in Africa that are sometimes considered part of civil society by some scholars, such businesses define their interests and roles in Africa narrowly and primarily to make profit without getting involved in the internal affairs of the country in reference (Makumbe 1996: 315–316). Although they support civil society groups and organizations by publicly donating money, it is obvious that they only support state-affirming civil society groups—those that maintain their status quo—whose agenda falls within the purview of the ruling elites, whatever it is.

With the preceding brief overview and critical analysis of the concept of civil society in general and its specific application to contemporary development in postcolonial Africa, the chapter proceeds to examine the role of Pentecostal churches in democratization and development processes in Africa. Doing so is pertinent because Pentecostal churches are an excellent example of civil society organizations and groups with respect to what they can do to contribute immensely to transforming society.

Pentecostalism and the Spread of Democratization in Sub-Saharan Africa: The Empirical Evidence

With regard to the political contribution of the church, there are several questions we can ask that can help us to answer the broader question of their impact on the political institutions and culture, and the civil society of a country. The questions are: how is power exercised within the churches? How accountable is the leadership of the churches to their members? How publicly transparent is the decision-making processes of the churches, especially with regard to the elites? If the churches have constitutions, to what extent do they observe and comply with the documents in their decision-making process? Finally, with regard to the members of the congregations, to what extent do they have equal opportunity to advance their social status?

Research findings indicate that the leaders of Pentecostal churches use committees to make decisions, but that the church leadership from behind the scenes manipulates the leaders of the committees. Sometimes the leaders use patronage to influence key decision-makers in the church, so that they can make favorable decisions. In some respects, there was little difference in the nature and quality of leadership in the church compared to the leadership provided in the wider society. Indeed, sometimes leadership in the church is even more authoritarian, which is just a reflection of the culture around them (e.g., the role of some chiefs in colonial and postcolonial African societies). Church leaders were also found to use the Bible and the Holy Spirit to justify limited or even no discussion at all on important issues affecting the church. These happenings in Pentecostal churches militate against the church being a strong agent for promoting democracy in society (Brouwer et al. 1996; Gifford 1998; Gifford 1995).

Internally, the organizational structure of Pentecostal churches in Africa is very authoritarian, because everything revolves around the "anointed man of God," who has presumably received special grace, and has charisma to lead. It is true that in theory, every member of a Pentecostal church can acquire the charisma from God and use it; but in reality, the charisma that God confers on some members (i.e., degree of anointing), specifically leaders, is supposed to be significantly higher. This then creates a hierarchy that is relatively unaccountable, since it is derived exclusively from God. Indeed, it is considered sinful to think negatively or raise critical questions about the validity of the actions, statements, or decisions made by the "man of God." Gifford describes how a Pentecostal minister in Kampala, Uganda, relates to the members of his congregation:

> It is often claimed that the born-again churches function as schools of democracy, since they are groups of brothers and sisters promoting equality. Many of those we considered were personal fiefdoms, held together by the personal gifts of their leaders. We noted the tendency to authoritarianism – in Uganda one pastor would not even allow members to call him Brother, and insisted on his own views being sacrosanct and unquestioned, unlike those of his followers (Gifford 1998: 344).

Such approach to congregational and denominational administration significantly negates accountability and the cultivation of the social skills of rational dialog, which are integral for the operation of a modern democratic society. The church is as much a social organization as it is a spiritual one. Clearly, decisions or policies in many Pentecostal churches in Africa do not come out of a process of rational democratic dialog such as the type that Jurgen Habermas desires to see in modern civil society (Morrow and Torres 2002). Thus, in many Pentecostal churches, there is no dialog but rather *communiqué* from the minister to the congregation, to use Paulo Freire's description of the nature of communication in anti-dialogical education, which is based on the desire to perpetuate hierarchy. The decisions are made by the "righteous" based on their absolute and exclusive access to truth, owing to the grace of the Holy Spirit. The main conclusion here is that an organization that is internally undemocratic and authoritarian in its decision-making and implementation process cannot promote democracy in the wider society.

The preceding point is eloquently argued by Robert Michels' study of European socialist political parties that claimed to implement egalitarian policies, but were not internally democratic as social organizations (Michels 1962). It may be argued that rational democratic decision-making and implementation does not absolutely guarantee that there will be no failure. The system can indeed be captured by a faction of the ruling elites or interest groups in society. However, if the rational democratic principle is adhered to, it reduces the chances of abuse because of the built-in checks and balances. While it is difficult to easily scrutinize the activities of ruling elites in general, it is indeed extremely difficult to do so with elites in social organizations that are not transparent and who are not compelled to do so by law, as is the case with much of the leadership of Pentecostal churches in Africa. An example of the lack of transparency in the decisions and policies of some Pentecostal churches in Africa is illustrated in Gifford's observation:

> Many of these churches tithe, and with the money collected, they embark on projects of which they can feel a sense of pride and achievement. But sometimes the people have had no say in what their money goes into. They own a project in the sense that it was built with their money; not in the sense that it was chosen and planned and operated by them for their benefit. The church-run bakery we met in Kampala was established with church money, but this effectively became a business of the pastor and his wife, who then employed church members (among others) in distribution. This certainly created jobs that would not have existed otherwise, but was not in any strict sense an activity owned by the church (Gifford 1998: 346).

In examining the observation above, one gets a sense that some of the ministers use the churches as strategy for capital accumulation and social mobility. Money is generated from the lay members of the congregation and is used by the church elite to support themselves. Indeed, there is quite an elaborate body of evidence from Africa and Latin America demonstrating that many Pentecostal churches have a class dimension to their practice of Christianity (Anderson and Hollenweger 1999).

The assertion above is justified because many Pentecostal ministers begin their ministry as entrepreneurs. Gradually, they accumulate wealth by making high financial demands on the members of their congregations and affiliating themselves with powerful and influential people in government as well as Pentecostal congregations in North

America (Brouwer et al. 1996; Gifford 1998; Gifford 1995). Although the money is generated in the name of God and the ministry, the decisions about how it is used and the ownership of the investment are significantly controlled by the leader of the ministry due to the personalistic and autocratic leadership style in the churches.

Furthermore, as members of the church become wealthier or attract relatively well-to-do people, they begin to develop a distinctive bourgeois class lifestyle that marginalizes church members who happen to be less fortunate. Such very successful Pentecostals feel no concern about their ostentatious display of wealth, because they rationalize their behavior as glorifying God for his blessings. In some respects, many successful Pentecostals insulate their sources of income and success from their faith, for without doing so, they would have to ask themselves serious questions about the system they are benefiting from. Simply because the system exists, and they benefit from it does not mean that their behavior is ethical, a fact they readily ignore. Marshall-Fratani documents this situation in one church in Nigeria:

> In 'prosperity' churches, it is most often wealth, which is the miracle designating God's chosen. Pastor Kris Okotie recently bought his wife a 0.8 million naira BMW to complement his own new Mercedes, quoting James 1: 17: 'Every good gift and every perfect gift is from above, and cometh down from the Father of lights' (Marshall-Fratani 1995: 256).

In a poor country like Nigeria, the monetary value of this minister's family automobile asset alone is extravagantly out of proportion with the reality of income distribution in the country. Interestingly, the minister quoted the Bible to rationalize his wealth. All the wealth is generated from the congregation. This portrays Pentecostal ministerial work in Africa as equal to, or more lucrative than being in business.

But beyond ministers like Chris Okotie, who has been described above, there is evidence that class consciousness is emerging among members of Pentecostal churches, who are either uppity or come from upper-middle class backgrounds in the context of Nigeria. Clearly, wealth and social mobility affect the consciousness and commitment of Pentecostals to the original egalitarian vision of their faith. Marshall describes the members of a Pentecostal church in Lagos, Nigeria as follows:

> The Pentecostal revival in its early period of the 1970s developed around a doctrine of radical anti-materialism, extremely purist personal ethics, and a withdrawal not only from dominant forms of popular culture, but an attempt to achieve both institutional and moral autonomy from the state. Yet as the movement expanded, developing stronger international ties, and entering into competition for clients, this localized, retreatist community expanded from its origin among socially dominated groups of the urban poor and youth, becoming more and more associated with leading businessmen, professionals, military men, and politicians. Fellowship breakfasts at the five star Eko Le Meridien Hotel, the inauguration of groups like Christ the Redeemer's Friends Universal, a fellowship organization of the Redeemed Christian Church of God which requires members to have a post-secondary school degree or diploma in order to join, and which publishes a monthly magazine recounting the conversion stories and received miracles of leading businessmen, military officers, politicians and civil servants, all these are part of a conscious strategy among Pentecostal churches to gain access to the "political nation" (Marshall-Fratani 1995: 253–254).

Hollenweger describes a similar situation with a particular Pentecostal church in Guatemala, Central America (Hollenweger 1999). So Pentecostals have not only undermined the traditional value constraints to aggressive wealth accumulation, but also the restraints in how wealth should be consumed. They engage in conspicuous consumption and create organizations that distinguish their lifestyles as an emerging *petit bourgeoisie* from other unfortunate members of the church and society at large. This issue raises the need for critical concern and reflection.

If Pentecostalism fosters the emergence and perpetuation of a *petit bourgeois* class as described above, what are the broad social-cultural consequences of this for society at large, and the mission of the church? First, one of the consequences of this is the uncritical acceptance of neo-liberal capitalism as an economic system with all the human cost that this entails (Mihevc 1995). The human cost of a capitalist system that has run amok is well-documented in advanced industrial and peripheral capitalist societies (Havery 2005). The situation is indeed worst in peripheral capitalist societies. Some negative consequences of the contemporary global capitalist system are: the production of arms and ammunition; laying off millions of workers who become unemployed for the sake of higher corporate profits; the super exploitation of workers in the Third World as a strategy for subsidizing the high cost of production and living in the developed world; and environmental degradation (Hollenweger 1999).

Surely, capitalism can benefit all people if values external to it regulate its excesses, especially in cases of market failure. But Pentecostalism as described above is diluting some of the basic egalitarian and social justice ethics of Christianity (Kelley 1972), instead of using it, among other things, to develop a discourse of social reform for justice, accountability and equity (Hollenweger 1999). Unless Pentecostals begin to ask questions about *economic and market fundamentalism* as a paradigm (Stiglitz 2002) with a view to providing viable alternatives to neoliberal hegemony, they will be co-opted, if this has not already taken place.

The second broader consequence of capitalism, which is absolutely supported by Pentecostalism, is summarized by Hollenweger (1999: 190):

> The competition between the races, the sexes, between the poor and the rich, between people in the Third World—this competition thought to be a blessing of God by Margaret Thatcher has economic root causes and results in people making war with each other. The church is not generally developing alternatives to the capitalist system; the only ones who made a beginning at this were Mennonites and Quakers, who in times past created alternative means of production, democracy in industry and co-ownership of capital and work-force.

Hollenweger is asserting that in trying to honor God and reap His blessings within the capitalist global economy as we know it, Pentecostals have supported a system that makes them wittingly or unwittingly enemies of each other because of competition in the labor market and the global economy. They naively assume that they can create a genuine "Christian community" by simply subsuming their vision within the broad framework of the global capitalist system. Yet, many people who have made no pretension of having the transcendental power that Pentecostals claim they have are assiduously laboring to reform and gradually transform the capitalist system.

Pentecostal Theology and Plural Politics

Pentecostal theology is not just anti-democratic in Africa, but also a threat to the sovereignty and integrity of multi-ethnic or culturally diverse nation-states. This assertion is justified because they perceive their role in politics in a missionary fashion. They want to colonize the state or win the election for Jesus. Claiming to be the righteous in society, they want to "decree" or "command" things to happen because of their being chosen by God. Marshall-Fratani illustrates this claim with a direct citation from a Pentecostal minister's sermon. Here are the words of the minister:

> Everybody must take orders from the commander-in-chief. No arguments, no debates. I told you last time you came, I said God is not a democrat... I want the Pentecostal Fellowship of Nigeria (PFN) to become an invading army. I don't want it to become a social club. I want to see a PFN by the grace of God that when the devil hears "P" he will begin to shake. That cannot happen if we go about it democratically. Because when God has spoken and we say this is the way we shall go, someone will say, let us vote. I can tell you, whenever you go to vote, the majority will vote for the devil (Marshall-Fratani 2009: 201).

One can imagine that if there are several religious groups in a society making claims such as the ones made by the minister in the quotation above, this can be a recipe for sectarian conflict as a result of religious particularism. It is a threat to the integrity of the modern democratic state when a civic association in civil society is not willing to have dialog on equal basis with other legitimate civic associations in order to produce a negotiated solution to public issues. Many Pentecostal churches prefer to decree their will because of their transcendental status as believers, which guarantees them access to absolute truth. Similarly, Pentecostal believers, by trying to colonize the nation-state for Jesus, are manifesting a colonial mindset. They want to colonize the public space, yet their moral values are not necessarily inclusive and universalistic, such that is accommodating of others in the public square of modern African societies. They do not see themselves as one civic association among others in civil society. Rather they perceive themselves as special citizens with a transcendental source of wisdom that warrants them to command and decree things to happen. Clearly, these are not attitudes and social skills that will aid the effective functioning of a modern democratic society that is inclusive of diverse people.

In a sense, one can argue that the Pentecostal movement is engaged in nation-building because it is creating a new identity, and a community that transcends the narrow tribal/ethnic identity. That this is happening is an indication of the failure of the postcolonial state's project of nation-building. Its failure has created room for an alternative project spearheaded by the religious groups (Juergensmeyer 2008). It is indeed a progressive move on the part of the Pentecostal movement, especially when one visits major African cities and notices how a new "brotherhood" and "sisterhood" identity is created among people who would hitherto hate or avoid each other. The problem, however, is that this new nation is a moral community of the righteous. It is so confident of its vision that it can subordinate or even oppress people outside its defined moral community, especially if the group constitutes a threat to the realization of the Christian moral agenda as defined by Pentecostal believers. Their cognitive understanding of the world is Manichean, since it assumes that people are divided into two camps: good and evil. This may be difficult to sustain in a modern industrial and democratic society, where social-cultural diversity is cultivated. In view of this, one can conclude that the Pentecostal movement is further complicating the extremely difficult task of postcolonial nation-building in Africa's plural societies.

One way this complication takes shape is the retardation of Africa's political development in situations that Susan Rose describes as "Christocentric Exclusionism" (Brouwe et al. 1996). Christocentric exclusionism is particularly serious in countries where the Christian and Muslim populations are sizable. In such a multi-religious society, moderation, tolerance and accommodation are necessary for the sake of peaceful coexistence. But in countries such as Nigeria, Pentecostals in the name of glorifying God make many public statements that show no respect or recognition of Islam as another faith. They portray Islam as "Satan's empire" and Muslims as agents of Satan. Surely Muslims, or any group of believers for that matter, are not going to find such comments complimentary. Yet the quote below, which extracts some sentences from a book used by Pentecostals to educate their members about Islam, suggests the belligerent approach to the "Other" by Pentecostals. Brouwer et al. describe G. Moshay's argument in his book titled *Who is this Allah?* Brouwer et al. notes:

> The devil is holding all Islamic countries 'in bondage of false religion and demonic influence,' he declares, and goes so far as to suggest that the evil spirit inspiring Mohammed was the same spirit that inspired Hitler. Published in July 1990, the book needed a second edition within four months (Brouwer et al. 1996: 174).

These statements, which suggest the reality of religious particularism, remind one of the wars that were fought in Europe because of religious intolerance during the reformation era (Thompson 1999). Can the extremely complex modern democratic society exist without tolerance? I doubt it.

Similarly, some Pentecostal churches and ministers affect Africa's process of institutionalizing the modern state. In the area of politics, Pentecostals often end up supporting corrupt political regimes that are suppressing citizens and denying them human rights. This takes place because of their over-spiritualization of issues, as well as the logical implications of being a "single issue" citizen (this refers to citizens who choose one issue and assign it pre-eminent importance, using it as the single criterion to evaluate a president or government of a country). For example, in light of apocalyptic and theological reasons, Pentecostals in most countries see evangelizing people as the main responsibility of an existing Christian. Consequently, even if a government is repressive and corrupt, in so far as it allows evangelism, it is considered to be legitimate, and Pentecostal leaders are willing to ignore all other things the leader does, such as human rights violation. For instance, in Kenya, when Moi visited the Gospel Redeemed Church, instead of the minister keeping focus on genuine teaching, he decided to assert the following in front of the congregation and in the presence of the president and journalists:

> In heaven it is just like Kenya has been for many years. There is only one party – and God never makes a mistake. President Moi has been appointed by God to lead the country and Kenyans should be grateful for the peace prevailing... We have freedom of worship; we can pray and sing in any way we want. What else do we need? That's all we need (Brouwer et al. 1996: 176).

The preceding statement does not only demonstrate a myopic and sycophantic situation, but also the lack of courage on the part of the Pentecostal minister to tell the truth about those in power. It demonstrates the way many Pentecostals in Africa have lost their original vision. How can ministers turn to be sycophants? This suggests either that they read the Bible uncritically or they were seeking accommodation at the corridors of power.

Conflict resolution is yet another type of involvement in public affairs by African Pentecostals. In theory, Pentecostals as Christians are supposed to be peace-loving people. But because of the simplistic way they interpret the Bible in many parts of Africa (i.e., simply based on the hermeneutic of faith), they arrive at a conclusion that is not just naive but also counter-productive to lasting peace at both the national and international levels. At the national level, their desire to be politically relevant results in them supporting oppressive and dictatorial regimes. They do so by either serving as goodwill ambassadors of human rights-violating regimes (e.g., Bishop Idahosa of Nigeria) (Gifford 1998), or serve as high-ranking public officials (e.g., in Zambia) (Freston 2001; Gifford 1998). Since they are not primarily concerned about institutional or structural changes, they focus primarily on spiritual issues and questions of direct influence on the government. Furthermore, Pentecostal Christians do not seem to have a coherent voice, vision or agenda with regard to the social transformation of society. Consequently, they end up being part of the problem rather than the solution. Presumably, based on their teachings, socio-historical and institutional analysis is irrelevant if one desires to spiritually transform a society.

Similarly, the narrow emphasis on teaching forgiveness as the basis for peace in historically conflict-ridden social relations (especially among ethnic groups) makes Pentecostal ministers come across as somewhat naïve (Christianitytoday.com 2004). This assertion is not meant to dispute or deny the importance of forgiveness in personal, national, or international relations, as was the case in South Africa's "Truth and Reconciliation Commission." Neither is it aimed at belittling the role of one's spiritual beliefs in shaping how they pursue justice. Rather, it is important that one is concerned about the need to balance spiritual reconciliation processes with rigorous analysis of the socio-historical and institutional conditions underpinning conflict, and the need to deal with it in a manner that lays the foundation for lasting peace. The idea that one can solve the historically vexed problem of community relations in Rwanda, for example, by having neighbors who killed each other's relatives simply forgive each other while failing to address the underlying historical and social conditions responsible for the massacre in the first place, is somewhat naïve, even though surely an act in good faith. One cannot see how the faith approach can be fundamentally contradicted by a systematic socio-historical analysis of institutions and social processes.

Conflict resolution by Pentecostals in Africa is also typically exemplified by their eschatological interpretation of the conflict between Israel and Palestine. Indeed, examining this eschatology helps us to understand not only their attitude toward conflict, but also how the international relations with Israel constitute a kind of discourse accounting for the continued underdevelopment of Africa. With reference to the situation in Zambia, Corten asserts:

> The Evangelical Fellowship of Zambia issued a press release on 7 February 1991 stating: 'The Bible is clear that God will bless those that bless Israel.' This may imply that those who oppose Israel can only expect the wrath of God. Some of the present difficulties experienced in our country can be attributed to a direct result of rejecting Israel… Christians shall only vote for a party whose foreign policy would strive to promote Zambia's relations with the international community …This shall include a diplomatic relationship with Israel above all… Zambia has cursed Israel in both word and attitude and we are still reaping the curse on our nation. God's word is final. By being against Israel we are standing up against God and his will … No wonder we lack progress (Gifford 2001: 76).

The citation above suggests how, based on their simplistic and uncritical reading of the Bible, African Pentecostal believers are willing to escalate conflict in so far as it is *biblically justified* to do so. This assertion is based on their unconditional support for Israel. Similarly, it is important to note how the ministers are willing to account for Zambia's or Africa's economic woes. African nations, they argue, are experiencing national and continental curse as a punishment from God because the nations have either cursed Israel or refused to maintain diplomatic relations with the country. It should be evident that because the Palestinians are human beings like the Jews of Israel, we should devote our attention to creating a broad-based peace plan that can ensure both groups live in peace with each other and prosper. The Pentecostal solution here fails to fully acknowledge Palestinians as human beings created in the image of God as stated in the Bible used by Pentecostals, and therefore deserving to be treated with respect and dignity. There is indeed a subtle presumption that the God of the Bible is not the God of the Palestinians actually, to the extent that even if it is initially conceded that He created them in His image like other people, He appears to have abandoned them. This suggests the need for the Palestinians to look for their own God or another God, who cares for them as human beings with dignity.

Civil Society Discourses in the Context of Pentecostal Christianity, Development and Democratization in Africa

In this section, the chapter intends to draw on certain themes, ideas and insights from the discourse on civil society to interrogate the role of Pentecostal Christianity in the development and democratization process in Africa, even while noting that there are varieties of Pentecostal experiences on the continent and in the world at large. First, when one situates the role of African Pentecostal churches within the broad debate about approaches to civil society and discourses, African Pentecostals emerge as not having a systematic and coherent vision for transforming the existing social structure and social order of African societies. They are rather satisfied with operating within the status quo but emerging spectacularly victorious out of it through the miraculous power and anointing of the Holy Ghost in their lives, while leaving the remaining African population to languish in misery because they lack spiritual anointing. The point being made here is relevant because it is impossible to think of Pentecostal churches or any civil society organization contributing seriously to transforming Africa for the better without fundamentally addressing the social structural causes of Africa's social maladies and problems. Indeed, Pentecostal Christianity in this case fails to measure up to both the liberal and Gramscian/radical ideal for civil society organizations as discussed earlier in the chapter.

Second, in order for civil society associations and organizations to contribute to the process of democratization and development, they need to operate outside the state and be autonomous. They cannot succeed in this mission if they are co-opted by the state. Yet the empirical evidence demonstrates how Pentecostal churches as part of civil society are more likely to affirm the state or seek recognition and affirmation from the state. This is in addition to the concern that many Pentecostal churches get their sources of revenue strengthened when corrupt members of the African middle class and ruling elites who embezzle public funds donate it to the church in order to earn recognition, legitimacy, and blessing from the anointed minister and members of their congregation (Winsor 2015). This surely makes the church part of the problem of Africa's struggle for development and democratization. Indeed there is, in some cases, evidence that some Pentecostal ministers collected money from corrupt leaders by promising to help the leaders win reelection (Sahara Reporters, 2016). Overall, the desire of many leaders of Pentecostal denominations to seek approval, affirmation and romance with the ruling elites suggests a naiveté on an issue that Abu Hamid Muhammad Al-Ghazali considered dangerous and worthy of issuing a warning in the medieval period. In regard to the relationship between ruling elites or princes and the clergy, Al-Ghazali warned as follows:

> Know that you can have three sorts of relations with princes, governors, and oppressors. The first and worst is that you visit them, the second and better is that they visit you, and the third and surest that you stay far from them, so that neither you see them nor they see you (cited in Emerson et al. 2011: 121).

Al-Ghazali provided this theological counsel based on empirical observation because he recognizes the potential of the clergy to lose their focus and autonomy to declare the truth at any historical moment without fear or favor because of the corrupting influence of being close to those at the corridors of power. His counsel resonates with the documented literature in Africa among Pentecostal ministers and denominations. Indeed, it is applicable even to the experience of the Religious Right in the United as documented by Martin (1996: 221–238).

Third, some Pentecostal ministers and churches in Africa can aptly be characterized as contributing to what Keane (1998) calls "uncivil civil society." They do so by promoting a discourse of exclusionary citizenship that is, Christocentric exclusionism. In this case, citizenship is not defined in terms of what the secular constitution of the country says, but rather, the criteria of Pentecostal Christian righteousness. In this case, anyone who is not a born-again Christian with baptism from the Holy Ghost is considered not to be part of the chosen ones and therefore a second-class citizen in a strict theological and therefore, social sense. Surely although this way of thinking provides a high sense of meaning, bonding and cohesion within the church group, if all social groups in a plural society behave that way, society would not function smoothly and peacefully. Given the religiously plural nature of many African societies with precarious peace, the fact that such discourses are publicly discussed can generate resentment and counter discourses among other religious groups leading to greater social alienation and conflict in society. This does not help in the creation of an inclusive civil society. In this case, as Larry Diamond asserted above, African civil society associations may be part of the problem even as they have the great potential to transform Africa for the better, by making it a more inclusive plural continent owing to the great variety of resources they can mobilize, assuming they become a social movement (Emerson et al. 2011: 106).

Fourth, given the brief literature reviewed on civil society organizations in Africa, Pentecostal churches and Christianity can be constructively critiqued for not demonstrating internally within their organizational structures and processes, good and exemplary ideals of participatory democracy, accountability, the struggle for social justice, and the promotion of rational civil discourse. In addition to that, in spite of their upwardly mobile members, many of their leaders and members lack an in-depth knowledge and understanding of how modern government and political systems work. And without such knowledge and sophisticated understanding of governance, and the subtle but persistent corrupting influence of power even among the clergy, they cannot provide a coherent critique of the state by producing well-informed and viable alternative solutions to problems and maladies of development in a democratic social order. If there are internal problems with accountability and social responsibility within the leadership of the church, they then lack the moral ground to reprimand the state on such problems. One would expect religious organizations that want to transform society to constitute a role model for what is accountable, socially responsible and constitute just governance. It is, however, unfortunate that Bishop Oyedepo in Nigeria slapped one of his congregants in front of his huge congregation and condemned her to hell (YouTube 2011). Another Pentecostal minister prayed publicly for the death of a public official whose public policy decision he disagreed with (Lindaikeji 2016). Surely there is nothing socially responsible about such acts even when committed by Pentecostal ministers who claim the guidance of the Holy Spirit, twenty-fours per day, 365 days of the year.

Finally, Pentecostal churches and Christianity play an ambivalent role with regard to direct effort to increase or improve the institutional capacity of African countries for the delivery of public goods. I characterize the role as ambivalent because in many respects, many leaders of Pentecostal churches are more concerned about building their religious and spiritual empire to out-compete their opponents in the competitive religious marketplace, than helping to build the common good in their societies. Yet it cannot be denied that Pentecostal denominations across Africa have invested heavily and commendably in building modern educational institutions from elementary schools to universities. Some of their universities are highly ranked in Africa, and considered better managed than state universities (e.g., Covenant University in Nigeria).

Unfortunately, access to the kind of public education they provide from elementary school to university is too expensive, to the point where many ordinary citizens and members of the denomination become outpriced. If one of the goals of civil society organizations is to improve the quality and delivery of public services, then Pentecostal churches and denominations may be woefully failing by contributing to the socially undesirable phenomenon of widening the chasm between the haves and have-nots. The inequality and lack of fair access to public goods and services is already high and a major source of social exclusion across Africa. What we need is innovation in the area of better, more efficient, fairer and more equitable distribution or access to such public goods that empower ordinary people. Ironically, many Christian educational institutions such as those created by Pentecostal denominations are too expensive for ordinary citizens, including the members of the denomination. Interestingly, this is happening in cases where ordinary members of congregations have extensively contributed money to build the university, secondary or elementary school. Even though the denominations offer some scholarships and tuition discounts to some members, such scholarships and discounts do not change the material fact that the cost of such an education is extremely expensive and inaccessible to many ordinary Nigerian families who are members of the denominations. If schools established by Christian organizations confront in a bigger way the problems that exist in public universities across Africa, then what difference are they making when they are just like any other organization? Are they not supposed to be role models?

To conclude this section, one would say that given their widespread influence in Africa Pentecostal churches are well positioned to use their social capital and other types of resources to contribute to the increased democratization and development of African institutions and societies. But what comes out of this depends on several mediating factors, processes and variables such as: what the leaders' values, aspirations, social and material interests are, and what they decide to do with them (Emerson et al. 2011: 109).

In this respect, one must note the lack of depth of theological thinking and reflection, especially with regard to how Pentecostal Christians can live out their faith within the context of a modern, rational world that is increasingly colonizing different spheres of public life (Ritzer 2014). That we are living in a modern-rational world dominated by instrumental rationality is an incontrovertible fact. The question of how one balances a faith orientation that sees miracle as an important component of a strategy to transform society and the world for the better, with a modern-rational tradition that is predominantly oriented toward the pursuit of efficiency, predictability, control and calculability as its overarching goals, is not an easy or enviable task for anyone who cares to explore this issue carefully. Max Weber, who has reflected deeply on this dilemma, had this to say about his fear for a world that is becoming increasingly dominated by instrumental rationality:

> Imagine the consequences of that comprehensive bureaucratization and rationalization which already today we see approaching. Already now … in all economic enterprises run on modern lines, rational calculation is manifest at every stage. By it, the performance of each individual worker is mathematically measured, each man becomes a little cog in the machine and, aware of this, his one preoccupation is whether he can become a bigger cog. … It is apparent that today we are proceeding towards an evolution which resembles [the ancient kingdom of Egypt] in every detail, except that it is built on other foundations, on technically more prefect, more rationalized and therefore much more mechanized foundation. The problem which besets us now is not: how can this evolution be changed? – for that is impossible, but: what will come of it? (cited in Coser 1977: 231–232).

The fear that Weber expresses is exactly one important challenge that confronts Pentecostal religious leaders and denominations in the twenty-first century with increased globalization and the spread of the use of information technology and business practices in many Pentecostal churches in pursuit of efficiency, predictability and calculability. This concern is accentuated by the fact that regions of the world that are least religious (e.g., Scandinavian countries) are ranked highest in the world in terms of human development compared to the most religious societies which are among the most unequal in the world (Grant 2011). Moreover, many countries in East Asia that are not Christian have made more progress in human development than African countries experiencing great Pentecostal and Islamic revival (World Bank 1993). One might ask: did the Chinese phenomenal success in economic development and drastic reduction of poverty, which drew positive international acknowledgment rely on religious revival? These are surely empirical questions that can create a sense of uneasiness among persons of faith, but they are legitimate questions given the issues at hand in the literature.

In the concluding part of this chapter, some preliminary insights on the divergent trajectories between Pentecostal and Islamic revival in Africa are highlighted.

Divergent Trajectories Between Pentecostal and Islamic Revival in Africa: Some Concluding and Critical Observations

Some commentators and observers always highlight the fact that even though both Christianity and Islam are experiencing revival, what is happening in the name of the two religions is a great contrast and a matter of concern (Jenkins 2009). Across Africa, but especially in the eastern, western and northern regions, sectarian groups that identify themselves as Muslims are using violence to spread their brand of religion, achieve supremacy and create a theocracy. On the other hand, Pentecostal Christianity, which is the most dynamic and successful in terms of evangelical outreach and conversion uses relatively peaceful methods to expand its influence. What then accounts for the difference?

For anyone familiar with the sociological study of religion and how fundamentalism manifests itself, this is a very broad and complex issue that is beyond the scope of this chapter because it is not the main purpose here. Moreover, fundamentalism in the West is different in substantive terms from fundamentalism in other regions of the world (Davie 2013: 185–206). But I will highlight in general some reasons that based on the literature can help us begin to ruminate on the differences. To begin with, both Islam and Christianity at some point and as religions that make exclusive claims have been involved in the use of force and violence to either spread their faith, justifying the domination of one group by others, or assert the superiority of their God over other Gods (Jenkins 2002; Trible 1984). Jenkins made an eloquent case in support of the fact that in both the Holy Quran and Holy Bible, there are verses that can be used to justify violence against the "other" and in some cases commit what in today's language would be considered "genocide." Trible, using the term "texts of terror" documents what, from a feminist perspective, is gender violence in the Bible. Given this, the serious questions to ask are: who are the people at the helm of affairs of the religion? What are their human interests and how do such interests affect their interpretation of the scriptures? What is their socio-cultural and historical context? In this respect, we can partially account for what is happening in Africa with the two religions by examining the pathway through which the two faiths' traditions came to settle on the continent and the content of the teaching at that time, and how it is interpreted in the current socio-historical specificities of the religious tradition today (Azumah 2001). But before doing that it is important to make this observation:

> The groundbreaking work, *Terror in the Mind of God* by Mark Juergensmeyer (2003) provides a sociologically rich perspective for understanding the links between fundamentalism and terrorism and violence. First, not all religious based violence is carried out by fundamentalists. Sometimes, in fact, religion is used as a justification for violence by people and groups without specific religious ties. Second, not all fundamentalist groups are violent. In fact, most are not. Even though there are many fundamentalist people and groups in the United States, for example, there has been less violence here than, say, in many nations of the Middle East. And when fundamentalist-based violence has occurred in the United States, it is often the work of an individual operating alone, without the organized support of a religious group (Emerson et al. 2011: 92).

Juergensmeyer's analysis clearly underscores the complexity of this topic which defies simple or straightforward conclusion. That said, Islam came to Africa through the Arabs in North Africa and the Middle East (Azumah 2001). In contrast, Europe and North America are the pathways through which present day Christianity came to many parts of Africa. It must be observed, however, that Europe and North Africa have gone through momentous transformations that include the scientific revolution, the Enlightenment, Liberalism and the secularizing effect of modern science, technology and capitalism, which necessitated the cultivation of pluralism as a survival strategy in a complex culture and society (Kagan et al. 1999: 396–418). The greatest source of inspiration for the Pentecostal movement in Africa comes from the Bible belt in the southern region of the United States (Mawell 2007). While there are surely conservative and even fundamentalist religious groups in the United States, because of the social and historical context and institutional structure of the state, even such movements opt for changing society through the existing institutional structures and provisions (Martin 2001). If they cannot, they often withdraw from mainstream culture and society that they consider secular and morally corrupt by creating cultural enclaves (Kraybill and Hurd 2006). Should they decide to engage in the use of violence to spread their faith or elevate its status in the society, the strong and efficient institutional capacity of the state, combined with a broad consensus among the citizens that violence is not a viable political option in the long run for any healthy and prosperous society, make it difficult for such violent sectarian groups to thrive and flourish (Rosewood and Walker 2015). They are therefore quickly isolated and brought under control.

Indeed, many of the Pentecostal denominations in the United States promote ideals of material success as an indicator of the validity of one's Christian faithfulness. But such an indicator encourages believers to embrace the material culture of modern capitalism and inspire themselves to succeed in it by being methodical within the existing social structure. In effect, there is a relative synthesis and overlap between the ideals of neoliberal capitalism and the measure of success in life in the Pentecostal tradition. Such Christians do not raise fundamental questions about the unjust structure of society or the unequal social order. This mode of religious revival and engagement is the type that is exported to Africa through Pentecostalism from the Bible belt in the United States (Brower, Gifford and Rose, 1996). It desires to achieve a better and prosperous life within the broad structure of existing society. The movement is less interested in social structural transformation of society; it is more about thriving and flourishing in spite of it. At worse, they verbally demonize persons who disagree with their beliefs but stop short of engaging in violent conflict with them. They therefore see themselves as winners or people having great expectations and hope about the future, which is an important stabilizing social force in society.

On the other hand, the groups that identify themselves with Islam and the use of violence in Africa are inspired, mentored and nurtured by some religious leaders and groups in North Africa and the Middle East regions (Azumah 2001; Larkin and Meyer 2006: 286–312). The groups within these regions that promote violence are in their cultural worldview, in many respects, not only traditional, but premodern in their vision of social order in a plural and complex society—an issue that Western societies tried to address long ago, even if imperfectly (Kagan et al. 1999: 396–418). The cultures of those groups in the regions that inspire Muslims in Africa to be violent have not gone through the socio-cultural, institutional and attitudinal transformation that accompanies modernity for whatever it is. They are thus exporting ideas that inspire and encourage violence in a plural society where even within the same religion, people have diverse expressions of faith and interpretation of scriptures (Bender 1999: 160–176). The kind of scrutiny that fundamentalist Christian interpretation and reading of the Bible has gone through in the West because of the scientific revolution, Enlightenment, secularization and the instrumental rationality of free market capitalism did not happen to sectarian Islamic traditions in North Africa and the Middle East (Bender 1999: 160–176).

This of course means that such groups are living in the twenty-first century with a medieval mindset. This situation is further accentuated by the fact that such violent Islamic groups often represent or come from regions that have experienced prolonged and steady exclusion from mainstream society (whatever it is) and inclusive development. They have been alienated and feel irrelevant in the scheme of things. They resent the prosperity and dominance of the West which to them is symbolized by Christianity and its adherents in Africa. Under such a great sense of loss of respect and dignity, it is easy for an articulate and charismatic leader with a violent agenda to persuade such people to hide under the canopy of religion to use violence in order to pursue their social and material interests, given their specific social and historical context. Of course such context has rendered them to be surplus people in the sense that they are irrelevant to the calculus of neoliberal globalization.

With no sense of hope and self-efficacy about a pathway out of their situation and about the future, death means nothing or is even a meaningful path, because they have nothing to lose but may earn respect and a new identity. At least their violent approach to religion makes them recognized as relevant and active players in the global political economy, as indicated by the attention they receive from influential international media outlets. Violence gives them recognition and a voice that they desired to acquire through conventional and legitimate ways but were denied (Siegel 2015: 299–314). Violence gives them relatively easy power over other people, which would otherwise be difficult to achieve. It also gives them relatively easy access to other people's material resources with a sense of moral exoneration to violate other people's human rights and get away with it because they use instruments of violence that others do not have. Unfortunately, often the state lacks the institutional capacity to effectively uproot them (Bates 2008). On the surface, such violence is religious fundamentalism but at its core it is a reaction against a sense of social alienation and hopelessness in a society that has rendered them to be surplus people and irrelevant (Siegel 2015: 299–314). Religion is just used as the easiest and available mechanism to justify and rationalize their anger and frustration.

In this respect, the difference between Pentecostal expansion and the violent brand of Islamic revival in Africa has to do more with the genealogy and evolution of the religious traditions, and their specific social and historical contexts. Many Pentecostal believers rush to church for the purpose of getting their terrible predicament and sense of alienation solved. Whether the predicament and sense of alienation are solved or not is not the key issue here, but rather, the ability of their faith to give them a sense of hope, self-efficacy and stability in life within their social context, thereby dissuading them from using violence. These are the key mediating processes and variables that help explain the differences. In this respect, there is some truth to Karl Marx's idea of religion playing the role of "opium to the masses". Marx's limitation is that he saw this only as the possible function of a religion. But religion is far more complex than playing such a stabilizing role, even in an unjust situation.

References

Anderson, Allan H., and Walter J. Hollenweger (eds.). 1999. *Pentecostalism After a Century: Global Perspectives on a Movement in Transition*. Sheffield, UK: Sheffield Academic Press.

Assensoh, A.B., and Alex-Assensoh Yvette. 2002. *African Military History and Politics: Ideological Coups and Incursions, 1900-Present*. New York: Palgrave Macmillan.

Azumah, John A. 2001. *The Legacy of Arab-Islam in Africa*. Oxford: Oneworld Publications.

Bates, Robert. H. 2008. *When Things Fell Apart: State Failure in Late-Century Africa*. Cambridge: Cambridge University Press.

Bender, David L. 1999. *The Spread of Islam*. San Diego, California: Greenhaven Press.

Blaney, D., and Pasha, M. 1993. "Civil Society and Democracy in the Third World: Ambiguities and Historical Possibilities." *Studies in Comparative International Development* 28 (1): 3–24.

Bratton, Michael and Van de Walle, Nicolas. 1997. *Democratic Experiments in Africa: Regime Transitions in Comparative Perspective*. Cambridge: Cambridge University Press.

Brouwer, Steve, Paul Gifford, and Susan D. Rose (eds.). 1996. *Exploring the American Gospel: Global Christian Fundamentalism*. New York: Routledge.

Chazan, Naomi, Peter Lewis, Robert Mortimer, Donald Rothchild, and Stephen John Stedman (eds.). 1999. *Politics and Society in Contemporary Africa*. Boulder, Colorado: Lynne Rienner Publishers.

Christiantoday.com, World Edition. 2004. *"Rwanda's Evangelical Churches Bring Revival to the Nation*."http://www.christiantoday.com/article/rwandas.evangelical.churches.bring.revival.to.the.nation/704.htm. April 26. Accessed on 2 April 2016.

Cooper, Frederick. 2001. *Africa since 1940: The Past of the Present*. Cambridge: Cambridge University Press.

Coser, Lewis. 1977. *Masters of Sociological Thought: Ideas in Historical and Social Context*. New York: Harcourt Brace Jovanovich.

Davie, Grace. 2013. *The Sociology of Religion: A Critical Agenda*, 2nd ed. Los Angeles: Sage Publications.

De Tocqueville, Alexis. 1969. *Democracy in America*, trans. George Lawrence and ed. J.P. Mayer, 512–517. New York: Harper Perennial Modern Classics.

Diamond, Larry. 1997. Prospects for Democratic Development in Africa. Paper presented to the University of Zimbabwe, Department of Political and Administrative Studies, Democratic Governance Project, March 1997, Harare, Zimbabwe.

Emerson, Michael O., William A. Mirola, and Susanne Monaha (eds.). 2011. *Religion Matters: What Sociology Teaches Us About Religion in Our World*. New York: Allyn & Bacon.

Freire, Paulo. 2000. *Pedagogy of the Oppressed*. New York: Bloomsbury Academic.

Freston, Paul. 2001. *Evangelicals and Politics in Africa, Asia and Latin America*. New York: Cambridge University Press.

Friedman, M. 1962. *Capitalism and Freedom*. Chicago: University of Chicago Press.

Gifford, Paul (ed.). 1995. *The Christian Churches and the Democratization of Africa*. New York: E. J. Brill.

Gifford, Paul. 1998. *African Christianity: Its Public Role*. Bloomington and Indianapolis: Indiana University Press.

Gifford, Paul. 2001. "The Complex Provenance of Some Elements of African Pentecostal Theology." In *Between Babel and Pentecost: Transnational Pentecostalism in Africa and Latin America*, eds. Andre Corten and Ruth Marshall-Fratani, 62–79. Bloomington: Indiana University Press.

Grant, Tobin. 2011. "Religion and Inequality Go Hand-in-Hand: Why Some Countries Are More Religious than Others" *Christianity Today* http://www.christianitytoday.com/ct/2011/septemberweb-only/religioninequality.html. Accessed on 2 April 2016.

Harvey, David. 2005. *A Brief History of Neoliberalism*. New York: Oxford University Press.

Hollenweger, Walter. 1999. "Critical Issues for Pentecostals." In P*entecostals After a Century: Global Perspectives on a Movement in Transition*, eds. Allan H. Anderson and Walter J Hollenweger, Sheffield: Sheffield Academic Press.

Horowitz, Donald. 2000. *Ethnic Groups in Conflict*. Berkeley: University of California Press.

Hutchful, Eboe. 1996. "The Civil Society Debate in Africa." *International Journal* 51 (1): 54–77.

Jenkins, Phillip. 2002. *The Next Christendom: The Coming of Global Christianity*. New York: Oxford University Press.

Jenkins, R. 2001. "Mistaking 'Governance' for 'Politics': Foreign Aid, Democracy and the Construction of Civil Society." In *Civil Society: History and Possibilities,* eds. S. Kaviraj, and S. Khilnani, 250–268. Cambridge: Cambridge University Press.

Juergensmeyer, Mark. 2003. *Terror in the Mind of God: The Global Rise of Religious Violence*. Los Angeles: University of California Press.

Juergensmeyer, Mark. 2008. *Global Rebellion : Religious Challenges to the Secular State, from Christian Militias to Al Qaeda*. Berkeley: University of California Press.

Kagan, D., S. Ozment, and F.M. Turner. 1999. *The Western Heritage: Vol 11: Since 1648*, 2nd ed. Upper Saddle River, New Jersey: Prentice Hall.

Kainji, N., C. Brag, and W. Mitullah. 2002. *Promoting Land Rights in Mozambique and Kenya: How Do NGOs Make a Difference*? London: Department for International Development.

Keane, J. 1998. *Civil Society: Old Images, New Visions*. Cambridge: Polity.

Kelley, Page H. 1972. *Amos: Prophet of Social Justice*. Grand Rapids, Michigan: Baker Book House.

Kraybill, Donald B., and James P. Hurd. 2006. *Horse-And-Buggy Mennonites: Hoofbeats of Humility in a Postmodern World*. University Park, PA: Pennsylvania State University Press.

Larkin, Brian, and Bright Meyer. 2006. "Pentecostalism, Islam & Culture: New Religious Movements in West Africa." In *Themes in West Africa's History*, ed. Emmanuel Kwaku Akyeampong, 286–313. Athens: Ohio State University.

Lewis, David. 2011. "Civil Society." In *The Encyclopedia of International Development*, ed. Tim Forsyth, 78–81. New York: Routledge.

Lewis, David. 2011. "Non-Governmental Organizations." In *The Encyclopedia of International Development*, ed. Tim Forsyth, 483–488. New York: Routledge.

Lindaikeji. 2016. "Kaduna Religious Bill: Pastor Suleiman Refers to El Rufa'i as Herod, Says He Will Die." http://www.lindaikejisblog.com/2016/03/kaduna-religious-bill-pastor-suleiman.html. Accessed on 2 April 2016.

Makumbe, John M.W. 1996. "Is There a Civil Society in Africa?" *International Affairs* 74 (2): 305–317.

Mamdani, M. 1996. *Citizen and Subject: Contemporary Africa and the Legacy of Late Colonialism*. Princeton: Princeton University Press.

Marshall-Fratani, Ruth. 1995. "God is Not a Democrat: Pentecostalism and Democratization in Nigeria." In *The Christian Churches and Democratization of Africa*, ed. Paul Gifford, 239–260. New York: E.J. Brill.

Marshall-Fratani, Ruth. 2009. *Political Spiritualties: The Pentecostal Revolution in Nigeria*. Chicago: The University of Chicago Press.

Martin, David. 2001. *Pentecostalism: The World Their Parish*. Blackwell Publishing.

Martin, William. 1996. *With God on Our Side: The Rise of the Religious Right in America*. New York: Broadway Books.

Maxwell, David. 2007. *African Gifts of the Spirit: Pentecostalism and the Rise of a Zimbabwean Transnational Religious Movement*. Athens, Ohio: Ohio University Press.

Michels, Robert. 1962. *Political Parties: A Sociological Study of Oligarchical Tendencies of Modern Democracy*. New York: The Free Press.

Mihevc, John. 1995. *The Market Tells Them So: The World Bank and Economic Fundamentalism in Africa*. London: Zed Books.

Morrow, Raymond A., and Carlos Alberto Torres. 2002. *Reading Freire and Habermas: Critical Pedagogy and Transformative Change*. New York: Columbia University, Teachers College Press.

Putnam, Robert. 1993. *Making Democracy Work*. Princeton, NJ: Princeton University Press.

Putnam, Robert. 2000. *Bowling Alone*. New York: Simon and Schuster.

Quadir, Fahim. 2011. "Governance." In *The Encyclopedia of International Development*, ed. Tim Forsyth, 139–156. New York: Routledge.

Ritzer, George. 2014. *The McDonaldization of Society*, 8th ed. Thousand Oaks, California: Sage Publications.

Rosewood, Jack, and Dwayne Walker. 2015. *The Waco Siege: An American Tragedy*. CreateSpace Independent Publishing Platform: Amazon.com

Schmidt, Elizabeth. 2005. *Mobilizing the Masses: Gender, Ethnicity, and Class in the Nationalist Movement in Guinea, 1939–1958*. Portsmouth, NH: Heinemann.

Siegel, Larry. 2015. *Criminology: The Core*. Stamford, CT: Cengage Learning.

Stiglitz, Joseph E. 2002. *Globalization and its Discontents*. New York: W.W. Norton.

Stiglitz, Joseph E. 2007. *Making Globalization Work*. New York: W.W. Norton.

Thompson, Stephen P., (ed.). 1999. *The Reformation*. San Diego, California: Greenhaven Press, Inc.

Todaro, Michael P., and Stephen Smith. 2015. *Economic Development*, 12th ed. Boston: Pearson.

Trible, Phyllis. 1984. *Texts of Terror: Literary-Feminist Readings of Biblical Narratives*. Minneapolis: Fortress Press.

Winsor, Morgan. 2015. "Nigeria Corruption Caused By Christian Churches? Pastor Sunday Adelaja Blames Religious Leaders For Immoral Values." *International Business Times* http://www.ibtimes.com/nigeria-corruption-caused-christian-churches-pastor-sunday-adelaja-blames-religious-2046170. Accessed 2 April 2016.

Wood, Terence, and Warwick E. Murray. 2007. "Participatory Democracy in Brazil and Local Geographies: Porto Alegre and Belo Horizonte Compared." *European Review of Latin and Caribbean Studies* 8: 19–41.

World Bank. 1993. *The East Asian Miracle: Economic Growth and Public Policy*. New York, NY.: Oxford University Press.

YouTube, 2011. "Bishop Oyedepo Slapped and Humiliated Girl." https://www.youtube.com/watch?v=RwGkornIh1k. Accessed on 2 April 2016.

CHAPTER 4

The Military, Militarism and State Integrity in Africa

Earl Conteh-Morgan

Introduction

Analyses of the role of the military in African politics is extensive. Since independence, the absence of the rule of law, and in some countries the observance of even basic human rights, as well as widespread poverty has resulted in *coups d'etat*, civil wars and instances of interstate conflicts. Accordingly, the perception and at times the reality has been that Africa is the most violence prone continent, where the military is often in an adversarial relationship with both civilian regimes, and society in general. Both domestic and external factors influence the military-related causes of Africa's propensity for violence. In other words, what are the societal reasons for coups, civil strife, and even the involvement of children in "irregular wars "?

The focus of this chapter is not to analyze internal and external factors, nor the contradictions that fuel militarism, *coups d'état* and irregular warfare. A vast literature exists on the African military's proclivity to intervene in politics since the 1960s (First 1979; Bienen 1989; Gurr

E. Conteh-Morgan (✉)
University of South Florida, Tampa, FL, USA

G.K. Kieh, Jr. (ed.), *Contemporary Issues in African Society*,
African Histories and Modernities,
https://doi.org/10.1007/978-3-319-49772-3_4

2000; Brecher et al. 1988; Kieh and Agbese 2004; Harbeson 1987; Rupiya et al. 2015). The history of Africa is characterized by constant interactions between different cultures, ethnicities and heritages. This, coupled with economic marginalization, has created an environment underlined by political instability and internal anarchy in some states. One aspect of this landscape of political instability was the preponderance of *coups d'état* between the 1960s and 1980s. For some countries post-colonial politics has been characterized by protracted periods of military rule. Most countries, with the exception of Gabon, Kenya, Tanzania, and Botswana have experienced at least one "successful" military coup in their brief post-colonial political history. South Africa was under Apartheid rule till 1994 and therefore does not fall into the category of newly independent states that did not experience military intervention.

Before 2000 both Ghana and Nigeria had either experienced many military coups or been ruled by military regimes for most of their political independence (Hutchful and Bathily 1998; Luckham 1994). Other countries, such as the Democratic Republic of Congo (then Zaire), Togo, Benin, Somalia and Mali, among others, have experienced a pendulum swing between civilian rule and military rule. The problem is not just the question of coups, but their frequency in Africa.

When the democratization process began in 1992 fewer than 20 countries were not ruled by military dictatorships. Some others continue to alternate between civilian and military rule. The majority of these states are in Southern Africa. In other regions that were coup prone, the democratization process succeeded in altering the political status of Ghana, Benin, Malawi, Zambia and others. In other words, Africa's penchant for military coups may have declined by the late 1990s only to be coupled with the irregular wars of the early 1990s spawned by the end of the Cold War and the impact of globalization austerity measures. The relative decline in coups could be attributed to the fact that civilian dictators or military leaders turned civilian dictators had largely disarmed their militaries in favor of paramilitary or security forces with ethnic loyalties to the President or incumbent regime.

In order to delve into the reasons for the frequency and inclination for militarism, military interventions and irregular warfare that have overtaken some states, there is a need for more rigorous analysis. Accordingly, the questions that guide this chapter are: (1) What are the internal and external contradictions that are associated with military intervention in politics and militarism in general? (2) How did militarism in turn combine with the unconventional (irregular) wars of the early

1990s to involve the participation of child soldiers? and (3) What are the possible solutions to the militarism-irregular warfare nexus in Africa?

Militarism and Irregular Warfare: Conceptual and Theoretical Issues

It could be argued that Africa is characterized by what Morris Janowitz (1975) referred to as "Unanticipated Militarism" which is manifested in the frequency and recurrence of coups, or the persistence of military rule because society lacks the values, political traditions and practices that can effectively keep the military establishment out of the political process. By extension it also means the failure of the civilian political elites to responsibly exercise political and economic governance in society. In Africa this militaristic tendency over time becomes entrenched because as the military repeatedly intervenes in politics due to the lack of democratic culture, it ends up undermining and even destroying the existing civilian institutions that are designed to produce greater civilian control of government. The consequence is the fostering of a political culture where military intervention in politics becomes institutionalized. Militarism in Africa is therefore the growth, recurrence, or persistence of practices which weaken military professionalism, and create ongoing tension between the civilian political sphere and the military sphere within a nation-state.

Militarism, as conceptualized by Alfred Vagts (1937), captures Africa's propensity for military coups which have undermined democratic culture in many states. In making the distinction between "militarism" and "the military way," Vagts (1937: 13) emphasized that:

> The military way is marked by a primary concentration of men and materials on winning specific objectives of power with the utmost efficiency, that is, with the least expenditure of blood and treasure. Militarism, on the other hand, presents a vast array of customs, interests, prestige, actions, and thought associated with armies and wars and yet transcending true military purposes. Indeed militarism is so constituted that it may hamper and defeat the purposes of the military way.

Internally, Africa's militarism has had adverse effects on domestic society. The economic changes brought about by neoliberal economic policies have increased the personal and corporate insecurities of armies in many parts of Africa. As a result some have abandoned their professionalism and even participated in irregular warfare.

Since the early 1990s, an increasing number of African conflicts have taken on an irregular character summed up in heinous war crimes, bloodletting and pillage, among others. A good deal of this type of warfare can be largely explained in terms of the frustrations of economically deprived soldiers, youth and child fighters. Whether or not their participation in war is voluntary or coerced, they end up committing violent acts mostly against the civilian population. In both the Liberian and Sierra Leone civil conflicts, children were forced to drink a mixture of cane juice (from sugar cane) and gunpowder in order to make them callous to bloodshed and increase their bravery at the war front (Jackson and Larsen 1998). In severely impoverished states, soldiers and chronically unemployed youth are forced into irregular warfare because, by its very nature, it is a self-help process in an environment of anarchy where basic needs are not accessible to many. A major consequence is the resort to looting, banditry and confiscation of property that belongs to others. According to White (1996: 60):

> Irregular forces are substantially less limited by logistic factors. Their needs for food and ammunition are simpler, and they normally do not move over great distances. They draw support from the local population. Much of their weaponry is easily transported, and they usually develop their own ability to service and repair simple weapons and vehicles.

Irregular Warfare ignores or relies on unconventional methods of fighting that discard basic human rights in place of looting, brutality against civilians and total disregard for the rules of warfare. Both professionally trained soldiers and rebel forces utilize children by forcing them to participate in such conflicts. Disloyal soldiers in the army are especially prone to engaging in criminality associated with irregular warfare.

Coup Propensity in Africa: An Overview

At risk of oversimplification, we can discern three general patterns between the 1960s and the 1990s in Africa's propensity for militarism and irregular warfare. In some states the multiparty constitutions were discarded after independence and replaced by single-party government. The institution of multiparty politics introduced a more democratic culture because it undermined the symbiotic relationship that had developed between the government, ruling party and army. The second pattern is the alternation between military rule and civilian government. This sometimes involves the military head of state legitimizing himself by shedding his uniform as was the case in Ghana, or it may be a situation of short-lived authoritarian and civilian regimes. The third pattern is where the state fails, as in Sierra Leone during the 1990s, or collapses as in the case of Somalia. State failure or collapse is marked by economic dislocation, misrule and an inability of government to deliver services to the people. Irregular warfare and multiple sovereignties could follow or involve state failure or collapse.

The combined effect of ethno-regional cleavages and factions in politics and the military, as well as the weakness of African economies also undermined the weak institutions established by departing colonial administrations. The process of reconciling the different ethno-linguistic and political groups in places like Uganda, Nigeria or Sierra Leone was done hastily and therefore not effective. A very good example of this was the serious cleavage between "stateless" societies and "kingdom" people in Uganda (Mazrui 1977). Accordingly, the first decade of African independence was plagued by *coups d'état* because no clear separation of state roles between civilian and military authority was nurtured by the departing colonial powers. For example, in the case of France, McNamara (1989: 19) asserts that:

> The army in Africa was ill-prepared for independence. A French-led colonial army had been created in the late 19th century to provide cheap manpower for the conquest of an African empire.... This colonial army continued to serve France well in two World Wars, in Indochina, and in Algeria.... Before 1959, no real effort had been made to create national armies in the future independent states.

The colonial powers failed to create new policies and institutions to control the new national armies. Besides, the African armies' functions, which involved maintaining peace for colonial administrations, ingrained in them the belief that their mission is one of maintaining and ensuring the integrity of the state by intervening in politics. The implementation of this acquired belief has led to the military's longevity in political rule compared to civilians in the majority of African states. The politicized military is now seen as having a preponderance of influence during times of uncertainty and disunity, or economic malaise in many African countries.

Several reasons have been discussed as justification for the military's incursions into politics. There have been instances when interventions were motivated by class divisions and ideological differences as in the case of North Africa. Marxism and its focus on class asserts that the "military is the repressive arm of the state" (Marx 2004; Wolpin 1992). However, disagreements between the civilian political elite and the military elite could be a reason for overthrow of the ruling class, or it could be because of intra-military conflicts between the military elites and those at the lower levels (captains, lieutenants, and non-commissioned officers) of the military hierarchy (Kandeh 1996). In the case of the overthrow of the civilian political elites by the military elites, the latter simply replace the former, rather than instituting fundamental changes. This era of globalization has often resulted in some level of deprivation, or loss of either political or economic privileges by groups in society, including the military. However, the military is likely to stage a coup, if the privileges it thinks it is entitled to are lost. The resulting political intervention is a way to try and recoup its privileges and ensure the continuation of its corporate interests. Its exclusive privileges in many African states have been reflected in excessive salaries relative to other groups, a steady and assured supply of basic food items and heavily subsidized goods, among others (Conteh-Morgan 1994). Since the Europeans had used the military extensively to intervene in support of their interests, the Africans came to see the military as an instrument for intervention in furtherance of personal and corporate goals. In the process, it plays both a restorative and transformative role. Restoring itself or a favored regime to power, or transforming the political system into one conducive to its interests.

Many coups have been perceived as the result of chronic systemic disequilibrium that triggers the corrective role and professional pride of a patriotic army angry at the anarchy produced by civilian rule. This anger results from civilian indiscipline in contrast to "the military mind which is disciplined, rigid, logical, scientific…." (Huntington 1967: 60). Lucien Pye also underscores these innate qualities of the traditional army, which may have led to many African coups. Regarding the Burmese Army, Pye (1962: 78) wrote:

> Many of the skills commanded by the army are particularly relevant to civilian, and particularly administrative abilities. The army thus takes a considerable pride in its ability to develop modern skills and believes that it is well fitted to manage all aspects of Government.

The discipline exhibited by the military as well as its cohesiveness compared to civilians has led many analysts to entertain the thought that in terms of effectiveness in implementing development policies, military rule may be more beneficial for developing countries than civilian rule. In other words, the discipline, hierarchy and obedience that is integral to the military is an advantage over civilian political behavior.

African armies have, however, often been described as divided by corporate, ethnic or personal grievances that lessen their effectiveness, and which reduce them to rival armed factions as opposed to cohesive and professional national armies. Their disunity is exacerbated by, and directly related to politicization in the form of nepotism, ethnic favoritism, regional balance, and other social cleavages reflected in each nation-state (Shils 1962). Such politicization may be directly due to the colonial policy of playing one identity group against another, and now utilized by unscrupulous politicians using ethnicity or identity as an instrument to gain power and win elections. On the other hand, the military's inclination for intervention in politics may just be a manifestation of a high level of political mobilization and participation in society whereby the military becomes so engaged in politics that it dilutes its institutional efficacy.

Other theorists may argue that the military's frequent involvement in politics is simply an indication of the legacy of the colonial state's undemocratic nature which deprived the African colonies of a democratic culture such that after independence they could not function as sovereign democratic entities. Similarly, the coercive but disciplined nature of the military means that most of civil society—labor unions, universities, women's associations and other civic associations—are unable to match its efficacy.

While military incursion into politics is a common occurrence, it is nonetheless disruptive of the principle of civilian control of government. In other words, Africa still needs to resolve the issue of appropriate roles for soldiers and civilians, or who should be in charge of running the state. Why is Africa still plagued by this perennial problem of coups, as well as irregular warfare in states experiencing conflict? In order to examine this question, the analysis will now focus on three competing explanations of violence in Africa. From the three explanations an attempt will be made to develop a synthesis as an alternative to the reasons for Africa's coup and irregular warfare. The synthesis will then be followed by suggestions on how to deal with the innate contradictions within African society that produce militarism and irregular warfare.

Africa's Militarism and Propensity for Coups: The External-Historical Factors

Historians and conflict theorists argue that violence in Africa is closely related to the heritages or civilizations introduced from outside the continent in the form of major religions like Islam and Christianity, as well as the politico-economic system introduced by the Europeans (Wallerstein 1974). These external civilizations conquered and even partitioned the continent into states in which there is no compatibility between geography and culture. The result has been the lumping together of groups whose differences make for more severe struggle for political power and scarce resources. Besides this, Africa is still the victim of interventionist activities by external powers thereby limiting the sovereignty of its states. Multinational corporations, neocolonial interest and interference in civil wars are part of politics on the continent.

In this age of globalization, the continent is being invaded by varied issues and actors in a more extensive manner. For instance, there is the issue of balanced budgets, austerity measures, and political liberalization with its attendant requirements of regular free and fair elections. With the end of the Cold War, some countries were affected by the spillover of civil strife from neighboring countries. The African continent is of great economic value to external actors. The result is a good amount of rivalry for its strategic minerals. Its civil wars are often aggravated and prolonged by the widespread availability of light arms supplied by external actors with vested economic interests within certain countries. Light arms contribute to the internecine conflicts within nations (Grundy et al. 1985; Rodney 1982).

The African military is often a part of the violence that ensues. As an institution it is also the victim of weak institutions and inept governance that do not cater to the welfare needs of citizens. Accordingly, when a faction of the military intervenes to correct misrule or promote its interests, the entire military is labeled as unprofessional. However, the military is in many countries often the only well-organized, hierarchical and effective institution within society. At times, the military is drawn into politics because of the interplay of external financial, ideological and strategic interests.

The Continuing Revolution of Rising Expectations

Since gaining independence many African nations have been undergoing "a revolution of rising expectations" or are influenced by the "demonstration effect" of the West. This means that African states crave modernization or rapid development reflected by skyscrapers, super highways and other institutions or infrastructure that effectively guarantee security, welfare and economic stability (Rostow 1991). The discrepancy between what Africans think they should have acquired since independence and what has actually been achieved causes disenchantment and at times rebellion, or intervention by the military to correct events. Instability is common in many African states because of their artificiality which aggravate the fast-paced modernization goals they want to achieve. The result is imbalances between sectors of society and increased stresses and strains on limited government budgets. Often imbalances occur between education levels and employment opportunities. The youth experience most of the frustration in societies with widespread unemployment levels and lack of other opportunities. While Europe and North America experienced centuries of slow but steady development, Africa's accelerated and lopsided development path is producing a great deal of frustration, inequality and disenchantment.

A situation of insufficient resources to support the process of development is often associated with a volatile, explosive and anarchic environment in many states. The consequence is regime illegitimacy, rebellion and a loss of authority by the government. Groups excluded from the neo-patrimonial benefits of government experience frustration and often welcome military intervention in politics to correct the situation.

The military's tendency to intervene in politics along with its attendant violence is due to the rivalry that comes with the artificial African state, ethnic diversity, lack of adequate resources and distributional inequity. The African states are characterized by cultural incompatibilities which are mirrored in the military.

Primordial and Instrumental Forces

In theories of ethnicity primordial explanations are at times used to explain ethnic conflicts because, it is argued, the differences in language, regional origins, and even physical characteristics are responsible for the persistence of civil strife, or factionalization in the military. Primordial attitudes are due to visible markers and endowments of groups and as such are enduring. On the other hand, others argue that it is politicians who use ethnicity as an instrument to struggle for power or limited resources. Political elites exploit the differences among groups for political gain during elections. At times the consequence is civil strife, or struggles for power within the military. The cultural diversity in Angola, Ethiopia, Sudan or Liberia, among others is no different from that of European nations. This African condition suggests that before peace is realized on the continent, intensive and extensive national integration should be realized.

Ethnic favoritism in Africa is just as enduring as corruption or nepotism. In reality nepotism is an integral part of ethnic or tribal favoritism. Culturally, Western notions of individualism, or what constitutes corruption are very antithetical to African notions of communalism, and the expectation to take care of kith and kin. There is often a fundamental clash between the two worldviews. Good governance, military professionalism, and strong state institutions in general are difficult to achieve in many African states because of the endemic nature of tribalism or sectarianism. In many states, political life becomes a constant struggle between ethnic factions in which favoritism plays a big role and in turn may spawn violence and coups.

The Three Perspectives: A Synthesis

In sum, external-historical factors, modernization/globalization imperatives, and the ethnic incompatibilities within African states all interact to produce civil strife, especially in the form of irregular warfare where child soldiers predominantly figure; and military intervention in politics tends to be rife. The political tensions inherent in civil-military relations are aggravated by an elite led development drive that often involves the deliberate politicization of social cleavages. A wide range of conflicts (insurgencies, secessionism, military mutinies, coups, etc.) have demonstrated this elite driven process grounded in the clash of incompatible cultures within artificial states. Some relevant examples are the Congo civil strife following independence in 1960, the Rwanda and Burundi genocidal conflicts since independence, *coups d'état*, genocide in Idi Amin's Uganda, or the case of Chief Buthelezi's instrumental use of Zulu historical warrior tradition to gain support. In terms of the clash of heritages or civilizations, Sudan and Nigeria are very good examples. In Sudan (before the establishment of South Sudan) one finds a violent interaction between race (Arabs and Blacks) and religion (Islam, Christianity and animism). Currently in South Sudan one sees a case of ethnic competition for control of the state and its resources. In Nigeria it is a case of religious violence and regional cleavage.

Many of Africa's *coups d'état* have had undertones of primordial ethnic loyalties, especially where the army has been "detribalized" through politicization by politicians in search of power (Magyar 1993). Primordial forces are likely to have the upper hand if political malaise or crisis persists, especially in cases where effective sovereignty is limited to the urban areas of a country. Furthermore, with globalization the social cleavages of religion, ethnicity, and other identities resurfaced with intensity because of the end of the welfare "social contract" between state and society.

In the case of the military, attitudes toward conflict may in fact be undergoing serious change for the worse in states that have either collapsed or are failing. Soldiers in such societies, instead of relying on the *coup d'état* may instead decide to prey on civilians just like rebel groups (Conteh-Morgan and Dixon-Fyle 1999). Much of the civil strife that rages in many African societies is little more than banditry in which the military is just as involved in lawlessness and indiscipline as rebel forces. As a result of irregular warfare which produces national insecurity because of the loss of faith in protection by the military, the attitude of respect for soldiers by ordinary Africans may be changing.

In essence, historical, external and internal categories of explanations offer insight. Although the Cold War came to an end, still military interventions are not free of external interference. Nation-building efforts are still plagued by external interference. This external factor coupled with the serious divisions within an African society can have profound effects on nation-building projects.

Escalation from Coup Frequency to Irregular Warfare

While coups were predominant between the 1960s and 1980s, the *fin de siècle* period saw a new kind of warfare because of its irregular nature. Liberia, Sierra Leone, Somalia and the Democratic Republic of Congo became notorious for the irregular nature of their wars. The dislocated and militarized nature of society in Africa has produced a new class of warfare based on criminality and perpetrated by both trained soldiers and rebel forces made up mostly of children.

Combatants on both sides, soldiers and rebels, lack discipline and most have received little or no formal military training, and often those with professional training (that is members of the national army) tend to join or behave like rebels with no training (White 1996; Arreguin-Toft 2005). Child soldiers form a substantial segment of the combatants in irregular warfare.

The Liberian Civil War and the conflict in Sierra Leone, for instance, were, due to the scope of violence and their character, good examples of irregular warfare. Motivations of the combatants were often based on several factors, such as grievance against the government, self-help in an environment of anarchy, coercion by others and retaliation, among others. For all of them satisfying their material wants was achieved through pillage and looting. In addition, villages were burned down and many innocent civilians killed in the process. In many instances rape became a common crime perpetrated by both rebels and trained soldiers. It is not surprising that there were no clear-cut differences between soldier and rebel fighter in terms of lawlessness and threat to civilians. In Sierra Leone soldiers played the role of rebels as well as that of trained soldier with the underlying motivation being economic self-enrichment. Roughly 50% of some 14,000 soldiers fell into the category of what has been referred to as soldier-rebels (sobels) (Jackson and Larsen 1998).

The actors in irregular conflicts are often diverse in terms of age, training and regional origin. Many have no training in counter-insurgency techniques. One of their major goals is to control a resource rich territory within a country. In particular, the rebels are often alienated and marginalized members of society excluded from the political patronage system that permeates African politics. They are excluded from the political and economic opportunities that others enjoy because of their connection to powerful politicians. The major reason for insurgency is no doubt economic, or the need to satisfy one's basic needs in particular. For example, in the Sierra Leone conflict, the Revolutionary United Front (RUF) rebel force never communicated a detailed and specific political agenda. Its strategy was more dominated by terror than by any well-articulated manifesto.

In irregular violent conflicts, both professional soldiers and rebel groups utilize the same strategies and perpetrate similar violence on the civilian population. Villagers and small town dwellers often bear the brunt of the violence which ranges from attacks on civilian mini buses, looting and pillaging villages and towns, attacks on aid convoys, forced recruitment of children, forcing women to become sex slaves, to extra-judicial killings in towns and villages seized by them. It is at times rare for both types of combatants to attack each other head on. This is because rogue soldiers and rebel groups become very preoccupied with looting and self-enrichment, and therefore would avoid confronting each other for extended periods of time. In irregular conflicts, there is often an element of frequent change in alliances among the fighters based on expediency. In the Sierra Leone conflict government soldiers often joined rebel forces when it was in their interest to do so.

The irregular violent conflicts at the end of the twentieth century were strongly associated with the deprivations brought about by IMF austerity which further disadvantaged those who were not connected to the political patronage system. These conflicts are therefore also due to both domestic and external factors. The domestic divisions within a country are especially susceptible to exploitation by ethnic elites. Globalization is strongly associated with the phenomenon of state failure and is linked to the state's inability to provide even a modicum of welfare to its population. The delivery of clean water, electricity, decent roads, among other services is often absent. In Sierra Leone, for instance, inept, corrupt governments, weak institutions and the threat to the traditional patronage system which impelled self-interested rulers to channel critical resources under private commercial interests, rather than traditional patronage clients, spawned widespread demonstrations, violent protests and revolts on several occasions. While irregular warfare may be associated with many factors, in the final analysis, it is dominated by economic motives and may end up being a struggle to control areas rich in resources like diamonds, gold or bauxite, among others.

Irregular warfare is different from other types of warfare. Rebellions, insurgencies, guerrilla warfare and civil war are all examples of fighting grouped at the lower end of the spectrum of conflict. These can be either regular or irregular in nature. The differences in the two lie, first, in the underlying causes of the conflict; second, in the manner in which the conflict is conducted; and third, by the very nature of the combatants themselves. In irregular warfare it is difficult to distinguish between the behavior of government soldiers and that of rebels. Both groups equally exhibit criminality, unnecessary violence and indiscipline (Gray 2005; Kiras 2008). Extreme violence is inherent in irregular warfare, and this violence is largely directed at the civilian population in an indiscriminate manner. One of the main objectives of both sides is to satisfy their fighters by redistributing as much loot as possible to them. Often it is the loot taken from civilians who have abandoned their homes or whose houses have been burned down after being looted. Both sides may not care very much about gaining the support or sympathy of the local civilian population. Moreover, disregard for civilian life and the rule of law is because of the deliberate choice by the military to ignore the tenets of professionalism for which a disciplined military is known.

Child Participation in Irregular Warfare

Both the Liberian civil war and the Sierra Leone conflict were characterized by the participation of child soldiers in the scope and intensity of violence. A good deal of irregular warfare (looting, amputations, banditry, etc.) could be examined via the treatment and role of child fighters. Their participation is largely coerced or based on positive incentives such as promise of a better life or possession of more material goods. The RUF sought to bolster its troop strength and size by recruiting large numbers of youth either by coercion or economic promises. To a large extent, it could be argued that the choice of children (at times below the age of 12) to participate is a quest to find a meaningful life or a survival strategy in an environment of anarchy.

First, the young are at times bullied into joining the war (coercion as a reason for participation), and to support the poorly defined objectives of the RUF. For example, Michael Johnny, an 11-year-old coerced participant said: "The rebels killed my mother and father and took me along with them to be carrying their looted items on my head" (Reuters 1998). Often to obtain their participation children are subjected to cruel treatment such as being beaten into submission and initiated into a life of heinous crimes such as rape or murder.

Second, the promise of economic incentives ensures child participation in war atrocities. It is often a promise to redistribute confiscated and looted goods, or a monetary promise from the rebel leadership which is a motivating factor for continued high morale to capture major towns. For example, a 22-year-old ex-NPFL fighter stated how easy it was to recruit young fighters for the Sierra Leone conflict because of the promise of economic gratification, after the end of the Liberian conflict found many of them idle and with no other opportunities. "President Taylor could not integrate us into the Liberian army and I thought coming to Sierra Leone to fight could have helped me out" (Reuters 1998). Other coerced youth soldiers said they had been promised diamond and gold by the deposed Armed Forces Revolutionary Council (AFRC) junta and Liberian officials. It was not surprising that the struggle to capture the diamond rich east and southeast of Sierra Leone was so very intense especially after the ousting of the AFRC in February of 1998. The RUF leadership targeted the diamond rich regions because it was using them as a resource base to entice and maintain the thousands of young boys who perpetuated most of the violence in the war. In the Sierra Leonean conflict, therefore, what began as a struggle against an inept regime continued as disputes over resources and fruits of victory.

Often the decision to volunteer for economic incentives is not exercised freely, but is driven by socioeconomic factors. Hunger and poverty may motivate parents to offer their children for participation in war. On the other hand, children may believe that this is the only way to make sure they satisfy their most basic need of food. Eventually, the child bonds with the rebel force and becomes a hardened fighter. Some argue that child soldiers are overwhelmingly recruited from abjectly poor families, disrupted family backgrounds and from marginalized segments of society. In Sierra Leone's conflict, the RUF was made up to a large extent of youth from dysfunctional and abjectly poor homes. Recruitment to the movement was open to all who volunteered to join the rebel cause. The majority of those who trained in Libya were either from very poor homes with no employment or other societal opportunities, or who had grievances against the ruling elite. Most of the RUF cadre and field commanders were from a category of society that could be described as deviants who often engaged in drug abuse and were rebellious to the cultural expectations of society. These are mostly troubled children who are prone to violate the mainstream values of society and thus welcomed the RUF behavior because it seemed to align with their own inclinations. It was also a way to boost their low self-esteem and thereby reverse their status in society.

For the young, war is soon perceived as a way of life. They have known very little else other than gun violence in the context of civil war. They grow up thinking and even believing that violence against others is the normal state of affairs. They have seen their homes destroyed, parents killed and they themselves may have participated in the killing of people they know. When this happens, war escalates into total anarchy characterized by lootings, banditry and senseless killings. For a young person, the power of a rebel force with near monopoly on violence provides a sense of security. In other words, in addition to economic security, being part of a rebel force for an impoverished child provides psychological gratification: companionship, excitement and respect. Psychological gratification also comes in the form of the prestige of wearing military uniforms and having a sense of doing something very important. Apart from the necessity to escape from desperate conditions at home, some children joined rebel groups and armed forces because of the prestige of wearing a uniform or for the feeling of doing something important. Joining rebel forces to avenge the killing of a loved one also falls into the category of psychological gratification, and is given by some child soldiers as the reason for their participation in war.

It is easy for young impressionable minds to be transformed into young killers, especially if they come from backgrounds with values that do not adhere to mainstream societal values. It is not surprising that the RUF was so successful in molding the minds of the unruly, impoverished and angry youth of Sierra Leone society. At an early age they exhibited untoward behavior often intensified by habitual drug abuse and a belligerent attitude toward many within their environment. The RUF leadership, in collaboration with these deviant, frustrated or angry groups, used both alcohol and drugs to maintain the obedience of the children. The argument apparently is that drugs and alcohol numb the senses and thereby produce fighters who are callous to corpses, and blood and are ready to kill themselves.

Irregular warfare, especially where the fighters are comprised of armed individuals or groups who are generally not members of the national army, has relied heavily on child soldiers. This is due to a number of reasons. First, children are more capable of effectively operating in the terrain where these conflicts take place. It also means that rebel leaders are inclined to use children as carriers of looted items in forest roads, or rugged paths from one town or village to another. Such terrain is usually not suitable for operations by regular vehicles because of their width and surface. Children were therefore often used to transport loads, or as messengers and cooks.

Moreover, the level of violence in irregular warfare corresponds closely to the spread of light weapons in developing countries. Children are better able to use light weapons such as the AK-47 or assault rifle, machine guns, mortars, grenades or land mines. The RUF was capable of withstanding regular armies because these light weapons were easy to use and carry. The training involved in using them is simple and not time-consuming. Because of the ease involved in operating these modern light weapons, even small children below ten can easily use them. The pervasive arms transfer process in the world makes light weapons easily available in even the poorest of societies. The consequence is that conflicts like the one in Sierra Leone became protracted and intense.

Children become an integral part of irregular warfare because such warfare is more heavily influenced by the individual personality of participants who comprise the rebel force. Whims, wishes or desires of participants were paramount to any well-articulated goals or objectives. For example, many Sierra Leoneans were baffled by the intensity of violence by the RUF against civilians. The rebel group did not in any way try to win the affection of ordinary people. Instead it engaged in a frenzy of killings, amputations and pillage. Thus one is tempted to conclude that the RUF's war was a war directed by a leadership based on purely idiosyncratic factors.

The lack of a coherent and well-articulated war objective by the RUF may have been responsible for the random, irrational and incredible atrocities committed by its fighters. The child soldiers, especially those in their preteens, may not have had a deep understanding of the political and economic reasons for the war. The RUF youth soldiers were masters of their own strategies and their participation was guided by their whims and caprices. This lack of a clearly articulated goal spelling out what they were fighting for was largely responsible for the terrible atrocities perpetrated by the child soldiers.

In the African context, the manipulation of child soldiers is enhanced because respect for elders is endemic to African cultures. Thus children become pawns in the hands of warlords and their immediate commanders because of this deeply ingrained respect for age in developing societies. In Liberia and Sierra Leone obedience is expected of those who are younger. Children have generally been raised to be obedient and to submit to the wishes of older people. This pervasive cultural trait made it easy to ensure maximum child participation.

Finally, the networks of social support for children in regions of irregular warfare have been undermined by the scope, intensity and duration of violence which further destroyed relevant institutions focused on child growth and education. In order to help reintegrate children into society, and prevent fresh eruptions of violence that directly affect children, the power elites need to: (1) help reverse abject poverty and marginalization of entire segments of youth; (2) institute a program of education with the objective of de-indoctrination so that child soldiers are fully rehabilitated into normalcy; and (3) re-establish the networks of social welfare between families and communities that have been destroyed by violence as well as the rapid implementation of austerity measures that has destabilized families and societies in general.

Possible Solutions

What would be the most feasible solutions to Africa's militarism, coups and irregular warfare, in light of the interactive effects of the three perspectives discussed above? At risk of sounding like an economic determinist, the first suggestion would be for African governments to encourage private enterprises that employ many people so that government is not seen as the most beneficial employer. This involves fostering a business/commercial climate that would produce successful firms capable of gainfully employing thousands and providing them income security. The development of such a vibrant economic climate would do away with all the sub-systemic imbalances prevalent in African economies, such as the imbalance between levels of education and levels of employment. The latter is usually low while the former is high, especially among college graduates. The problem of Africa's low economic performance is strongly related to the transitional nature of African societies characterized by a dialectical tension between traditionalism and modernity (Fieldhouse 1986). In other words, Africa is neither bourgeois-capitalist (advanced industrial) nor totally rural/agrarian in terms of values. Africa, to a large extent, has been yearning for modern material items faster than it can afford them.

Second, and related to a sound economic base, is the role of education in transforming African societies into one predominant mode of thought. Currently, African societies are still steeped in traditional values. With widespread education, the communal, ethnic and kinship orientation and behavior that characterize African ethno-linguistic groups and society in general, and which are so often easily manipulated by ambitious and greedy politicians, will be transformed into modernization values characterized by impersonal behavior based on the rule of law and in particular, respect for civil and political rights (Palmer 1985). The lingering influence of pre-colonial and colonial legacies and traditionalism has a strong hold in the African military and may be responsible for many *coups d'état*.

A third possible solution to Africa's militaristic behavior is the establishment of a diarchy, or the setting up of civil-military political rule in states that have serious problems with the military. This involves legally incorporating the military into government so as to prevent it from intervening in politics. Diarchy has been referred to as the middle course between two extremes because it does not entail outright civilian or military rule

(Dixon-Fyle 1989). Rather, it involves the participation of the armed forces and politically includes them thereby weakening any incentive they may have to seize power. Its supporters believe that this makes for a healthy relationship between the civil realm and the military arena.

A fourth suggestion is for governments to resort to privatized military security and then take away guns from soldiers in order to ensure that national armies do not intervene in politics. This will be quite in line with the current emphasis on economic issues, privatization of security and the emergence of private armies like Sandline International that offer military services to NGOs, and some governments around the world. Globalization at times means that the state has lost its monopoly on the use of coercion. As a result, states are increasingly depending on the military security provided by private armies in order to contain the violence that can be unleashed by ethno-nationalism based on either religion, regional or language differences and blatant inequalities. However, the main question should be whether peace and stability could be sustained in a non-bourgeois society.

In addition, African governments should continue to have zero tolerance for *coups d'état*. Since the 1990s, with the introduction of multiparty politics, coups became less frequent. The strategy of refusing diplomatic recognition to a military junta was very effective between May 1997 and February 1998, when the AFRC effected a *coup d'état* against the civilian regime of President Kabbah of Sierra Leone. Besides widespread denial of diplomatic recognition to the AFRC, the ECOWAS Cease-Fire Monitoring Group (ECOMOG) forces enforced an embargo on the junta until it was removed from power. Moreover, in February 1998, 12 battalions of an ECOMOG force of approximately 8000–9000 soldiers from Nigeria and Guinea, accompanied by loyal soldiers from the fractionalized Sierra Leone Army and national police force, engaged the AFRC/RUF junta and removed it from power (Jackson and Larsen 1998). The outstanding success of the operation can be attributed to the multilateral determination of member states in the region not to encourage the illegal overthrow of a legitimate civilian regime by the military. The first decision to reject military coups was made in 1999 by the Organization of African Unity (OAU) , and again in 2002 the AU underscored its opposition to all unconstitutional changes of government. Term limits have enhanced the democratic process in African states making for more frequent elections and thereby obviating the necessity for coups.

Finally, many African states do not really need armies because they are not under any threat, nor are they able to afford them. Armies are designed largely for international conflicts or to defend the state from external attacks. Many mini-states in Africa would function just as effectively with a well-trained police force to maintain law and order in cases of civil disturbance. Abolishing armies will most likely end the military coup propensity in many states.

Conclusion

The chapter has attempted to examine the problems of military intervention, military rule and irregular warfare in Africa. Prior to the 1990s, the military intervened recurrently in African politics. Only a few African countries were spared the scourge of military *coups d'état*. Military intervention in African politics was caused by societal, corporate and external factors. Since the 1990s, with the dawn of the "Third Wave of Democratization," the incidence of military intervention has decreased, although the scourge has not ended, as is evidenced by the recurrent civilian and military elite clashes in Guinea Bissau, and the recent military coup in Guinea following the death of its president, as well as the even more recent attempt by top soldiers in Burkina Faso to take over power following the ouster by the people of its long-ruling leader. Clearly, the decrease in the incidence of military intervention has been precipitated in some measures by the current intolerance of the international community for military putsches. In particular, the African Union (AU), ECOWAS, the UN and the United States have all clearly expressed their current policy of intolerance to coups. The AU Peace and Security Council quickly condemned the September 2015 coup in Burkina Faso and even imposed sanctions on the coup leaders. This is all part of the AU's determination since 2002 to promote democracy in Africa by ostracizing and sanctioning coup leaders.

On the issue of military rule, soldiers have performed very poorly as governors. This has exacerbated the development crises in the affected African states. Despite the poor performance of military regimes, some of them have consolidated power by civilianizing. For example, the late General Gnassingbé Eyadéma civilianized his rule and maintained an authoritarian stranglehold over Togo until his death in early 2005. Similarly, President Blaise Campaoré civilianized his military junta, shortly after ousting Captain Thomas Sankara from power.

Another major security challenge facing Africa is the burgeoning increase in the rate of irregular warfare. The chapter discussed the nature and dynamics of this phenomenon by examining several cases, including Liberia and Sierra Leone. Irregular warfare, by and large, has involved the efforts by warlordist militias to wrestle away state power. In the cases of the Democratic Republic of the Congo, Liberia and Sierra Leone, irregular warfare is fueled by the avarice for minerals—diamond, gold and rutile, among others.

Finally, the chapter outlines various ways in which African states could address the problems of coups and irregular warfare. The suggestions include the following: There is the need to invigorate the private sector in various African states so that it can, among other things, create well-paying jobs. This would help to make the public sector less attractive as a source of private accumulation. Also, given the nature of conflicts in Africa, there is no need for a standing military force. That is, many African states could do without armed forces. It is also important to ensure that African presidents keep to term limits as stated in the national constitutions. Both civil society and the international community should make sure they abide by what is stated in the constitution, and not be allowed to amend clauses in order to prolong their stay in power. In particular they should not be allowed to use phony elections rigged in their favor to indefinitely cling on to power. In places such as Nigeria, Mali, Niger and Guinea, among others, both military coup leaders and civilian presidents have been guilty of violations of human rights as well as corrupt practices, misrule and intolerance of dissent. The only safeguard is opposition mounted by a very strong civil society and backed by a vigilant international community to ensure good governance.

References

Arreguin-Toft, Ivan. 2005. *How the Weak Win Wars: A Theory of Asymmetric Conflict*. New York: Cambridge University Press.

Bienen, H. 1989. *Armed Forces, Conflict and Change in Africa*. Boulder, CO: Westview Press.

Brecher, M., J. Wilkenfeld, and S. Moser. 1988. *Crises in the Twentieth Century*. Vol. 1. Oxford: Pergamon Press.

Conteh-Morgan, E. 1994. The Military and Human Rights in Post-Cold War Africa. *Armed Forces & Society* 21 (1): 69–87.

Conteh-Morgan, E., and M. Dixon-Fyle. 1999. *Sierra Leone at the End of the Twentieth Century—History Politics and Society*. New York: Peter Lang.

Dixon-Fyle, M. 1989. Reflections on the Role of the Military in Civilian Politics: The Case of Sierra Leone. *The Australian Journal of Politics and History* 35 (2): 211–219.

Fieldhouse, D.K. 1986. *Black Africa, 1945–80: Economic Decolonization and Arrested Development.* London: Allen & Unwin.

First, R. 1979. *The Barrel of a Gun.* New York: Penguin.

Gray, Colin S. 2005. *Another Bloody Century: Future Warfare.* London: Weidenfeld & Nicolson.

Grundy, K.W., G.M. Carter, and P O'Meara. 1985. "The Impact of Region on Contemporary African Politics." In *African Independence, The First Twenty-Five Years*, eds. G.M. Carter and P. O'Meara, 97–125. Bloomington, IN: Indiana University Press.

Gurr, T.R. 2000. *Peoples Versus States: Minorities At Risk in the New Century.* US Institute of Peace: Washington, DC.

Harbeson, John W. 1987. *The Military in African Politics.* New York: Praeger.

Huntington, S.P. 1967. *The Soldier and the State.* Cambridge, MA: Harvard University Press.

Hutchful, E., and A. Bathily (eds.). 1988. *The Military and Militarism in Africa.* Dakar, Senegal: Codesria.

Jackson, B., and J.A. Larsen. 1998. *Analytical Study on Irregular Warfare in Sierra Leone and Liberia.* Englewood, CA: Foreign Systems Research Center.

Janowitz, M. 1975. *Military Conflict: Essays in the Analysis of War and Peace.* Thousand Oaks, CA: Sage.

Kandeh, J. 1996. "What Does the 'Militariat' Do When It Rules? Military Regimes: The Gambia, Sierra Leone and Liberia." *Review of African Political Economy* 23 (69): 387–404.

Kieh, George K., and Pita O. Agbese. 2004. *The Military and Politics in Africa: From Engagement to Democratic and Constitutional Control.* London: Ashgate.

Kiras, James D. 2008. Irregular Warfare. In *Understanding Modern Warfare*, ed. David Jordan, et al., 224–228. Cambridge: Cambridge University Press.

Luckham, R. 1994. "The Military, Militarization and Democratization in Africa: A Survey of the Literature and Issues". *African Studies Review* 37 (2): 13–75.

Magyar, K.P. 1993. "Culture and Conflict in Africa's History: The Transition to the Modern Era". In *Conflict, Culture, and History*, eds. Stephen J. Blan, et al., 229–289. Montgomery, AL: Air University Press.

Marx, K. 2004. *A Critique of Political Economy.* New York: Penguin.

Mazrui, A. 1977. "Soldiers as Traditionalizers." In *The Warrior Tradition in Modern Africa*, ed. Ali Mazrui, 236–258. Leiden: E.J. Brill.

McNamara, F. 1989. *France in Black Africa.* Washington, DC: National Defense University.

Palmer, M. 1985. *Dilemmas of Political Development.* Adelaide, Australia: Peacock Publishers.

Pye, L. 1962. "The Army in Burmese Politics". In *The Role of the Military in Underdeveloped Countries*, ed. L. Pye, 231–251. Princeton, NJ: Princeton University Press.

Reuters Business Briefing/Inter Press. 1998. Feb. 6.

Rodney, W. 1982. *How Europe Underdeveloped Africa.* Washington, DC: Howard University Press.

Rostow, W.W. 1991. *Stages of Economic Growth: A Non-Communist Manifesto.* Cambridge, UK: Cambridge University Press.

Rupiya, M., G. Moyo, and H. Langesen (eds.). 2015. *The New African Civil-Military Relations.* South Africa: The South African Policy and Research Institute.

Shils, E. 1962. "The Military in the Political Development of New States". In *The Role of the Military in Underdeveloped Countries*, ed. J.J. Johnson, 7–67. Princeton, NJ: Princeton University Press.

Vagts, A. 1937. *A History of Militarism.* New York: Free Press.

Wallerstein, Immanuel. 1974. *The Modern World System: Capitalist Agriculture and the Origin of the European World Economy in the Sixteenth Century.* London: Academic Press.

White, J.B. 1996. "Irregular Warfare: A Different Kind of Threat". *American Intelligence Journal* 15 (8): 57–63.

Wolpin, M. 1992. *Militarism and Social Revolution in the Third World.* Ottawa, Canada: Allanbold, Osman and Co.

CHAPTER 5

Ethnic Conflicts in the Great Lakes Region of East Africa

Theodora O. Ayot

Introduction

The purpose of this chapter is to investigate the synergistic effects of the resistance to the agitation for multi-partyism and democratization process, as an attribute of the fear of losing the one-party political power structure by some of the leaders in the Great Lakes region of East Africa namely, Daniel Arap Moi, the former Kenyan President, Juvenal Habyarimana, the late Rwandan President and the late Mobutu Sese Seko of the Democratic Republic of Congo. In this connection, the chapter also investigates and looks at the synergy of the effects of the Anglo-French rivalry, which not only created the fear of losing cultural, political and economic influence and dominance in the region but, also culminated into propagating, propelling and creating the rivalry which eventually infiltrated into the Rwandan internal political landscape. This move eventually led to the internationalization of the crisis in the Great Lakes.

T.O. Ayot (✉)
North Park University, Chicago, IL, USA

G.K. Kieh, Jr. (ed.), *Contemporary Issues in African Society*,
African Histories and Modernities,
https://doi.org/10.1007/978-3-319-49772-3_5

Therefore, the chapter posits and asserts that the Rwandan genocide was a function of a combination of negative synergistic forces of opposition to political pluralism and the democratization process, first and foremost in Kenya, Congo and Rwanda, and the change of government in Uganda where Museveni literally transported the Ugandan crisis into Rwanda and diverted attention from Uganda (Mamdani 2001). On the one hand, the continued external interests and activities of some of the international powers such as France and Belgium culminated in the interplay between the regional and international forces. Thus, in an attempt to address this multifaceted and intricate aspect of the Rwandan genocide the following questions are posed:

First, was the Rwandan genocide a self-internally propagated act of destruction and violence against the people or was it partly propelled by the already existing undercurrents of events including regional ethnic cleansing that was eminent in some of the states in the Great Lakes region such as Kenya and the Democratic Republic of Congo? Second, in terms of internalization of the crisis in the Great Lakes region, did the militarization of Rwanda by some international powers enhance and create an atmosphere that proved more conducive and lucrative for the genocide in that country?

By using the term synergy, this chapter employs the following definitions of the word: First, the interaction of two or more agents or forces whose combined effect is greater than the sum of their individual effects. Second, the cooperative interaction among groups, especially among the acquired subsidiaries or merged parts of a corporation, that creates an enhanced combined effect and finally, the creation of synergy when things work in concert together to create an outcome that is in some way of more value than that of the total of the individual input.

Authoritarian Rule and Ethnic Conflicts: A Background

The Travails of Autocracy

In their desire to maintain the dictatorial regimes and the one-party state system, Presidents Daniel arap Moi, Mobutu Sese Seko and Juvenal Habyarimana manipulated the political climate of their own governments and created an illusion of victimization by "multi-partyism" or opposition and therefore used it as a justification for ethnic cleansing and violation of human rights of their own people. Martin (2007) has pointed out that as far back as 1966 and with the abolition of the post of the prime minister in the Democratic Republic of Congo, the executive powers became effectively concentrated in the office of the presidency. He goes on to explain further that "Single party state soon followed when Mobutu founded the *Movement Populaire dela Revolution* (MPR) in 1967. In 1974, the MPR became the nation's only political institution. Through tight centralized control, the progressive elimination of the *Binza Group*, and direct appointment of high-level party and state officials, Mobutu then proceeded—from late 1967 to 1970—to establish an increasingly authoritarian and personal rule, based on terror, political assassination and co-optation. In typical patrimonial fashion, all power derived from the presidency, and all decisions were made by Mobutu" (Martin 2007: 93). And for a period of thirty years, Mobutu's dictatorial one-party state regime was maintained by US support.

In Rwanda, on the other hand, Habyarimana's fifteen year one-party state dictatorial regime had been sustained by France. Habyarimana had formed the National Revolutionary Movement for Development (NRMD) in 1975. This became the single ruling party in the country which formulated the constitution in 1978 that ensured that Habyarimana would be the sole candidate and would be returned to power when elections took place. Therefore in order to strengthen his position, "a military co-operation and training agreement was signed with Paris, and over a period of fifteen years, France slowly replaced Belgium as the foremost foreign ally, offering financial and military guarantee which Belgium could not provide" (Melvern 2000: 24).

This was also true in the case of Kenya where the Kenya African National Union (KANU), as a single political party, strengthened Kenyatta and later Moi's authoritarian and personal rule, especially after the opposition political party in the country, the Kenya Peoples Union (KPU), was stripped of its power in 1966, the same year Mobutu made drastic changes in the Congo. As Gecaga (2007: 67) has pointed out, "Kenyatta used his monolithic powers to destroy or push into oblivion all pro-democracy people centered movements that had been involved in the struggle for independence and land rights, thereby emasculating institutions meant to provide checks and balances on the executive." She goes on to explain that by the time Moi came to power in 1978, the country was "essentially a politically corrupt society in which most of the institutions and notion of democratic governance had been subverted to personal rule." And by 1982, Kenya had become a *de jure* one-party state. Moi then proceeded to govern the country "through violence, harassment, intimidation and increased use of state security organs for self-preservation" (Gecaga 2007: 67).

It was the extreme personalization of power that led Moi and his government to orchestrate genocidal acts by scheming, planning and hatching the final solution for the removal of non-Kalenjin speakers from the entire Rift Valley Province and thereby creating what became known as KANU zone where the opposition party was not allowed to operate. This came about after Moi and his dictatorial one-party government were forced to accept the restoration of multiparty politics after twenty two years. The change took place on December 2, 1991 with the repeal of Section 2(A) of the constitution that had made Kenya a *de jure* single party (Troup and Hornsby 1998: 86–87).

The 1990s witnessed the highest level of Moi's authoritarian leadership under the auspices of KANU with the elite supporters within the party. As a reaction to political pluralism, Moi maintained that Kenya would be better off operating under a one-party political system, giving his own political rationale that the country would be faced with ethnic conflict if political pluralism was allowed. This is why some of the "Kalenjin leaders apparently judged that the incidents (of ethnic cleansing) would confirm President Moi's predictions that multiparty democracy would ignite ethnic animosities and discredit opposition leaders and the advocates of the multi-party competition" (Troup and Hornsby 1998: 198). Troup and Hornsby go on to quote the International NGO's *Human Rights Watch and Africa Watch*:

> President Daniel arap Moi of Kenya confidently predicted that the return of his country to multi-party system would result in an outbreak of tribal violence that would destroy the nation. His prediction has been alarmingly fulfilled. One of the most disturbing developments in Kenya over the last two years has been the eruption of violent clashes between different ethnic groups. However, far from being spontaneous result of a return to political pluralism, there is clear evidence that the government was involved in provoking ethnic violence for political purposes and has taken no adequate steps to prevent it from spiraling out of control (Troup and Hornsby 1998: 198).

By the same token, in 1990, Habyarimana introduced new measures that were aimed at changing Rwanda's political landscape, making it a democratic state through the introduction of political pluralism. In the meantime, Museveni had denied the Rwandan refugees in Uganda citizenship status, a move that subsequently culminated in the Rwandan Patriotic Front (RPF) invasion of Rwanda, leading to a civil war in the country. It is also interesting to note that in the same way that Museveni had denied the Tutsi citizenship status, Mobutu Sese Seko had also denied the Bunyamulenge citizenship status in the Congo (Adekunle 2003: 222).

Up until the 1990s, Kenya, Rwanda and the Democratic Republic of Congo had been operating as single-party states under dictatorial regimes. And even in the midst of the discussion on the power sharing arrangement at Arusha, Tanzania, after the civil war in Rwanda, ethnic cleansing was taking place in Kenya and the Congo respectively. For instance, by August 1992, ethnic violence had erupted in the Democratic Republic of Congo between the most dominant group, the Lunda and the Luba-Kasai, and this went on until well into 1993. According to Adekunle "Mobutu's repression of the protests was ethnically motivated because the Luba-Kasai people who lived in the Shaba region were systematically expelled and politically marginalized" (Adekunle 2003: 222).

Likewise, during the 1990s, some of the prominent KANU ruling elites in Kenya "invoked the *Majimbo* card in response to the mounting tide of the multi-party crusade. They changed the majimboism from the policy of regionalism to an ideology of ethnic cleansing" (Kagwanja 1998a: 10–11). Therefore, the events that occurred between November 1991 and April 1992 witnessed Kalenjin warriors targeting non-Kalenjin Kenyan communities that were living in the Rift Valley Province namely, the Luo, Gusii, Luyia and the Kikuyu.

The mission of the warriors was to carry out the instructions that were given by President Moi and his government. The first was to silence the ruling elite's critics within the Kalenjin community as was the case of the moderate Hutu in the Rwandan society. The second motive was to create a confusing situation and provoke a mass reaction in support of President Moi and KANU within the group, and prevent the populous Nandi and Kipsigis from joining the opposition. And finally as Kagwanja (1998a: 6) argued "the warriors were expected to drive away thousands of non-Kalenjin workers from the Kericho District's plantations, who were associated with the opposition. Next, guns were turned on the Kikuyu in Molo, Rongai, Narok North, Eldoret North, Eldoret South and Eldoret East constituencies and the Luhya in Eldoret South, Trans-Nzoia and Bungoma. This was the most violent and horrifying phase that generated the most profound humanitarian crisis in independent Kenya".

Accordingly, *Human Rights Watch/Africa Watch* had this to say about the situation in Kenya:

> The government has relied on different tactics, such as extra-legal intimidation and violence, to silence and disempower critics. The change in tactics appears to be a deliberate move on the part of the government to avoid international censure. A growing culture of state-sponsored harassment and vigilante violence against opposition leaders and other critics is being encouraged and fostered by the government. The chilling aspect of the violence is that the government denies any knowledge of or responsibility to it, attributing it instead to unknown vigilantes.

Subsequently, two political rallies were held at Kapsabet in the Nandi District and Kapkatet in the Kericho District, where Joseph Misoi, a member of parliament representing Eldoret South, made it very clear that "What we are saying is that unless those clamoring for political pluralism stop, we must devise a protective mechanism by launching this movement" (Kagwanja 1998b: 12). What followed was a call to the Kalenjin-speaking people to "arm themselves with bows and arrows to destroy any multi-party advocate. The powerful KANU elite, Nicholas Biwott, was quick to add that the members of the opposition would subsequently be 'crushed,' and that the KANU youth wingers would fight to the last person to protect President Moi's government" (Kagwanja 1998b: 12). By this point, there was already in place a coalition of the entire Kalenjin, Maasai, Turkana and Samburu (KAMATUSA).

This coalition constituted 60.7% of the Rift Valley Province's eligible voters. Therefore, agitation for political pluralism by members of the opposition was interpreted as a political movement that was directed against the head of state by the mere fact that he was a Kalenjin hence, the opposition members were the enemy of the entire KAMATUSA coalition and the KANU government. By the same token, the opposition in Rwanda and the RPF were also portrayed as being against the head of state and the enemy of the existing Rwandan government headed by Habyarimana.

The newly cultivated attitude by the KAMATUSA coalition meant that the proponents of political pluralism were viewed as outsiders, "'aliens' or 'foreign' oppressors of the 'natives' or 'indigenous' owners of the Rift Valley—KAMATUSA" (Kagwanja 1998b: 12–13). Therefore, the only way to protect the members of KAMATUSA as an ethnic entity was to eliminate all the non-Kalenjins and/or drive them from the Rift Valley. Therefore, on October 29, 1991, ethnic cleansing began in Miteitei farm in the Nandi District, an area that borders the Rift Valley,

Nyanza and Western Provinces. The non-Kalenjin groups that were targeted were the Kikuyu, the Luyia, the Luo and the Gusii since they were considered to be outsiders, foreigners or aliens who must be killed or totally driven out of the Rift Valley Province.

The Kikuyu became the major target "for special retribution throughout the Rift Valley" (Kagwanja 1998b: 8). For instance, the Kikuyu farms in Rukini, Kondoo, Lokwania and Ya Mumbi in the Burnt Forest were attacked and the people either killed or driven away. Some of the names of these places were changed and given Kalenjin names and then allocated to other Kalenjins. On September 2, 1993, President Moi declared what he had termed "Security Operation Zone" in the ethnic conflict areas of Molo, Burnt Forest and Londiani. On October 15, 1993, Maasai *morans*, security forces and Narok County Council Game Rangers attacked the Kikuyu settlers in Enoosupukia, killing at least 30 people and displacing 30,000 others. Instead of taking meaningful steps to bring an end to the ethnic cleansing and vigilante war in the country, the steps taken by Moi opened a new chapter in human rights abuses against the displaced, members of the press, civil society, church leaders and foreigners, who attempted to visit the areas that were affected by ethnic cleansing or genocide.

Furthermore, in March 1994, just one month before the beginning of the Rwandan tragedy, a vicious vigilante attack in Burnt Forest left 18 people dead and displaced nearly 25,000, most of them Kikuyu. Ripples of Kikuyu backlash were felt as far North as West Pokot. In so doing, the existing demographic composition of the multi-ethnic groups would be tilted to favor the Kalenjin groups especially during the elections of 1992. Thus, the Kenyan genocide, also referred to as ethnic clashes, tribal clashes, land clashes or ethnic cleansing were partly meant to fulfill President Moi's 'prediction' that Kenya's return to a multiparty system would plunge the country into tribal violence. But having succeeded in carrying out the state-sponsored genocide, where the Kalenjin and Maasai warriors used bows, arrows, spears, machetes and clubs to kill mercilessly, burn houses and destroy farms, the hegemonic KANU ruling elite managed to win a political victory in the 1992 elections.

President Daniel arap Moi had cried foul, that he and his government were the victims of the opposition. But in reality, it was Moi's own making, being afraid of the winds of change that were blowing in the Great Lakes region through the agitation for multiparty politics and democratic liberal constitutionalism. Nevertheless, the spirit of change remained solid despite the killings that took place.

On the other hand, in the Democratic Republic of Congo, especially as a result of the end of the Cold War, the Western powers and donors pressurized and urged Mobutu Sese Seko to introduce political pluralism and a democratization process in the country. Thus, by April 1990, Mobutu bowed to external pressures and "agreed to end one-party rule … and initiate a process of democratization. In August of 1990, a Sovereign National Conference (CNS) was inaugurated in Kinshasa— The CNS finally concluded its work in December of 1992, without succeeding to unseat Mobutu, who had manipulated its participants and proceeded to stay in power in the same way that Moi had manipulated and undermined the opposition to stay in power" (Martin 2007: 96). Martin quotes Nzongola:

> In the face of overwhelming popular desire for radical change, Mobutu and his entourage decided to pretend that they were in favor of democratic reforms, while doing everything possible to obstruct the democratization process … As so many parties were being created, the regime found it useful to dilute the strength of the real opposition by setting up its own opposition parties. Financed by the regime, these artificial creations consisted of a few individuals who were mostly interested in money … (2002: 186, 188)

The political activities in the Democratic Republic of Congo and Kenya influenced events in Rwanda under Habyarimana and his dictatorial regime, even in the midst of the international discussions in Arusha. In both Kenya and the Democratic Republic of Congo, ethnic cleansing was going on. Habyarimana had hoped that he too would be able to manipulate the political situation in Rwanda the way his two friends and fellow dictators, Moi and Mobutu, had done to consolidate their powers in Kenya and the Democratic Republic of Congo after the 1992 elections respectively. But Habyarimana had run out of options, owing to international pressure on power sharing.

In retrospect, the Rwandan genocide did not occur in isolation. The country was hedged in and totally encircled by the events that were taking place in Kenya, the Democratic Republic of Congo and Uganda where Museveni had betrayed the very people who had helped him to oust Milton Obote and take over the country. Museveni denied the Rwandan refugees citizenship. Therefore, there were regional and international forces at work that made the genocide in Rwanda inevitable. Moreover, there were definitely certain similarities between what was going on in Kenya, Rwanda and the Democratic Republic of Congo. Moi, Mobutu and Habyarimana vowed to fight the opposition build-up and multiparty politics at all costs in each of these three countries.

The governments of Kenya and Rwanda were engaged in extensive training of some of their citizens for the sole purpose of carrying out ethnic cleansing and unprecedented mass killing. Both governments used armed militias and machetes extensively, killing and maiming the targeted groups. Thus, the mass murder in Kenya was disproportionately of a genocidal nature. It was orchestrated by the state, well-planned and systematically executed with a lot of precision. It was meant to be the final solution carried out by the government of Kenya under President Moi. On the other hand, the genocide in Rwanda was equally well-planned and the extermination was systematically well-executed. In Rwanda, the list of those who had to be eliminated had been drawn well ahead of time.

By the same token, in Kenya the list of the ethnic communities that had to be eliminated had already been drawn up so that the Rift Valley would be left purely under the control of the KAMATUSA coalition. These ethnic communities included the Kikuyu, the Luo, the Luyia and the Kisii, among others. All of them had lived in the Rift Valley for a very long time, even though they had originated from Central Province, Nyanza Province and Western Province. Many of those who were not killed became categorized as Internally Displaced Persons (IDP), and therefore refugees in their own country. The difference between the Kenyan situation and the Rwandan one is that in Rwanda, it was the Hutu against the Tutsi, and the moderate Hutu became the victims of the genocide. In Kenya, on the other hand, it was the nature of ethnic pluralism and ethnic composition (approximately forty communities) that saved the country from total countrywide genocide. This ethnic composition made it more complex and difficult to coordinate. As a matter of fact, this is the main reason why Moi and his government turned their attention to the Coast Province, where the state sponsored an ethnic conflict between the coastal and the upcountry people, which led to KANU victory in the 1997 elections.

Moi and Mobutu had successfully managed to disorganize the opposition and were able to gain very easy political victory in the 1992 elections in their respective countries. Habyarimana, on the other hand, had also hoped to derail the opposition to his dictatorial regime in order to establish firm, secure control and consolidate his political power in

Rwanda. However, the intermittent civil war that had erupted in Rwanda had caught the attention of the international powers that now pushed for a political solution. As was the case with Mobutu, who had been pressurized by the international powers to accept the multiparty system, the international pressure forced Habyarimana to accept the concept of power sharing with the RPF hence, the signing of the Arusha Accords of 1993. But peace accords can sometimes become increasingly frightening in regard to their outcome. Ahmed Rashid talks about his desire and intention to write a book about Afghanistan after spending time "in Geneva covering the excruciating UN sponsored negotiations in 1988, which ended with Geneva Accords and with withdrawal of the Soviet Union troops from Afghanistan." (Rashid 2000: viii). But rather than bringing peace to their land and in the broken places, "the Afghans drove straight from Geneva into a bloody, senseless civil war that still continues to this day" (Rashid 2000: viii). It is this kind of an outcome that made the events in Kenya, and the search for a solution for the alleged stolen election victory in 2007 more frightening, placing the country and its people in a vulnerable position.

On the other hand, it is the Arusha Accords that sealed the fate of Habyarimana, as his supporters viewed him as a traitor for having given into the idea of democratic governance and power sharing. Instead of embracing the new political arrangement based on the provisions of the Arusha Accords, the dictatorial government of Rwanda cried foul and portrayed itself as the victim of opposition and decided to eliminate Habyarimana for agreeing with the terms of the Arusha Accords. According to Melvern (2006: 127), "Bagosora told Marchal that the RPF had no intention of sharing power, and that its only motivation was to take power by force. For Rwanda to enjoy even one day of peace it was necessary to 'eliminate the Tutsi.'" What surprised Machal was the fact that Bagosora was brave enough to speak so openly even in the presence of Major-General Dallaire, the Canadian commander of the UN Peacekeeping Force. Melvern (2006: 127) explains further that Marchal later stated that "Everyone knew, even in Belgium, what was going to happen for the plan of the genocide was in place for a long time." The Rwandan situation took a different turn and gradually incorporated an international outlook.

The same international powers that had pushed for the Arusha Accords now turned their backs on Rwanda and abandoned the Rwandan people in their hour of need. Even when the Western powers and the US realized that the killing of the ten Belgian peacekeepers and the Rwandan Prime Minister Agathe Uwilingiyimana, was meant to ensure the exit of the international forces as had been the case in Somalia, leaving the extremists to go on a free killing spree, the West forgot all about the Arusha Accords and Rwanda. The leaders of the interim government pointed fingers at the RPF, which they hoped would be held responsible for the state action and a justification for carrying out the genocide in Rwanda. This is exactly what Moi had done in the Rift Valley of Kenya. Through the state-sponsored genocidal killings using well-trained militias and morans, who were armed with both sophisticated weaponry as well as machetes, he placed the responsibility on the opposition as a way of diverting attention from the government action.

Subsequently, the political events of the 1990s in Uganda under Museveni, in Kenya under Moi, in the Democratic Republic of Congo under Mobutu and in Rwanda under Habyarimana occupied the center stage of the regional political climate. And when on October 1, 1990, the RPF launched an attack on Rwanda, the Mutara Crossing, like the crossing of the Rubicon, became a point of no return, the defining and deciding moment in the history of Rwanda. Consequently, the regionalization of the crisis in the Great Lakes region took on a new phase. Fred Rwigyema was killed on just the second day of the attack, his friend Kagame stepped in and was assisted by Colonel Alexis Kanyarengwe, a Hutu whose appointment signified the link between RPF and the Habyarimana opposition in Rwanda (Melvern 2004: 29).

At the regional level, support for Habyarimana became readily available from the neighboring states. For instance, troops were sent from the Democratic Republic of Congo, from where President Mobutu dispatched his own Presidential Special Division (DSP), and from Kenya, President Daniel arap Moi also sent an undisclosed form and nature of assistance. This is supported by the fact that the Moi government gave refuge to some of the most notorious extremist killers even after the genocide had ended in Rwanda. It was not until the then Vice President Paul Kagame visited Kenya in 1997 that the Moi government handed over to the ICTR nine of the ten individuals who had been protected by the Kenyan government. (Kagame's words when he visited the country on this particular occasion would later prove prophetic for the 2007 parliamentary elections!) However, just as Mobutu had his own Presidential Special Division, Habyarimana also had his Presidential Guard, and President Daniel arap Moi of Kenya had his own personal security force which was termed *Jeshi La Mzee*, literally the "Old Man's Army". Thus, each of the trio, Mobutu, Moi and Habyarimana had his own personal armed forces.

Jeshi La Mzee was a new vigilante force that was not part of the Kenyan Armed Forces. The vigilante group had become more and more visible in Kenya's political arena in 1992. According to Kagwanja (1998b: 16), the vigilante group "brought together some members of the notorious KANU (Kenya African National Union, the ruling party) youth wing and fresh recruits drawn from the burgeoning *lumpen*, the unemployed, impoverished and disillusioned youth who thronged Kenya's main cities." Some of these groups had come into existence as far back as the 1980s for the sole purpose of being instruments and agents of the government in hunting down 'anti-party' elements, monitoring and punishing "public dissent through indiscriminate violence, thuggery and extortion" (Kagwanja 1998b: 17).

Again, in the 1997 parliamentary elections, the *Jeshi La Mzee* became instrumental in carrying out violent acts against those whom the KANU ruling elite designated as a threat to the government of Daniel arap Moi, especially the members of the opposition. Kagwanja (1998b: 17) explains further that:

> …squads of Jeshi La Mzee stalked the main towns of Nairobi, Mombasa, Nakuru, Kisumu, Eldoret as well as smaller ones like Wudanyi, Machakos or Muranga. Private militias of some KANU bigwigs also went under the rubric of Jeshi La Mzee. For instance, the KANU Secretary-General, Mr. Joseph Kamotho, was reported to have a hit squad in his Mathioya constituency in Muranga's District. Similarly, another KANU leader, Darius Mbela, was reported to have a private militia, Jeshi La Mbela {Mbela's army) in Taita-Taveta, Coast Province.

The *Jeshi La Mzee* militia worked together with some Kenyan police, as well as the most dreaded General Service Unit (GSU) to violently break "the first constitutional reform rally that had been convened by NCEC at Kamkunji ground in Nairobi on May 13, 1992" (Kagwanja 1998b: 17). At this rally, police shot people at close range and even went as far as storming the Anglican Cathedral in Nairobi and used tear gas on the congregation. Another confrontation took place in Mombasa between those who supported the opposition party and *Jeshi La Mzee* (Kagwanja 1998a: 18). More serious was the attack on the first woman presidential hopeful, Charity Ngilu, whose political popularity in Ukambani pitted her against the ruling KANU party that considered Ukambani a KANU zone. Out of the various ***Jeshi La Mzees*** of the Moi-Kibaki era emerged the Mungiki, who carried outright killings even in Kibaki's backyard in Kikuyuland, and while the powerful John Michuki, a fellow Kikuyu, was the man in charge of internal security for the entire Republic of Kenya.

The Regional and Global Enablers of Autocracy

Thus, the Rwandan genocide was influenced and precipitated by both regional and international factors which were all waiting to converge on the Rwandan political arena. And with the invasion of Rwanda by the RPF, the regional crisis took on an international outlook. The RPF was now fighting against both the influence of the regional leadership from neighboring states and military assistance that was made available to Habyarimana and his government by the international community.

To this extent, the Belgians sent 400 paratroopers and the French sent in troops and included French spotter planes to locate the retreating RPF soldiers. "For France to have abandoned Habyarimana would have been tantamount to handing Rwanda over to the English-speaking rebels" (Melvern 2004: 30–31). The French referred to Uganda as "Tutsiland" and maintained that President Museveni's long-term ambition was channeled toward building a Tutsi empire. This was paradoxically the most interesting statement coming from the French considering the fact that Museveni had denied the Tutsi citizenship status in the same way that Mobutu had denied the Bunyamulenge citizenship status. It would appear that in reality, France was fighting not only against the RPF, but also against Uganda and by extension, against the British and American (Anglophone) influence in the Great Lakes region of East Africa.

According to Melvern (2004: 30–33), by October 4, 1990, French troops were dispatched to Rwanda; 300 French Paratroopers, who were stationed in the Central African Republic. More than 600 French troops were already in the country. There were two companies of parachutists and paramilitaries from the French Secret Service and combat helicopters. Two weeks later, Egypt began to supply Rwanda with weapons after negotiation with Egyptian Foreign Minister Boutros-Boutros Ghali, who would later become the UN Secretary-General in 1991. The first consignment included 60,000 grenades and some 2 million rounds of ammunition, 18,000 mortar bombs and 4200 assault rifles and rocket launchers. The arms deal was kept secret between the two governments. Thus, Rwanda had become the third largest importer of weapons in Africa behind Nigeria and Angola.

Melvern (2004: 33) has indicated that Rwanda spent an estimated $100 million on arms alone. As for the funding, this was as follows: about US $216 million of international funding had been earmarked for Rwanda; some of it came from the European Union, with sizable bilateral contributions from France, Belgium, Germany, and the US. Rwanda's status had changed and the country's economy was now in the hands of the world's most powerful international institutions—the World Bank and the IMF. The Rwandan army expanded virtually overnight from 5000 to 28,000 men. The arms that were used during the genocide, ranged from machetes to rocket launchers, all came from France, Belgium, South Africa, Egypt and China. "The governments of both France and Egypt were intimately involved in arms deals with extremists in Rwanda" (Melvern 2004: 33).

The Rwandan government was able to utilize the funds that had been provided by the international financial institutions namely, the World Bank and International Monetary Fund, to purchase arms. According to Melvern (2005: 5), "World Bank officials were fully aware of the militarization of Rwanda, but failed to share their knowledge even with the UN Security Council. Documents held in Kigali, as well as hitherto unpublished evidence of the UN Security Council deliberations in New York, revealed a sequence of events that is as agonizing as it is shocking". In her account of the Rwandan situation, Melvern laments the fact that "there were some who covered it up and that there is also some evidence that points not just to negligence, but also to complicity. The combination of revelations about the scale and intensity of the genocide, the complicity of Western states, the failure to intervene and the suppression of the information about what was happening, is as shocking an indictment, not just of the UN Security Council, but even more so of governments, and individuals who could have prevented what was happening but chose not to do so" (Melvern 2004: 4–5).

Moi and Mobutu continued to give their support to the Rwandan government to the extent that their governments protected some of the perpetrators of the genocide. At the international level, starting with the RPF invasion in 1990, the Rwandan government received arms from certain world powers, and this assistance continued during and even after the genocide. To this extent, the RPF was actually fighting a war of offense and defense, both on the home front and against the international powers, which made sure that the Hutu extremists had a constant and adequate arms supply. According to Waugh (2004: 170–171), even long after the genocide, Moi and Mobutu still posed a threat to Rwanda. He goes on to explain:

> The region's old guard of rulers obstructed the process too (Arusha Tribunal): Zaire's (DRC) Mobutu and Kenya's dynastic Daniel arap Moi were more in the mold of, if not loyal to the memory of, the deceased Habyarimana and his extremist successors. The pursuit of the criminals in Zaire (DRC) was complex, muddied by continuing war and numerous factions struggling for power and resources within its borders. (Waugh 2004: 170–171)

However, the Kenyan situation became very different as the government continued to protect the extremists who had sought refuge in the country. In July 1997, the Rwandan Vice President, Paul Kagame, made a bold statement during his state visit to the country. According to Waugh:

> ...Vice President Kagame took matters in his own hands...making an issue of the fugitive killers who were still being harbored in the aging ruler's republic. At that time Kagame spoke of "a feeling of betrayal, even by our own African brothers." "What happened here can happen elsewhere – it can happen in these other countries – and then I am sure they will run to us... Things have happened and they can happen again". (Waugh 2004: 171)

Soon after Kagame's state visit to Kenya, nine suspects were transferred to ICTR by the Kenyan government. They included Jean Kambanda, the former prime minister of the interim government in Rwanda. Melvern (2004: 1–2) states that "On the run for three years after the genocide was over, Kambanda was arrested in the early morning of 18 July, 1997 in Nairobi. He was taken to Arusha in Tanzania by plane the same day, accompanied by Pierre Duclos and Marcel Desaulniers, two investigators for the International Criminal Tribunal for Rwanda, the ICTR." Also apprehended in Nairobi were the editor of the Hutu Power Kangura magazine, Hassan Ngeze and the Belgian broadcaster for the RTLM, George Ruggiu (Waugh 2004: 171).

The Impact of the Ethnic Conflict in Kenya

The Socioeconomic Dimension

In Kenya, the violent conflict which started in the 1990s, had far-reaching consequences for the people of the country. "People are still living in squalid, unhygienic camps without proper sanitation or shelter. Many of these unsettled people have become refugees in their own country," observed Nthamburi (1993: 6).

Considering that Kenya's rural women are the backbone of the country's subsistence farming, the ethnic conflict of the 1990s denied them the tools and services for sustainability. This had far-reaching effects not only on Kenyan society but particularly on the health, education and security of the children as well as young women and girls who had been traumatized by these conflicts. Women and girls became victims of genocide, rape, torture, displacement and other abuses. These women should have been empowered through access to productive resources, which should include the repeal of restrictive laws regarding land ownership; adequate housing, alternative sources of energy, credit schemes and simple technologies, such as farming tools, hand plows, tractors, irrigation schemes, improved seeds and fertilizers. Also, some of these rural women, especially in the Rift Valley, Western and Nyanza provinces had been rendered homeless.

The women's once self-reliant approach to life had been shattered and reduced to the level of displacement and helplessness. Also disrupted by the so-called "land clashes" were the various development activities in these areas. Support mechanisms which had been available and enhanced women's effectiveness, such as inter and intra-community cooperatives, marketing, transportation, networking systems and storage facilities for daily use (as well as during emergencies), and such systems that enhanced peaceful coexistence between the various Kenyan ethnic groups, suddenly became immobilized and destabilized; the hard hit areas being the Rift Valley and the Western and Nyanza provinces.

These women had been denied a chance to participate in social, economic and political development of their country, as they continued to rely on relief, food, undefined shelter and humanitarian contributions, which included articles of clothing. Even those who had raised their level of understanding through the acquisition of basic education and who were trained in various skills, and even literate ones had been displaced. The civil education for participation in community decision-making processes, which had begun to have a positive impact on these rural women, especially in terms of empowerment and human development, suddenly became stalled and halted. The sorry state of conflicts led to the withdrawal of the United Nations Development Program (UNDP) which pulled out of a program of rehabilitation of ethnic clash victims (Daily Nation 1995).

The Other Dimensions

According to the "Kiliku Report," there were two root causes of the ethnic conflict in Kenya: the clashes were politically motivated and fueled by some officers in provincial administration and second, the clashes were instigated through misconceptions that some ethnic communities intended to drive away other ethnic communities in order to acquire their land. As a result, the violent ethnic conflict spread to a wide area in Kenya including Koru, Chegaiya, the settlement scheme in Timboroa, Turbo, Kamasai, Londiana, Saboti, Endebess and Kwanza divisions, Molo, Eronge and Sotik, all in the Rift Valley at the height of the so-called "land clashes" in Kenya. The Dailies reported horrifying stories: Three children and a woman were burned to ashes. These were Mrs. Louise Wanjiku who died with her 2 and a half-year-old son Harun still strapped to her back (The Daily Nation 1993: 1).

Mrs. Wanjiku reported how her neighbor's children were "slashed on the neck by the attackers" (The Standard 1993: 2). The same paper reported that "dogs were feasting on bodies rotting in several farms in Molo south." (The Standard 1993: 2). And Finance (1992: 17) explained: "Children have been killed by the police on their mother's backs. Others while on the backs of their elder sisters". Other children had died of malnutrition in places such as Kamwaura and Molo camps (The Daily Nation 1993: 5). Also reported in The Standard (1992: 2):

> A woman who gave birth a day ago was seen seated along the Kisii road with her children crying and obviously hungry. Other areas that were affected by the ethnic violence included some schools where in places such as Enosopukia, Enaibalbel and Mau Narok twenty three primary schools had to be closed as about 400 teachers fled to safety. Reflecting on the situations at the various schools, Father Louis Elungata remarked: "This is the saddest, most unfortunate and barbaric thing that has ever happened to the school. Tribal sentiments should never be allowed to infiltrate schools as they are the only places where the youth can be taught in harmony as Kenyans."

On the political scene, the issue of ethnicity and ethnic clashes had far-reaching consequences. The December 1992 multiparty elections were a culmination of ethnic national patriotism, and they were either won or lost "on the basis of personalities rather than issues, ethnic rather than party affiliation" (Nzomo 1994: 6). The elections turned out to be a reaffirmation or reinforcement of the divisions based on ethnicity and the Balkanization of Kenyan society along ethnic lines. Oyugi (1993: 23) explains that the December 1992 elections did not in any way push the democratization clock ahead, but that the elections merely disturbed its rhythm… the birth of multi-partyism in Kenya in its present form is only conducive to anti-democratic tendencies. All the political parties as currently constituted are essentially ethnic parties. This held true even for the December 1997 elections. Thus, among the major ethnic communities in the country, voting was carried out along ethnic lines. As had been observed by Nzomo (1994: 12):

> …women across ethnic groups have been, more so than men, most opposed to politically-instigated ethnic clashes. Indeed since the ethnic clashes started, women across ethnic groups have been most vocal in condemning the violence. They have issued many press statements in the local media and organized prayer meetings for peace. Significantly, their appeal has been directed at men in general, to stop the genocide. They have made their appeal in their capacity as mothers of this nation, than as spokeswomen of given ethnic communities.

The other factor that emerged from the ethnic conflict was the issue of refugees and persons displaced in their own country. In 1993, the late Professor Wangari Maathai observed that: "Women have had their wombs opened to kill even their unborn offspring, and dead bodies have been fed to dogs" (Society 1993: 9). The Standard (1991: 1) reported that "a 50 year old woman at Oromotit Village in Tinderet was raped and killed before her body was set on fire." These and many more are some of the effects of violent ethnic conflicts that have continued to afflict Kenyan society, as it regresses from the birth of nationhood and the development of nation-state to ethnic loyalty. Instead of owing allegiance to the national flag and the people of Kenya for which it stands, one witnesses a situation where ethnicity has been manipulated for political and economic gains.

Nthamburi (1993: 9) sounded a warning as he reflected on the Kenyan situation:

> A situation like the one that exists in Kenya is potentially explosive. To counteract the potential evils of ethnicism it is necessary to engage in an open and frank discussion on the political order in which every person

and tribe would have a stake in nation building. There must be built-in checks and balances to ensure that no single community can predominate in leadership. Whatever the future holds for Kenyans, one thing must be made clear. While tribes will continue to exist and make their contribution as citizens of this nation, it must be emphasized that every person has the inalienable right to live and work in any part of the country without being discriminated against. Indeed, it is a subtle form of discrimination to treat a Kenyan as an outsider in his/her own country. The constitutional right of every Kenyan to live and own property in any section of this country is non-negotiable. This right must be protected by all leaders. While we belong to different ethnic groups, we must feel that first and foremost we are Kenyans. Indeed this is our unity in diversity.

The Concept of Regionalism or Federalism in Kenya

Background

The political transformation led to hostility among the various ethnic groups in Kenya. Apart from political manipulation by the elites, the issue of land and property ownership must be considered as the root cause of the violent conflicts in the Rift Valley, and the Western and Nyanza provinces. The land issue as a major economic factor was camouflaged into political sensitization of ethnicity. It was because of this development that the German Ambassador rightly observed that "Sometimes one gets the eerie feeling that the notion of federalism is used by some politicians here as a justification for ethnic strife; namely as a pretext ***to create ethnically pure regions by pushing unwanted tribes out***" (emphasis mine) (Society 1994: 34). Thus, some of the politicians attempted to incite ethnic sentiments among the diversified groups of people who had lived together for several decades in these sections of the country namely, the Rift Valley and the Western and Nyanza provinces.

According to information obtained from the Internally Displaced Persons Program, the Kenyan situation may be summarized in this manner:

> Serious ethnic violence began in Western Kenya in late 1991. In the next two years, it spread to other parts of the most fertile and productive regions of Kenya. In this period, various ethnic groups, who had previously lived in peace and with a degree of interdependence, were brought into violent conflict. Subsequent ethnic clashes caused deaths and injuries,

> internal displacement, destitution and extensive destruction of resources in the affected areas. Substantial damage was inflicted to agricultural, economic and social infrastructures – including education and health care. At the national level, loss of crops and livestock was one cause of national food shortages. At household level, it is estimated that, at the height of the disturbances, some 250,000 people were affected, either by internal displacement in the short or long term or by social and economic disruption. People had to abandon their farms, houses were burnt and many lost everything they had— tools, livestock, household effects, food stocks. Since then, further clashes, notably in Enosopukia and Burnt Forest, have displaced thousands and more (Internally Displaced Persons Program 1995).

For a long time, indeed since independence, Kenya was ranked as one of the few African countries that had remained sober and sane. The Kenyan people continued to remain patient, applying reason and logic where they could easily have been driven to madness. The beginning of the twenty-first century has been the most trying time in Kenya's historical development, being characterized by chaotic transition from one party to the multiparty era. In their desperate attempt to realize some form of prophecy that the advent of multi-partyism would lead to chaos, some leaders went out of their way to inculcate into the minds of their people the feeling that there were some groups in Kenya who were referred to as foreigners in their own land. This spirit of indigenous ethnic patriotism led to what commonly became known in Kenya as "ethnic clashes", "tribal clashes" or simply "land clashes".

This kind of patriotism invoked and lit the fire of economic, political and cultural superiority that sent hundreds of thousands of people fleeing the Rift Valley. There was a sudden discovery that there were some "foreigners" who should not have been living in this vast province of Kenya. It all started with the pronouncement of some highly placed individuals in Kenya's government. The ethnic clashes involved attacks, fighting and actual killings that were made by people who appeared to be unknown to the victims as they armed themselves with bows and arrows. The major victims were the Agikuyu, Kalenjins, Abaluyia, Luo and Abagusii. The groups that are believed to have committed this crime against humanity were the Kalenjin, which comprises the Nandi, Tugen, Marakwet, Kipsigis and Sabaot.

On September 8, 1992, two Kenyan cabinet ministers, Biwott and Misoi, one assistant minister, some members of parliament and several civil servants or civic officials met at Kipchoge Keino Stadium, Eldoret, and issued threats that culminated in the main cause of ethnic eruption in the Rift Valley and the Western and Nyanza provinces. The government officials meeting at the Kipchoge Keino Stadium was reported to have urged the young people in the Rift Valley to take up arms and drive out of the Rift Valley non-Kalenjin-speaking peoples, non-Maasai speakers and non-Pokot speakers. The officials further stated that they would eventually table what they called the Majimbo Bill in the august house with a view to making all non-indigenous residents of the Rift Valley quit the area. The advocates of multiparty democracy were banned from the province (Kangwanja 1998b: 11).

The Structural Tapestry of Political Power

Majimboism is derived from the Kiswahili word for a region. Therefore, in the historical development in Kenya, majimboism, regionalism and federalism have all been used interchangeably in expressing a political arrangement that is based on ethnic patriotism as opposed to national patriotism. According to Kibwana (1994: 1), "Majimboism or regionalism refers to a political system or organization in which the country is divided into semi-autonomous regional units presided over by weak governments, which in practical terms, resemble local authorities government". He looks at such governments as being a halfway house between a centralized state and a federal state. Still others tend to think of majimboism or regionalism as somewhat "quasi-federalism, nominal federalism and sometimes as bogus federalism" (Kibwana 1994: 1). He goes on to explain:

> Federalism is a system of government in which two distinct governments exist in a country, that is, a central government and a state government or a government at the periphery or local level. Powers are constitutionally and legally shared between the two governments so that, on the whole, overlap of functions is avoided. Each local unit is usually distinct by way of history, culture, economic organization and viability, politics, linguistic characteristics, etc. Often, the local unit could be a country in its own right; it has the ability to be self-reliant. However, the local unit will favor being in union with others so as to reap the advantages of economies of scale e.g., as is the case with the many states which form the United States of America. (Kibwana 1994: 2)

It is noted that federalism as a structure of government gives room for democratic realization in the sense that the central government shares power with local units, which tends to perform the duties and tasks best done at the "grassroots" level. This system ensures that local units can actually exercise their powers independently and that the people would have more say in day-to-day activities and the running of the affairs of these units, as well as political, economic and social development. On the whole, federal structure tends to promote and enhance democratic ideals if and when applied as a balance between "a central government and state government or a government at the periphery or local level" (Kibwana 1994: 2).

The above would seem to imply that there exists a system whereby there is equitable distribution of power between the two units, namely the center and the periphery. Its major objective would be to ensure that marginalization of one group by another does not exist or would be safeguarded. We learn from De Smith (1965: 253), in his reflections on federalism as a structure of government in relation to the American, Swiss, Canadian and Australian governments, that it is "…a manifestation of democratic constitutionalism, it involves the division and limitation of governmental power, the demarcation of forbidden zones, the frustration of the will of the majority on the issues deemed to be of special importance to regionally grouped minorities; it implies political pluralism, decentralized policy decisions as well as decentralized administration, a readiness to hasten slowly by means of bargains and compromises and to acquiesce in legalistic solutions to governmental problems".

In Kenya, the issue of federalism, that is, majimboism, came about in the 1950s and early 1960s, where the minority groups, Asians and white settlers advocated for federalism. They argued that majimboism or regional structure was best suited for the protection of their interests and aspirations. To them, KANU was a party of majority ethnic groups, namely the Luo and the Agikuyu. Just as in the early 1950s and early 1960s, the proponents of majimboism in the 1990s argued that this structure of government would, no doubt, safeguard the interest of the minority and would ensure that minority groups are not politically, socially and economically oppressed by the majority, who comprise the larger population in the country. In the 1990s, both the minorities and majority had come to view regionalism in terms of ethnic nationalism. Thus, the concept of regionalism was seen as "a ploy used by the political elite to ensure sharing power and wealth via the use of ethnicity" (Kibwana 1994: 7). Reacting to the issue of majimboism in Kenya, Kuria (1994b: 2) remarked:

> Kenya's majimboism is not federalism. The central theme that its advocates have pursued is power at any cost. They are disinterested in democratic

> theory of federalism, which divides power between the center and the region. Indeed these advocates supported one-party rule, and did not show interest in federalism until September 1991 when they realized that the impending pluralism threatened their hold on power…

In the Kenyan situation, the prevailing winds of change which brought about the advent of multi-partyism created an atmosphere of fear, anxiety and animosity. The return to multi-partyism seems to have coincided with the eruption of ethnic violent outbursts in the Rift Valley, and Western and Nyanza provinces. All of a sudden, the proponents of majimboism saw nothing wrong with negating the Kenya Constitution, which had safeguarded the rights of its citizens by stating that all Kenyans were free to live and, indeed, own property anywhere within the republic. Suddenly, the people of Kenya seemed to have forgotten that by joining the United Nations organizations, they had, in actual fact, nurtured the Universal Declaration on Human Rights "which affirms that human beings have an identical nature" (United Nations 2015: 1). Contained in this article in part is the statement that "all human beings are born free and equal in dignity and rights" (United Nations 2015: 1) that "they are endowed with reason and conscience and should act towards one another in a spirit of brotherhood" (United Nations 2015: 1) and sisterhood.

Indeed, the nineteenth-century revolutions in Europe led to the overthrow of tyrannical governments, following the famous American Declaration of Independence. In 1891, one of the most important outcomes of the French revolution was the Declaration of the Rights of Man. This followed the 1776 American Declaration which said in part that "We hold these truths to be self-evident that all men are created equal and they are endowed by their Creator with certain inalienable rights among these life, liberty and pursuit of happiness" (Sunstein 2003: 3). Kuria (1994a: 3) explains further that "all constitutions of independent African countries have been founded on this truth which one-party regime and the military have departed from."

The advent of multi-partyism challenged the political power brokers who had monopolized the political and economic scenes for decades since independence. Some believed that the political transformation which was taking place on the African continent meant the loss of their political and economic powers. Such threats culminated in real and imaginable fears. A new type of nationalism emerged. This new ethnic nationalism had faded away with the establishment of the colonial state and its articulation with the indigenous political, social and economic systems, since the people of Kenya viewed the colonial state as the enemy. There was, therefore, a unifying factor to the extent that when the colonial state banned political parties, the ethnic political associations of the 1920s led to nationalist political parties that steered Kenya toward the road to independence. The ethnic political associations were important in the sense that they resulted in the realization by the masses of Kenya of the advantage of coming together to fight the common enemy, that is, the colonial regime.

However, in the 1990s, three decades after independence, political elites from certain sections of the republic began to call for the establishment of regionalism. With time, the constitutionally guaranteed right of every Kenyan to own property anywhere in the country was also violated. Leaders began to play on ethnic emotions; ethnic consciousness began to replace that feeling of national patriotism as people moved steadily toward ethnic patriotism. The proponents of majimboism or regionalism, in fact, advocated for the revival of ethnic loyalty and consciousness in order to show how some had gained from the fruits of independence, while others had been marginalized or simply remained at the periphery. This peripheralization had been blamed on those who had monopolized power relations and power politics (Kagwanja 1998a: 3).

The agitation for majimboism did not in any way symbolize what federalism is all about. Indeed, the central theme of this new awakening was that its advocates wished to protect their political and economic powers at all cost. Therefore, the agitation for regionalism was based on two major issues: ***land and power***. The political power would be a means to reinforce economic power through land control. Thus, majimboism was envisaged as a means to an end; and majimboism would protect the individual's political power as well as economic and cultural base. The advocates of majimboism used these ideas to appeal to people's support, the people on whose behalf they talked without their mandate. It was a coincidence that the proponents of majimboism only seemed to have realized the need to appeal to ethnic nationalism or patriotism by September 1991, especially as the impending political pluralism seemed to have gathered momentum thus threatening their own power base! This is what eventually led to the violent ethnic conflicts in the Rift Valley, and Western and Nyanza provinces of Kenya.

The other factor in the complex nature of the violent ethnic conflict in these regions of the country was that once violence erupted, many former inhabitants of the Rift Valley were forced to flee the area, their properties were confiscated, their land was taken and their houses were burned. Such developments were meant to rid the area of any opposition elements. Eventually, the Rift Valley Province was declared the zone for the ruling party, KANU and the opposition was not allowed in the area. The importance of this development was that in the event of future elections, the whole area would vote for the ruling party, KANU. Indeed, in the Rift Valley Province, multi-partyism was demonized as anti-Kalenjin movement, which was aimed at removing Daniel arap Moi from power not necessarily because of his ineffectiveness and incompetence as a leader, but owing to the fact that he was a Kalenjin and from the Rift Valley Province, and the Kalenjin felt they had to protect their interest even if it meant bloodshed through genocidal ethnic cleansing. According to Nthamburi (1993: 6):

> At first these clashes were portrayed by the government as a result of long-standing conflict over land or spontaneous response of ethnically divided communities to the challenges of election campaigns. It soon became clear that the violence was actually coordinated in September 1992, a Parliamentary Committee confirmed reports that high-ranking government officials had been involved in the training of the attackers. Everyone hoped that these clashes would cease soon after the elections. That has not, however, proved to be the case… There is in these areas a growing atmosphere of hatred and suspicion between communities that have lived together peacefully for many years. This is bound to be an area of tension and possibly retaliatory attacks for a long time. Once an area has been affected by violence, the people's lives are indefinitely disrupted.

Thus ethnic violence preceded the 1992 and 1997 elections in Kenya, leading to a very easy election victory for the ruling party, KANU. The ethnic violence was state-sponsored as an attempt by the government to thwart the ever-growing and increasing demands for multi-partyism and a democratization process in the country. The multiparty democracy had returned to Kenya amidst the joyous celebrations and hope for a new approach to governance in December 1991. But this democratization process was soon clouded by a new wave of widespread violence that the ruling party had baptized ethnic clashes, land clashes, border disputes or simply gangsterism.

The government enlisted the services of invisible but very powerful groups of warriors, whose mode of dressing reflected traditional African attire that distinguished them from the modern Kenya's armed forces.

They were armed forces with authentic weaponry such as spears, swords, bows and arrows and machetes that contrasted interestingly with, and yet, differed remarkably from, modern weaponry. The two forms of weaponry found expressions and met in one person, who used them interchangeably to shatter the dream and visions of many Kenyans for the establishment of a possible democratic institution in Kenya.

By the turn of the present century, Moi embarked on his disastrous and failed "Uhuru Project" with a hope of a political marriage between his children and the son of the first president of the republic, in an attempt to monopolize political leadership in the country. But by this time, Moi's days were numbered. He was dislodged by Mwai Kibaki in the 2002 election, where Raila Odinga played a major role in bringing the various ethnic communities together by simply uttering "Kibaki Tosha,—We are the unbwogeable." The Kenyan people had tasted the fruits of democracy through a peaceful democratic movement that transformed and utilized ethnicity for a positive result. Nevertheless, it is the same Daniel arap Moi, who had formed an alliance with Kibaki, and by extension, with Museveni against Raila Odinga's ODM Party. Shortly before his visit to the US, just as Kenyans were preparing for the 2007 election, Museveni publicly stated that he would not be comfortable with Raila Odinga's leadership in Kenya. Therefore, it was not surprising that Museveni's security forces appeared in Western Kenya in the midst of the reaction to Kibaki's stolen election victory. These forces, including an undisclosed number of the Mungiki, were meant to create a scenario of ethnic conflict that would make it appear as though it was one ethnic community against that of Kibaki. Contrary to this expectation, the spontaneous and explosive reaction from Lake Victoria across the Kenyan landscape to the Indian Ocean on the coast proved that this was not a Kikuyu-Luo conflict. Thus, Museveni's hurried and unplanned visit to Kenya in the midst of the violence that engulfed the country was meant to save face and divert attention from the Ugandan leader's involvement in the Kenyan crisis.

On January 4, 2008, Gwynne Dyer wrote an article reflecting on the turbulent situation in Kenya. She stated that: "More than two years ago, when Kenyan opposition leader, Raila Odinga, quit President Mwai Kibaki's government, I wrote: 'The trick will be to get Kibaki out without triggering a wave of violence that would do the country grave and permanent damage… Bad times are coming to Kenya." She goes on to emphasize the fact that "The bad times have arrived; but the violence that has swept Kenya since stolen election on December 27 is not just tribalism. Kikuyus have been the main target of popular wrath and non-Kikuyu protestors have been principal victims of the security forces, ***but this confrontation is about trust betrayed, hopes dashed and patience broken***" (emphasis mine). The confrontation between the people of Kenya was more of the "broken faith, not tribalism" (Dyer 2008: 1). The crisis, and eventual killings that followed, were basically prompted by the Kivuitu-Kibaki orchestrated surprise win and the hurried swearing in of Kibaki in secrecy.

In December 2003, Mutahi Ngunyi wrote an article that appeared in Sunday Nation under the title "Why our second liberation is yet to be completed." By then, Kibaki was only a year old in political leadership as the President of Kenya. Ngunyi stated:

> This week I want to give a suggestion to President Mwai Kibaki: He should fire his speechwriter! If we lived in a "banana republic" these people would have actually been charged with sabotage. What they gave the President to read on Jamhuri Day was flat and shoddy. In fact, his speech on this day sounded like recycled material from Madaraka Day addresses. And what is worrying is that his speechwriters did not seem to notice repetitions. The question we should ask here is why? The answer to this is simple: May be they also slept through the speeches! The long and short of things is therefore that someone is being negligent.

Mwai Kibaki was elected as the President of Kenya in 2002. Like his predecessor arap Moi, he continued the practice of the instrumental use of ethnicity. Unfortunately, this culminated in ethnic conflict in Kenya after the December 2007 elections. It is these developments that have changed the trajectory of Kenya's political landscape. Achebe (1999: 7) laments the fact that:

> "We live in terrible times when an individual tyrant or small clique of looters in power can destroy the lives and the future of whole countries and whole populations by their greed. The consequences of these can be of genocidal proportions." But Wole Soyinka (1999: 27) consoles us with "what was planted can also be uprooted, and that the grip of dissolute military power over the landscape of African nations will also be scrapped off inch by inch to restore vibrant culture as people of the continent embark on a process of self-renewal. If this has to be the last phase of decolonization, then let it be."

The mission and objectives of the warriors were to create a situation where any form of political pluralism would not exist, and in so doing, they would protect the privileges of the hegemonic dominant ruling elites in Kenya. The impact of the ethnic violence in the country both in 1992 and 1997 cut across regional, ethnic, clan, gender and religious boundaries. Among the hardest hit were women, children, the young and the old alike. Thus the 1990s historical development in Kenya took a different shift from the ideology of nationalism and the development of the nation-state to **"majimboism,"** which is derived from the Kiswahili word for a region (Kuria 1994b).

This concept of regionalism was the manifestation of a political leadership that was based on ethnicity. It was a reaction to the advent of multi-partyism in Kenya in 1991–1992. Instead of placing emphasis on the maintenance of a sense of unity in diversity, and cohesion among the various ethnic and religious groups in Kenya, cultivating, as it were, a sense of national identity buttressed by national ideology, ***majimboism*** embraced ethnic patriotism and loyalty (Kuria 1994b).

The ethnic violence that emanated from the early 1990s had far-reaching implications for social, economic and political relations in the country. In the Kenyan polity, various groups of people began to perceive one another differently. As a result, ethnic suspicions had been deeply planted and well nurtured through the design of the state. Thus, the harmony that had existed in the Kenyan body politic, and the harmony that characterized national development had been disrupted and replaced with ethnic antagonism. Even ethnic relations in which inter-marriages were encouraged, and which enriched reciprocal existence of communities in Kenya, had been adversely affected.

Indeed, the over-politicization of ethnicity had adversely affected social relations in the country. Both men and women became victims of the inter-ethnic hostilities. Earlier marriages across ethnic boundaries had been disrupted. In fact, certain cultural practices had been imposed on some female members married in different ethnic groups other than their own. Some of these females, who got married into communities that practice female circumcision, had been forcefully circumcised. Moreover, in the Rift Valley, and Western and Nyanza provinces of Kenya, households had suffered as a result of the conflicts. Most households had been ejected from their lands, their houses and household belongings either destroyed or burnt altogether. Lives had been lost in the process. But perhaps the most important is the fact that ethnic violence had great implications for gender relations.

Issues of Ethnicity in a National Perspective

Background

In the past few decades, the historical development in Kenyan society has tended to shift from the ideology of nation-state to a debate on the concept of regionalism. Regionalism has been a manifestation of political leadership that is based on ethnicity, where the group in power places economic benefits in its own ethnic community. Instead of trying to maintain a sense of unity and cohesion among the various ethnic and religious groups and cultivating a sense of national identity, majimboism has been based on ethnic patriotism and loyalty. The political, economic and social impact of this concept has been felt in almost every part of the country.

The Ubiquity of Ethnicity in Power Relations

Yet, ethnicity is an issue that cannot be ignored when articulating and deliberating on the country's political relations, because it forms part of the continent's heritage in which strong kinship ties still do exist. It is for this reason that there is a tendency for most African people to interpret their aspirations and interests in ethnic terms. Moreover, the process of development and the provision of service by the government also tend to be interpreted within the framework of ethnic advancement.

Various theories have been advanced in an attempt to explain ethnic eruptions in Africa. Apologists of imperialism view ethnic eruptions as a resurgence of pre-colonial barbarism and savagery, akin to that stage of human political development, the state of nature which had been described by Hobbes (1651). In this view, Africans are presented as a people, who blindly identify with their own ethnic communities to the detriment of other groups and their interests. Consequently, ethnic relations are characterized by hostility and violence. Some African leaders have harped on this, creating ethnic tensions within the general polity.

The second view postulates that ethnic eruptions could very well be traced back to the colonial period. Within this scope of argument, it is explained that colonial administrators carry the blame for the introduction and creation of what they termed "native reserves." These reserves and the whole process of Balkanization and land alienation in turn solidified ethnic barriers. They further isolated the so-called inward-looking communities who were portrayed as a people who were incapable of integrating themselves into larger social units, especially in the colonial state.

In the process of this isolation, there emerged ethnic tension between the privileged loyalists and the dispossessed ethnic groups (Murungi 1995). It is therefore, not surprising that ethnic groups such as the Maasai of Kenya were dispossessed of their lands, an event that created grave economic imbalances and disequilibrium between regions and ethnic groups. The impact of this was political, social and economic disparity among the various regions that form the nation. Indeed, in the case of Kenya, the British colonialists pushed the Maasai out of the high potential areas of the Laikipia Plateau at the turn of the twentieth century to marginal lands south of present-day Kenya.

Even with political independence, the Maasai did not recover their lost lands. Instead, the affluent and well-educated communities and individuals emerging out of the colonial dispensation either bought or were reallocated land on the basis of political patronage of the first independent republic. Sometimes this was done in collaboration with the elites from those communities. Nasongo (2006: 14) makes the following observations:

> According to Ntimama, the Maasai have historically been the victims of oppression, first, by the British colonialists, and second by the Kikuyu, who allegedly marginalized their people by encroaching on their ancestral homeland. At a conference in Vienna on indigenous peoples, he claimed that the Maasai were becoming an "endangered species" and would have to fight to protect themselves. Ironically, it was Ntimama, as Chairman of the Narok County Council at the time, who allowed the Kikuyu access to the land around Enoosupukia in the first place. For this he expected political support (Weekly Review 1993: 8–9). He espoused the view that settlers must vote with the local Maasai or move out of his district, even though the Kenyan constitution guarantees the right of all Kenyans irrespective of their ethnicity to move, settle, and own property wherever they choose.

By this same maneuver, the Kalenjin communities have had to go through the same type of treatment in the Rift Valley of Kenya, which had been the scene of ethnic violence in 1991–1992. The violence was directed against those referred to as invading communities since the 1992 multiparty elections in Kenya. In this group are the Agikuyu, Abaluyia, Abagusii and the Luo of Western Kenya.

There is yet a third view which postulates that ethnic conflicts are a product of political opportunism expressed by some unscrupulous, often selfish and unprincipled politicians. Within this framework, political leaders become inclined to exploit the "*laissez-faire*" of a multiparty political dispensation with the express purpose of taking advantage of the existing cultural differences of ethnic groups for their own interest. It is this conceptual framework that often leads to the call for ***majimboism*** , that is, federalism (Kuria 1994b). ***Majimboism*** raises ethnic tensions and fear of those who have been branded as invading communities. This is often followed by the call to expel such groups from regions, which are thought not to be their original homes. As a matter of fact, the ethnic tensions and conflicts in the Rift Valley and Western Kenya in 1991–1992, and the coast and other parts of the country in 1997, were all related to the issue of invaders from without.

The other school of thought that has tried to analyze the ethnic conflicts in Africa sets forth the argument that ethnic eruptions can be explained as a product of underdeveloped politics of Africa's un-captured peasantry by intellectuals and politicians (Ochwada 1995). In this fourth category, there is the notion that the intellectuals and politicians are embroiled in competition for the support of the peasantry; that in the process of the struggle for not only support but also control of the peasants, politicians usually emerge as the victors. This, it is argued, is due to the fact that politicians understand rural politics better and are more practical than the intellectuals.

It is further stated that the politicians have been able to endear themselves to a segment of peasants simply because the politics of peasants are predominantly local with a political vision that is terribly circumscribed to immediate, and, in most cases, parochial interests. Put another way, this school of thought sees the peasants as having no problem with corruption, nepotism, looting of the treasury, undermining national interests, singing false praise or even short-charging other ethnic groups if this were to bring immediate and tangible material benefits to them. Indeed, this explains why Africans have had no attachment to dominant ideologies in conventional liberal democratic practice. The ethnic conflicts dogging Africans are an offshoot of this kind of thinking. However, one would argue that the 2007 elections in Kenya seem to negate this notion, judging from the reaction of the people, as they believed that their democratic rights had been impeded upon.

The last of these schools of thought interprets ethnic tension in Africa as stemming from ethnocracy, that is to say, the unfair, inequitable distribution of economic and political power along ethnic lines. Therefore, ethnic conflicts are thought to be about the status quo. This would imply the control of ownership and management of the national resources, including the state parastatals. This aspect revolves around the idea of benefiting from ***Matunda ya Uhuru***, that is, the control of the fruits of independence—"the national cake."

Thus, in presenting the complex issues of ethnic conflicts in Kenya, and for that matter, the African continent, it becomes almost imperative that an explanation of the various conceptual frameworks be articulated. This is done solely for the purpose of coming to grips with the ethnic question in Africa, and how this has impacted on social, political and economic relations on the continent.

Conclusion

This chapter has tried to address the factors that contributed to the ethnic cleansing in the Great Lakes region in the 1990s. It contrasts the regional with the international involvement in the crisis in the area. The trio, namely Mobutu Sese Seko, Daniel arap Moi and Juvenal Habyarimana worked tirelessly and in concert with each other to preserve their autocratic personal rule against the agitation for political pluralism. Habyarimana died in the process, Mobutu's dictatorial regime came to an "inglorious end," and as for Moi, the writing was already on the wall, and it was just a matter of time as the events that ushered in the twenty-first century would reveal. Nevertheless, Moi actually managed to lead the hegemonic dominant KANU elite to a political victory in 1997, having engineered ethnic conflict in the country, especially in the Coast Province, where the upcountry people became the target.

The Rwandan genocide shocked the whole world, but the world kept silent and watched on, hoping that someone else would step in and end the tragedy. The neighboring African states waited for some outside force to come in and save the situation while some of the Rwandans simply sat there waiting, waiting for divine intervention or simply waiting for death.

As Ayot (2003: 4) asserts,

> When people have lost a sense of direction, let us say so. I have seen it happen before. It starts with the gathering storms and the light gives way and the heavens become dark, very dark. But it is not the normal darkness; it is pale, subdued and frightening because you can feel that the rains will be severe, very severe with the resultant flood sweeping everything on its way to some unknown destination. And rivers with tributaries begin to form in places where none have ever existed before. These newly created rivers begin to overflow their banks, you know, the banks that had never existed before. It is these that cause panic as they become agents of death and misery. Fear then sets in, and you can tell that something is terribly wrong when you look at the faces of terrified people and even the helpless animals and birds drowning in this huge form of the deluge.

References

Achebe, Chinua. 1999. *African People in African Markets.* Address Delivered at the IMF/World Bank Annual Meetings. Washington, D.C. September 25–30.

Adekunle, Julius. 2003. Conflict and African Politics. In *Contemporary Africa*, vol. 5, ed. Toyin Falola, 219–239. Durham, NC: Carolina Academy Press.

Agenda for Peace. 1994. *Women's Volunteer Contributions.* New York: United Nations Volunteers.

Ayot, Theodora, O. 2003. *The Quest for New Directions in Humanities in Africa: Conflict and Human Rights Violations in Africa.* Paper presented at the Humanities Conference Held at the University of the Aegean, Island of Rhodes, Greece. July 2–5.

De Smith, S. 1965. Federalism, Human Rights, and the Protection of Minorities. In *Federalism in the New Nations of Africa*, ed. W. Currie, 279–341. Chicago: University of Chicago Press.

Dyer, G. 2008. Broken Faith, Not Tribalism, Rends Kenya. *The Columbus Dispatch.* Jan 4, pp. 1–2.

East African Women Conference. 1993. *Gender Transformation and Empowerment.* Conference Report. Kampala, Uganda.

Editorial. 2003. When Blood Flowed Like River in Kenya. *The Nairobi Law Monthly* 84: 4–48.

Gecaga, Margaret, G. 2007. Religious Movements and Democratization in Kenya: Between the Sacred and Profane. In *Kenya: The Struggle for Democracy*, eds. Godwin Murunga and Shadrack Nasong'o, 58–89. London: Zed Books Ltd.

Hobbes, Thomas. 1651. "The Leviathan." http://www.Ttu.ee./public/m/mont. Accessed on 15 October 2017.

Internally Displaced Persons Program. 1995. *GOK/UNDP/KEN/94/009-17.* Nairobi: United Nations Development Program.

Kagwanja, Peter, M. 1998a. *Politics of Marionettes.* Working Paper. Nairobi, Kenya.

———. 1998b. *Killing the Vote: State Sponsored Violence and Flawed Elections in Kenya.* Nairobi, Kenya: Kenyan Human Rights Commission.

Kampala Action Plan on Women in Peace. 1994. Kampala, Uganda.

Kibwana, K. 1994. *Constitutional and Political Issues Surrounding Regionalism in Kenya.* Working Paper. Nairobi, Kenya.

Kuria, G.K. 1994a. *Democracy in a Multi-Ethnic Society.* Working Paper. Nairobi, Kenya.

———. 1994b. Majimboism, Ethnic Cleansing and Constitutionalism in Kenya. *Thought on Democracy Series.* Nairobi, Kenya: Kenya Human Rights Commission.

Mamdani, Mahmood. 2001. *When Victims Become Killers.* Princeton: Princeton University Press.

Martin, Guy. 2007. Diplomacy and Peace Operations: The Case of the Democratic Republic of the Congo. In *Stakes in Africa-United States Relations*, ed. Abdul Karim Bangura et al., 85–112. Lincoln, NE: iUniverse.

Melvern, Linda. 2000. *A People Betrayed: The Role of the West in the Rwandan Genocide.* London: Zed Books.

———. 2004. *A People Betrayed: The Role of The West in Rwanda's Genocide.* New York: Zed Books Ltd.

———. 2005. *Conspiracy to Murder: The Rwandan Genocide.* New York: Verso.

———. 2006. *Conspiracy to Murder.* New York: Verso.

Murungi, K. 1995. *Ethnicity and Multi-partyism in Kenya.* Nairobi: Kenya Human Rights Commission.

Nasong'o, Shadrack Wanjala. 2006. *Ecological Roots of Social Conflict in Kenya: Pastoralism, Land and the Development Paradox.* Paper Presented at the 24th Annual Conference of the Association of Third World Studies. Winston-Salem, N.C. November 2–4.

Nthamburi, Z. 1993. *Tribalism in Kenya Today.* Working Paper. Nairobi, Kenya.

Nzomo, Maria. 1994. *Ethnicity in a Multiparty Democracy: WHITHER GENDER?* Working Paper. Nairobi, Kenya.

Ochwada, H. 1995. Tribal Political in Kenya. *The Weekly Review*. July 28.

Oyugi, E.H. 1993. *Ethnicity in Electoral Politics: The 1992 Multi-party Elections.* Paper presented at the Seminar on Elections and the Democratization Process in Kenya.The Place, Nairobi, Kenya. August 19–21.

Rashid, Ahmed. 2000. *Taliban, Militant Islam, Oil and Fundamentalism in Central Asia.* New Haven: Yale University Press.

Republic of Kenya. 1992. *Report of the Parliamentary Select Committee to Investigate Ethnic Clashes in Western and other Parts of Kenya, 1992.* Nairobi: Society Magazine Weekly, various issues.

Soyinka, Wole, 1999. *Culture, Democracy and Renewal.* Keynote address delivered at the IMF/World Bank Annual Meetings. Washington, D.C. September 25–30.

Sunstein, Cass, R. 2003. *The Declaration of Independence and the Constitution of the United States.* Washington D.C.: Georgetown University Press.

Temple-Raston, Dina. 2005. *Justice on the Grass: Three Rwandan Journalists, Their Trial for War Crimes, and a Nation's Quest for Redemption.* New York: New York Free Press.

Troup, David, and Charles Hornsby. 1998. *Multi-Party Politics in Kenya.* Athens: Ohio University Press.

United Nations. 2015. *The Universal Declaration of Human Rights.* New York: United Nations.

Waugh, Colin M. 2004. *Paul Kagame and Power, Genocide and the Rwandan Patriotic Front.* Jefferson, NC: McFarland and Co.Weekly Review. Weekly Magazine, Nairobi, Various Issues.

Yaker, Layashi, 1994. *Statement.* Fifth African Regional Conference on Women Experts Meeting. Dakar, Senegal.

The Nairobi Dallies 1991–1993: The Daily Nation

20th March, 1992.

23rd March, 1992.

26th March, 1992.

15th March, 1993.

17th March, 1993.

22nd March, 1993.

9th September, 1993.

18th October, 1993.
19th October, 1993.

Finance

31st May, 1992.

Kenya Times

7th October, 1993.
21st October, 1993.
24th October, 1993.

Monthly News

April 1992. Manpower Publishers.
Nairobi.

Society

20th September, 1993.

Sunday Nation

15th March, 1993.

Sunday Standard

15th March, 1992.

The Standard

4th November, 1991.
5th November, 1991.
7th November, 1991.
11th November, 1991.
12th November, 1991.
18th March, 1992.

24th March, 1993.
8th April, 1993.
12th November, 1993.

Weekly Review

25th September, 1992.

CHAPTER 6

The African Union and the Conflict in Sudan's Darfur Region

Kelechi A. Kalu

Introduction

The organization of the international political system as it currently exists, privileges the rights of the state over those of individuals. The state and its government with the capacity both to protect and constrain citizens' rights reigns supreme over its territory—sometimes with coercion and at other times through peaceful institutionalized procedures. This relationship between the state and the citizens has made it possible for governments to claim sovereign authority over their territory—including the sovereign right to relate to their citizens peacefully or through coercive force. The latter has frequently resulted in gross violations of human rights across the globe. In the case of African states (Democratic Republic of the Congo (DRC), Sierra Leone, Liberia, Nigeria, South Africa, Sudan, Ethiopia, Rwanda, etc.), these violations were intensified during periods of autocracy and dictatorships. The policy of *non-interference in the internal affairs of member states* by the then Organization of African Unity also meant that violators of human rights

K.A. Kalu (✉)
University of California, Riverside, CA, USA

G.K. Kieh, Jr. (ed.), *Contemporary Issues in African Society*,
African Histories and Modernities,
https://doi.org/10.1007/978-3-319-49772-3_6

were not censored by their peers. Large-scale violent conflicts, especially the Rwandan genocide, awakened Africans to a central cultural norm across the continent—the inviolable essence of human life.

Many of the states that are experiencing this awakening are currently ravaged by violence, disease, poor public policies and, in many instances, an unwillingness or incapacity of the state to carry out its basic function of maintaining law and order. Consequently, Africans and members of the international community continue to call for the restoration of basic human rights. However, both groups have largely failed to implement viable and sustainable solutions to the intractable crises in many African states. The problem is not whether some Africans and their external supporters see human rights protections, stable political systems with a free market economy and constitutional liberalism as positive variables for ending endemic crises like those in southern Sudan, Darfur; but rather the lack of sustainable and institutionalized strategies for effective governance.

This chapter offers a strategic vision for reducing, and hopefully, ending gross human rights violations within the context of intrastate crises that have ravaged much of sub-Saharan Africa. The expected peace-dividend from the end of the Cold War never materialized in sub-Saharan Africa where Western governments' preference for stability continues to privilege autocratic strong men as leaders who ascend to power through fraudulent electoral results in places like the DRC, Nigeria, Burundi and the Sudan.

The international community stood by in 1994 while over 800,000 Rwandans were slaughtered with the full knowledge and support of the Rwandan government. Unlike Rwanda, the international community has responded to the crisis in Darfur. But that response has been grossly insufficient as women, children and men are raped, dehumanized and killed on a daily basis while the major powers debate the semantics of genocide.

The Context of the Darfur Crises

Historical Development

In Sudan, like most other multi-ethnic states in Africa, the struggle for political independence rendered ethnicity quite fluid as the goal for the nationalists was the attainment of political independence from

Britain and Egypt. Sudan gained its independence in 1956. However, "seeking... first the political kingdom," as Kwame Nkrumah asked Africans to do in the 1950s, did not result in statewide development because political independence revealed the dark side of ethnicity. In Sudan, and consistent with colonial practices elsewhere, the result was sustained development in one part of the country, the northern part and the intensification of underdevelopment and marginalization in the southern part of the country. Given the scarcity of resources and uneven development policies and strategies of the Sudanese government, the western part of Sudan, the Darfur Region, became the most neglected region.

M.W. Daly notes that Sudan's first scientific and only nationwide census was conducted in 1955–1956. Population data yields information that should give policymakers knowledge about the magnitude of the problems of development, and therefore serves as a basis for policy planning and action. But the data, as revealed in the 1955–1956 census in Sudan, was fraudulently interpreted and used to privilege the Muslim north by giving northerners disproportionate representation in the national population and institutions of government. This was done by playing down ethnic differences, and therefore under-reporting the proportion of other groups for purposes of power and resource allocation. The resulting tension was not resolved through the political process and led to the intractable civil war in contemporary Sudan. According to Daley (2007: 179–180),

> The census reported the Sudan's population as 10,263,000. Darfur's 1.35 million ranked third only to Blue Nile (2.7 million) and Kordofan (1.76 million); the six northern provinces comprised about 7.5 million, or 72 percent of the total, and Darfur therefore almost 18 percent of the north's and 13 percent of the Sudan's population. Of females over puberty but of childbearing age, Darfur had the highest percentage of any province – 24.6 percent – and between the ages of five and puberty also the highest – 11.4 percent.... The census found that a bare majority of Sudanese (51 percent) spoke Arabic at home, followed by Dinka (11 percent). Arabic was also the majority language in Darfur (55 percent); Fur (classified for census purposes as three dialects of one language, North, South and West Darfurian), was spoken at home by 42 percent (5.6 percent of the Sudan's population), and the rest spoke other languages, none of which accounted for more than 1 percent of the province's total.

Furthermore, in terms of ethnicity or "nationality," the census found that 375,000 of Darfur's people were Arabs (of whom 269,000 were Baqqara) and 758,000 "Westerners" (Fur, Masalit). Among many things, these figures indicate that Arabic had become the first language of roughly a third of those considered ethnic Fur. These and other figures relating to ethnicity, tribe, and language would later assume much more prominence in contemporary Sudanese politics (Daley 2007: 180; Republic of Sudan 1958: 4–7 and 10).

Population distribution was not the only factor contributing to instability in Sudan. Education and employment statistics are also relevant to contemporary events. Daley (2007: 180) further asserts,

> In terms of the highest school attended (by people over the age of puberty), no province of the Sudan, including even the South, had a lower percentage for intermediate school than Darfur: 0.2 percent; the figure for female was 0. Likewise for secondary school attendance, no province had a worse record: the Bahr al-Ghazal and Upper Nile matched Darfur at 0.1 percent. For the Sudan as a whole, 78 percent of males over the age of puberty had received no formal schooling, and 97.3 of females; for Darfur, the figures were 65 and 99 percent respectively.

The data provided the government with the ammunition that it needed to produce an effective national policy aimed at enhancing the well-being of all its citizens. The data should have been used for development planning that included the creation of jobs and the building of an intellectual infrastructure that would sustain not just Darfur and southern Sudan, but the entire country. Moreover, as Daley (2007: 179–180) posits,

> Of Darfur's 350,000 males over the age of puberty, 232,000 were farmers, 38,000 nomadic animal owners, and 31,000 shepherds. There were 158 male and 37 female primary and intermediate school teachers in the entire province. Among medical practitioners, 2 were classified as "professional" and 281 as "semi-professional" (including 63 women). There appear to have been 783 policemen and prison wardens (4 of whom were women), 1 professional accountant, and 2 (males) in the field of "entertainment." Most women – 79 percent – were classified as "unproductive," and the only field in which they outnumbered men was "Unemployed, beggars."

No national census has been taken since 1955–1956, and given that civil war has been the norm in southern Sudan for these last few decades, it is reasonable to assume that not much has changed in terms of development. The discovery of crude petroleum in southern Sudan has not improved the situation. However, as with other African states, the industry is largely based on expatriate employment—in this case, Chinese. Consequently, over time, with the lack of external and internal support, the historical neglect of Western Sudan by the central government ignited and intensified ethnic consciousness and a sense of marginalization. The strong nationalistic consciousness that preceded independence died because of poor development and implementation of policies by the central authorities, especially their lack of vision for building a truly nationalistic Sudanese state. The personalization of power by the Muslim Arabs in Khartoum and their efforts to create a homogenous Sudanese culture without requisite developmental infrastructure exacerbated the needs and desire for ethnic ties and consciousness. These expectations for ethnic unity were manifested in the formation of different groups, which hoped to achieve for themselves what the dominant group within the central government historically denied them—effective participation in making decisions that impact their well-being as Sudanese citizens.

The Ethno-Communal Frame

The 2003 formation of the Sudan Liberation Army/Movement (SLA/SLM) in loose association with the Justice and Equality Movement (JEM) intensified the use of ethnic consciousness as a framework for demanding a seat at the national decision-making table. However, SLA/JEM strategy has changed from engaging the political process to violent attacks on government targets outside of Khartoum. Arguably, the changed strategy from negotiation to violence by peripheral groups like SLA/JEM can be explained by their fear that Darfur and the western region would be left out of the power-sharing agreements that the government of Sudan was negotiating to end the civil war in southern Sudan. Such fear was based on the fact that the central government had repeatedly ignored their requests for meetings on how best to include the development of the Darfur region on the national development agenda.

The intensified ethnic consciousness born of political struggle for scarce resources expanded to include charges of racism against the central government and violence targeting government facilities by the "rebels," who defended their actions by accusing the government of oppressing *black Africans* in preference to *Arabs.* In response to the informal politics and strategies by the rebels, the government of Sudan responded with crushing air raids targeted at villages believed to be the source of rebel power and protection. The government also enlisted the assistance of former criminals, bandits and members of tribes with land conflicts against *non-Arab* populations in Darfur. In addition to providing arms, the government did not object to other groups and individuals with different agendas who sought to exploit the crisis by joining the "Janjaweed" in terrorizing the Darfurians. The Janjaweed, or "devils on horseback," have been labeled "Arab" because the majority of their ancestry is more Arab than African—further intensifying the rigidity of the alliances in the conflict.

Originally created and supported by Libya in Western Sudan for attacking Chad, the Janjaweed are responsible for the burning and looting of villages across Darfur as well as raping, murdering and kidnapping civilians. There are reports of instances where air raids by Sudanese government forces are strategically followed by mop-up operations by the Janjaweed—an indication of coordination between the government and the Janjaweed, contrary to government claims that the killings in Darfur are mostly committed by armed criminals. Due to the overall fear of the Janjaweed and its methods of violence against unarmed civilians, internal displacement has become a serious issue in Western Sudan. Darfuris have been forced to leave their possessions and homes and relocate to camps for Internally Displaced Persons (IDPs), mostly in northern Darfur and some in neighboring Chad. The rise in IDPs and refugees has created what numerous groups have labeled the worst humanitarian crisis in the world. Due to the racial and ethnic slogans, chants and motivations of the Janjaweed as they taunt, capture and kill the Darfuris, many, but especially the US government, have also gone so far as to label what is going on in Darfur as genocide. A United Nations Security Council (United Nations Security Council) (2007: 1) report on Sudan highlights the awful results of the conflict:

> The humanitarian situation in Darfur has suffered from persistent violence and overall insecurity. Over two million people are now internally displaced, while 1.9 million conflict-affected residents remain largely dependent on external aid. Approximately 107,000 civilians were newly displaced by insecurity [in] fighting between 1 January and 1 April [2007].

Thus, the Sudanese government's policy in Darfur is to bring the conflict to an end on its own terms—largely homogenizing all the ethnic groups consistent with the cultural, language and ethnic consciousness of the ruling northern elite. But more significantly, given the government's willingness to negotiate a comprehensive peace treaty with the south to end the civil war, it seems clear that the strategy adopted by the Darfurians for a share of the national wealth and the government's heavy-handed response suggests the government might be more concerned about regime stability than ethnic cleansing or genocide. In this sense, the government's violent reaction to the Darfuri rebels might be a calculated strategy to discourage other potentially marginalized and neglected groups from taking up arms against the government. And, to ensure that the Darfurians are not protected from the government and the Janjaweed, the violence sponsored by the government is not limited to the Darfuris, but extends to the aid and humanitarian workers in the region whose work is directly aimed at assisting civilians and providing succor.

Given the odious principle of *non-interference in the internal affairs of member states* by the now defunct Organization of the African Unity (OAU), resulting in conflicts which beset African states—DRC, Rwanda, Somalia, Sierra Leone, Liberia, Nigeria and Sudan—in the 1990s, the emergence of the African Union (AU) to replace the OAU was greeted with a sigh of relief by the international community. The AU is seen as a new body with a new philosophy and responsibility toward citizens whose governments have failed to protect them in the midst of violent conflicts. This so-called humanitarian intervention thesis is addressed later.

Darfur and the African Union

Background

The AU was established in 2002, as the successor to the OAU, which was established in 1963. Consistent with African leaders' general tendency to emulate Africa's former colonizers, the AU was the natural successor to the OAU similar to the European Union succeeding the European Community; in a sense, the question has to be raised whether the AU is truly African in spirit and form. The OAU was established in 1963 by 31 newly independent African states in a spirit of pan-Africanism that aimed to promote economic unity and collective security (Zweifel 2006: 147), and eventually, political unity. Its main strategy for dealing with African problems was to stress the principle of "peaceful settlements of disputes" (Murray 2004: 118). Without effective and viable institutional structures, or strategic and visionary leadership, its poor record on conflict resolution and management was compounded by financial, logistical and political problems. Much of the OAU's failure was due to its policy of non-interference in member states' internal affairs which weakened its ability to prevent and manage conflicts, especially civil wars.

Now, with 53 African states as members of the AU, the added features of intervention, independence, checks and balances, and monitoring make the AU potentially a "more effective, democratic, and autonomous organization" (Zweifel 2006: 148). According to the former OAU Secretary-General (and current AU Special Envoy), Dr. Salim Ahmed Salim, the promise of the AU is its objectives of "enhancing unity, strengthening co-operation and coordination as well as equipping the African continent with a legal and institutional framework, which would enable Africa to gain its rightful place in the community of nations" (Francis 2005: 29–30). These hopeful objectives are rooted in a desire and motivation to "enhance the cohesion, solidarity and integration of the countries and peoples of Africa" (Francis 2005: 29–30). The core instrument for achieving the above objectives is the Constitutive Act of the African Union.

The Constitutive Act empowers states to intervene in cases where a country has failed to protect its citizens from internal conflicts. Specifically, Article 4 (h) of the Principles empowers the "Union to intervene in a Member State pursuant to a decision of the Assembly in respect of grave circumstances, namely war crimes, genocide and crimes against humanity." This Act must not and cannot be impeded by the excuse of sovereignty which has been used to avoid responsibility and action in past instances where such intervention would have saved millions of lives (African Union 2000). Some argue that member states have essentially accepted external intervention in their internal affairs in times of serious or extreme crisis by signing this Act that runs against the standard practice of non-intervention as included in the UN Charter (Murithi 2005: 97). This document, however, while continuing to reiterate the importance of promoting peace, security, and stability for individuals and the continent also contains clauses which affirm the sovereignty and territorial integrity and independence of states exclusive of grave violations of human rights and goes so far as to prohibit the use of force or the threat of use of force under the basis of non-interference (African Union 2000). Despite these many improvements, the AU has inherited many of the same problems of its predecessor; precisely why skeptics warn against prematurely assuming that this new organization will "significantly enhance the project of uniting Africa or strengthen the capacity of states to respond to peace and security issues on the continent" (Francis 2005: 30). Perhaps this fear is why the AU established the Peace and Security Council (PSC or AUP-SC) as the organ to prevent, manage and resolve conflicts in the continent. As is profoundly evident in the case of the ongoing massive slaughter and displacement of certain sections of Sudanese citizens or crimes against humanity in Darfur, the strategic question—how to mobilize and deploy collective resources on the continent for realizing the goal of conflict prevention and management—remains substantively unresolved.

Comprised of 15 rotating members (for either two or three-year terms), the PSC has

> powers to anticipate events that may lead to genocide and crimes against humanity, recommend the intervention of the Union if there were war crimes, genocide and crimes against humanity, impose sanctions on unconstitutional changes in government and follow up in terms of conflict prevention issues of human rights, among other things. (Murray 2004: 125)

Intuitively, given the hegemonic intent in establishing the Peace and Security Council of the AU and its expressed powers, what significant and substantive instrument does the PSC have if it is to carry out its functions without constraints? That is, what functional or institutional power does the PSC have over the sovereign leaders of states who may not wish close scrutiny of their actions? That Article 7 forces African leaders to realize that sovereignty does not forever remain a "shield from intervention" (Levitt 2005: 26) is not sufficient without compelling strategic military and political instruments of statecrafts at the disposal of the AU to realize its stated goals of ensuring peace and security and the promotion of individual human rights. Through the PSC, the AU has also authorized the creation of the African Standby Force (ASF) made up of strictly African soldiers whose responsibility, among others, is to intervene in member states where crimes against humanity as outlined in Article 4 (h) above occur (African Union 2000). Again, we must ask: based on what vertical decision structure and with what kind of logistical and human resource base will the ASF carry out its functions? Indeed, given its current role, which is limited to that of humanitarian assistance and "alleviating the suffering of civilians in conflict areas" (African Union 2002), it is most urgent that the AU with the full endorsement of African governments, clarifies the strategic vision it hopes to deploy for its lofty goals before it becomes irrelevant from incapacity as the case of Darfur is already demonstrating. However, the establishment of the PSC shows the AU's commitment to ending conflicts through the legal and political processes which protect civilians against governments and government-sponsored violence. Thus, while political and financial enforcement mechanisms in the AU and PSC guidelines are clearly specified, the test of the AU's effectiveness will be the extent to which these important steps are implemented and show tangible results. More significant however, is the strategic process that moves key actors from violence to political negotiation, for example in the case of Darfur.

Given that the current structure of the AU-PSC and Standby Force places state sovereignty above the obligation to protect individuals, it is doubtful that the PSC will be able to carry out its functions or that the AU can intervene in a state where genocide is occurring if the government refuses such an intervention. Consequently, to achieve the goals of protecting individuals against state violence, the African Union is more likely to succeed if it establishes an African Security Command (AU-SC) with a standing rapid reaction force for military intervention where the AU identifies genocide and/or other state-sponsored crimes against humanity in Africa as the first step toward engaging the political process. The AU-SC can stand alone or complement other activities by the AU-PSC and the ASF. Armed and under the command of a reputable and competent leader, the rapid reaction function of the AU-SC is more likely to result in the realization of the AU Charter by elevating citizenship (or human rights?) over state rights, thereby ensuring consistent protection of human rights in the continent.

Substantively, while state sovereignty remains essential against non-AU threat, sovereignty and human rights are enhanced within the continent to the extent that a struggle between individual and collective rights, and citizenship and human rights are not blocked by autocratic claim of state sovereignty over human rights issues. Put differently, for a political process that privileges peace and robust resolution of issues of human rights, force has to be compelling in situations where government-sponsored violence remains a major obstacle for getting the actors to the negotiating table.

The AU's Intervention in Darfur

The effective functioning of the AU and its constitutive units is needed to curb the conflict in Darfur. Thus, while the AU worked closely with the international community, primarily the UN, in attempting to alleviate some of the humanitarian conditions, and convince the al-Bashir Government to allow a peacekeeping force in Darfur, the AU has only served in reality as a monitor of ceasefire since 2004. This is because the AU lacks the robust logistical and personnel presence to be effective. Anyway, since 2007, the AU and the UN have established a joint peacekeeping force in Darfur. The argument for a more robust AU through the AU-SC is in recognition of both African governments' desire and the international community's professed preferences for collective action to end genocide and government-sponsored violence against innocent civilians.

While the capacity for collective action in the international community, especially the UN, has always existed, it has not been deployed for the protection of individuals against their governments in Africa. It seems, however, that the UN has been awakened from its slumber about the suffering of Africans at the hands of their own governments, for "at the United Nations World Summit on September 17, 2005, world leaders agreed, for the first time, that states have a primary responsibility to protect their own populations and that the international community has a responsibility to act when governments fail to protect the most vulnerable." (Jentleson 2007: 582). The Responsibility to Protect international doctrine pledges "to take collective action if national authorities manifestly fail to protect their population from genocide, war crimes, ethnic cleansing and crimes against humanity." (Jentleson 2007: 583–584). While the international "responsibility to protect" doctrine gives us hope and an enabling framework for collective action to hold those governments that claim sovereignty without responsibility accountable for the atrocities committed against unprotected citizens within their territories, the question is: How can this collective responsibility be achieved in situations where governments fail to protect their own citizens or are complicit in the atrocities committed against them?

I argue that at the core of realizing the UN and AU's desire to protect citizens against government-sponsored violence is the recognition that the self-empowerment of African states, regional African organizations, nongovernmental organizations, citizens and the AU is the first line of defense against government and government-sponsored atrocities against their own citizens. Internal initiation of an accountable process for the maintenance of sovereignty would make it possible for non-African states, organizations and citizens to offer effective aid for bringing genocide and other human rights violations in places like Darfur to an end.

While the AU has its peace security functions and the desire to form a union government, it seems conflicted on the nature of the relationship between African states and their citizens. And, although the AU appears quite desirous of ending crimes against humanity in Darfur, it currently lacks the logistical and political will to do so. Cognizant of the international reality that the UN Security Council is responsible for global security and stability, African states formed the African Union Mission in the Sudan (AMIS) in 2004, and a second one in 2005. However, because of poor capacity and lack of resources, the two AMIS peacekeeping missions failed to competently execute their mission as evidenced by the continuing atrocities against women, children, aid workers and men both in the Darfur region and the refugee camps in neighboring states. But the most important fact about AMIS was that for the first time since decolonization, African leaders appeared cognizant of their responsibilities to Africans as evidenced by their decision (albeit poorly executed) in Darfur.

While the issues in Darfur as illustrated below are mostly economic and political in nature, they lend themselves to verifiable efforts through negotiation in good faith followed by national policies aimed at their effective resolution, if the political will exists in Khartoum to do so. We will first identify the intersecting issues—national and international—in the conflict in Darfur and then offer robust strategies on how African states and the AU can start the process of protecting the victims of human rights abuses and other atrocities on the continent.

Intersecting Issues in the Darfur Conflict

Weaving the Major Threads of the Darfur Conflict

The conflict in Darfur is born of several intersecting, yet separate conflicts. As Straus (Straus (2005: 126) insightfully notes, "the crisis is traced to the civil war between the Islamist, Khartoum-based national government and two rebel groups—the Sudan Liberation Army and the Justice and Equity Movement—based in Darfur." As previously noted, the rebel groups are fighting because of economic and political marginalization by the national government. In a sense, if the government in Khartoum had engineered a national economic and political development plan that did not marginalize any section or group in the Sudan, the SPLA/JEM would not have had verifiable reason to attack government facilities in 2003 resulting in the national government's arming of irregular militias to quell the violence that escalated to the ongoing despicable slaughtering of human beings in Darfur.

Similarly, the conflict in Darfur is related to the civil war that raged in Sudan following its political independence in 1956, in which the Arab-dominated national government and its policies of cultural and linguistic homogenization in Sudan created a dyadic civil conflict that has been simplistically explained as North-South and Arab-Christian conflict in contrast to the core issue of economic and political marginalization of the south by the northern-based government of Sudan. Under the auspices of the Intergovernmental Authority on Development (IGAD), the Sudanese government entered into negotiations with the southern rebel groups—which did not include representatives from Darfur. The peace negotiation resulted in the Comprehensive Peace Agreement that ended the longest civil war in Africa, and subsequently led to the creation of the new state of South Sudan. Consequently, the Darfuri rebels attracted attention to their own cause of marginalization as a strategy to mobilize ethnic, regional, continental and global attention to the poor economic and political condition.

The other dimension of the crisis is the localized nature of the race/ethnic dimensions of the conflict. As Straus (2005: 126–127) notes:

> Darfur is home to some six million people and several dozen tribes. But the region is split between two main groups: those who claim black

> "African" descent and primarily practice sedentary agriculture, and those who claim "Arab" descent and are mostly seminomadic livestock herders. As in many ethnic conflicts, the divisions between these two groups are not always neat; many farmers also raise animals, and the African-Arab divide is far from clear. All Sudanese are technically African. Darfurians are uniformly Muslim, and years of intermarriage have narrowed obvious physical differences between "Arabs" and black "Africans." Nonetheless, the cleavage is real, and recent conflicts over resources have only exacerbated it. In dry seasons, land disputes in Darfur between farmers and herders have historically been resolved peacefully. But an extended drought and the encroachment of the desert in the last two decades have made water and arable land much more scarce. Beginning in the mid-1980s, successive governments in Khartoum inflamed matters by supporting and arming the Arab tribes, in part to prevent the southern rebels from gaining a foothold in the region. The result was a series of deadly clashes in the late 1980s and 1990s. Arabs formed militias, burned African villages, and killed thousands. Africans in turn formed self-defense groups, members of which eventually became the first Darfur insurgents to appear in 2003.

That

> Khartoum instructed the militias to 'eliminate the rebellion,' as Sudan's President Omar al-Bashir acknowledged in a December 2003 speech.... [And that] army forces and the militia often attacked together, as *Janjaweed* leaders readily admit... and in some cases, government aircraft bomb areas before the militia attack, razing settlements and destroying villages (Straus 2005: 126)

clearly establishes the connection between the government decision to eliminate a segment of its population by virtue of who they are perceived to be—black African farmers. That these Muslims or Christians are unable to protect themselves against such massive government violence qualifies them as either objects of ethnic cleansing or massive human rights violations and indeed, genocide that calls for international protection consistent with the expressed goals of the United Nations and those of the African Union. Indeed, documents in the possession of the AU peacekeeping force in Darfur indicates the Sudanese government is directly involved in organizing and supporting the violence against the Darfuris.

According to Nicholas Kristof, one document directed the regional commanders and security officials to ensure the

> execution of all directives from the president of the republic .... Change the demography of Darfur and make it void of African Tribes ...[by] killing, burning villages and farms, terrorizing people, confiscating property from members of African tribes and forcing them from Darfur. (Jentleson 2007)

From all accounts, while Darfur like the rest of Sudan has been involved in various levels of conflicts since the 1950s, the intensity of the current conflict measured by the number of casualties estimated at over 300,000 deaths and over one million IDPs with hundreds of thousands more in various refugee camps outside of Sudan, was ignited by the Sudanese Liberation Army's "surprise attack on the airport at El Fasher, the capital of North Darfur State. They destroyed seven military planes and killed about 100 soldiers in late April 2003" (Kasfir 2005: 196). It was the swiftness and intensity with which the ignited by the Sudanese Liberation government of Sudan responded to the SLA attack in 2003 that led to the outcry of genocide in Darfur.

> As Prunier (2006: 200) notes, several explanations have been advanced to explain the massive killing in Darfur: (1) ancient tribal conflicts reignited by droughts; (2) counterinsurgency campaign by the government of Sudan gone wrong; (3) deliberate policy of ethnic cleansing of African tribes to make room for Arab nomads; and (4) "genocide ... supported by evidence of systematic racial killings."

Substantively, while these explanations are important singularly, collectively the timing and intensification of the killings suggest deliberate policy, strategy and motive by the Sudanese government to consolidate its power within the country by using the SLA/Darfuris' rebellion to demonstrate its resolve against other marginalized groups' future efforts to demand peace negotiations and therefore a share of national wealth and power similar to the generous provisions in the Comprehensive Peace Agreement with the Christian south. And, as Kasfir (2005: 197) succinctly summarizes,

> One problem in isolating the government's motives is that the Darfur crisis grows out of many conflicts at the local, regional and national levels. These conflicts involve responses to diminished natural resources, to ethnic and cultural conflict, to negotiations and the peace agreement in southern Sudan, and to the relationship of the national government with impoverished and marginalized groups throughout the country.

In light of the foregoing, it is clear that the government of Sudan organized and aided the Janjaweed—drawn mostly from marginalized Arab/Muslim communities in Darfur—to attack, slaughter and displace the non-Arab Darfuris; mostly Africans but predominantly Muslims. It is clear from the foregoing that the government adopted such a high-handed approach to the rebels from western Sudan because it was already engaged in a peace negotiation process in 2003 with mostly Christian southerners with whom it had fought against since 1956 and did not want to be drawn into a similar process by other marginalized groups and regions in the future.

The Centrality of Politics

Interestingly, the *political* dimension of both the Darfuris' rebellion and the government's response hold the key to an effective solution to the crisis in Darfur if the regional and national groups and the international community have the political will to engage the core issues of economic and political marginalization of minority ethnic groups in Sudan. And as articulated by intellectuals from southern Sudan,

> the central problems that pose a threat to peace and unity in the Sudan are attributable to three basic causes: (1) the dominance of one nationality over the others; (2) the sectarian and religious bigotry that has dominated the Sudanese political scene since independence; and (3) the unequal development in the country. (Akol 1987: 15)

The question is how to proceed toward realization of peace and stability throughout Sudan to enable individuals and communities to pursue their respective lives and interests. Given the intensity of the violence in Darfur, the Comprehensive Peace Agreement signed in January 2005 between the north and south, as well as the commitment of the government of Sudan to preserving its hold on power, resolving the Darfur crisis and indeed, upholding the CPA to its full implementation would require robust international and regional mediation between the various factions in Sudan.

Toward Resolution

The Efforts of the International Community

The international dimension of the Darfuris' rebellion and therefore, its partial solution, is evident in the fact that the peace settlement between the Muslim government of Sudan and the Christian southern rebels was already in the minds of US political leaders (with the appointments of Andrew Natsios in May 2001 as Special Humanitarian Coordinator for Sudan, and Senator John Danforth on September 6, 2001 as Special Envoy for Peace in Sudan—both part of President George W. Bush's conservative Christian constituency). Any hesitation on working together to resolve the age-old civil war on the part of both Washington and Khartoum was shelved following the terrorist attacks against the US in 2001, which provided President Omar al-Bashir's government—whose human rights record was largely seen as repugnant to civilized standards—with an unprecedented but grotesque opportunity to play the hero's part in the fight against terrorism. The Sudanese government's enthusiastic offer of support for the anti-terrorist policy can only be read as al-Bashir's desire not to repeat its earlier strategic error of siding with the late Saddam Hussein in the first Gulf War, and therefore, avoiding the polarization of its civil war into Arab-Muslim government versus Christian-southern rebels that would have increased global support of the rebels, especially from Washington if it did not make the correct choice of denouncing terror and terrorists on the global stage. As Adibe (2007: 26) notes,

> When September 11 attacks occurred... President Bashir firmly denounced Osama bin Laden and al Qaeda and pledged to cooperate with Washington in rooting out the terrorist menace. In Washington, Bashir's unsolicited support, like Ghaddafi's, was especially well received by Powell's State Department which was saddled with the task of putting together a 'coalition of the willing' on a very short notice. ... [And] "Since 9/11, Bashir

> has provided the US with a steady stream of much-vaunted intelligence" which has been used to track and target al Qaeda networks and funds.

Consequently, the Bush administration rewarded the Sudanese government by supporting

> ...the lifting of UN sanctions against Sudan on September 28, 2001... and quietly quelled pending legislation for imposition of capital market sanctions... [and for] the next two years, the Bush administration treated Khartoum as an ally in its war on terror while Bashir's security forces and the Janjaweed roamed Darfur with greater impunity. (Adibe 2007: 27)

The foregoing indicates that the United States has the moral and military force capability and credibility—when it chooses to use them in concert with others or unilaterally—to nudge others toward resolution of conflicts such as the Darfur crisis. I would argue that the United States fails to consistently use its capacity to enhance peace and security missions in Africa; or more specifically, fails to forcefully use regional and international organizations such as the United Nations and the AU in such projects because there are no consistent *national interest* imperatives for the foreign policy decision-makers in the United States. And certainly, there is no consistent African constituency with voting power at the congressional district levels to compel action on behalf of Africa.

Similarly, the United Nations and the former OAU did not, as collective action institutions, intervene in the internal affairs of an African state in protection of the rights of individuals as individuals or as members of a group. Even when such intervention would profoundly have saved hundreds of thousands of lives as the cases of Biafra and Rwanda showed, the two institutions did nothing beyond engaging in rhetorical debates over state responsibilities to their citizens and whether the atrocities qualified as genocide, because the interests of the elites in these institutions are largely devoid of compassion and commitment to the resolution of issues on behalf of the marginalized and disorganized victims of both structural and state-supported violence. It is against this background of previous collective inaction that the role of the AU can be more constructive than the conflict-avoidance strategies employed by much of the Western world in Africa; but especially that inaction is true of the veto-hobbled Security Council organ of the United Nations and the non-interference excuse for inaction by the defunct OAU.

Progressive Responsibility to Protect Argument

While sovereign states are notorious for protecting their rights to internal action, multilateral institutions such as the United Nations with collective security principles in their charters have been notorious for insisting on invitation from states before they could intervene in a nation's internal affairs to protect entrapped citizens facing extermination as was the case in Rwanda and the former Yugoslavia. But while powerful states such as the United States in collaboration with military alliances such as the North Atlantic Treaty Organization (NATO) will, if their interests are at stake, violate the UN principles as was the case in Kosovo in 1999, less powerful states and organizations such as those in sub-Saharan Africa are left to fend for themselves based on the inviolability of the principles of sovereignty at the expense of unprotected citizens as the case of Rwanda in 1994 demonstrates. It is illuminating that the US-NATO action in Kosovo in 1999 resulted in

> ... an unusual distinction when an independent international commission called the U.S.-NATO intervention *illegal* in the sense of not having followed the letter of the UN Charter but *legitimate* in being consistent with the norms and principles that the Charter embodies (my italics). (Jentleson 2007: 439; Independent Commission on Kosovo 2000)

Perhaps the foregoing insight led to the formation of the *International Commission on Intervention and State Sovereignty*, whose 2001 report provides a theoretical basis for the argument for the "responsibility to protect" doctrine. This argument (Jentleson 2007: 439; Independent Commission on Kosovo 2000) is based on the core principles that "state sovereignty implies responsibility" and that the primary responsibility of a state is the protection of people within its territory. In situations

> where a population is suffering serious harm, as a result of internal war, insurgency, repression or state failure and the state in question is unwilling or unable to halt or avert it, the principles of non-intervention yields to the international responsibility to protect. (Jentleson 2007: 439)

The "responsibility to protect" argument further provides for the *prevention* of "large-scale loss of life" as its priority with as little coercive measures as possible; and that the motive for intervention should be to avert human suffering. Furthermore, the five permanent members of the UN Security Council should agree not to use their veto powers to obstruct the passage of resolutions authorizing the use of military force when their interests are not involved. Specifically, it says,

> The Security Council should take into account in all its deliberations that, if it fails to discharge its responsibility to protect in conscience-shocking situations crying out for action, *concerned states may not rule out other means to meet the gravity and urgency of that situation*—and that the stature and credibility of the United Nations may suffer thereby (my italics). (*The Economist* 2007: 1)

Given that the "responsibility to protect" argument was accepted by the United Nations after both genocide and ethnic cleansing occurred in Rwanda, Bosnia and Kosovo, the Darfur conflict was the first test case for this important international norm and obligation. Unfortunately, the international community has failed this test because Russia and China have material interests in Sudan and/or because the United States has a verifiable national interest in working with the President Omar al-Bashir administration, whose support for the United States' "war on terrorism," compels the United States to be soft in its diplomatic engagement with its allies. An added dimension here is the negotiated peace between the Sudanese government and the southern rebels to which the United States, the United Nations and the AU were party to. The problem is that the AU which adopted the argument that there must be "African solutions to African problems" in Darfur frees the United States, China, Russia and, by extension, other Western powers from doing much beyond diplomatic talk. And, with its 7000 troops, who lacked logistical capability in Darfur, the AU was not able to provide robust and credible protection for the Darfuris and for its troops, some of whom were killed by Sudanese government forces, rebels and the Janjaweed.

What Must Be Done?

Background

Clearly, the "responsibility to protect" argument lacks "teeth." However, it is not a cliché to say the failure to protect the Darfuris is the failure of African governments to assume full responsibility for the peoples of

Africa. If we assume the AU is serious about privileging African peoples over state and sovereignty claims, the right to protect does provide for an effective role for a regional organization such as the AU in cases where the UN Security Council proves ineffective.

Toward Concrete Action

The question becomes what does the AU need to do? First, there has to be a peace to keep, before peacekeeping forces can be brought into the region. Therefore, the constraint on reaching and keeping peace in the Sudan is directly related to the asymmetry of force between the government of Sudan and the Janjaweed on the one hand; and the fragmented and disorganized Darfuris and the various splinter groups on the other. For the Darfuris, economic development and political justice constitute the core issues, which unarguably lend themselves to political negotiation. Therefore, creating the space for political negotiation requires a ceasefire between the combatants. Strategically, then, deploying troops (Africans and non-Africans) with robust logistical support to force an end to the fighting is the first step to engaging in peace negotiation and implementation. In this sense, force activation (in all its majestic presence), and deployment is predicted to lead to acceptance of ceasefire by both the Sudanese government and its collaborators and the Sudanese Liberation Army and their collaborators as a precondition for peace and therefore negotiation/resolution of issues about justice. For an effective outcome, neither the government nor the rebels should have the power to veto the source of the troops and/or the type of logistical support available to the military intervention force.

Following the military intervention force, the AU should take decisive steps toward bringing the government of Sudan, the Darfur representatives, the Sudanese Liberation Army, and the Justice and Equity Movement groups together to negotiate and correct whatever identified problems exist within the framework of Sudanese law and public policy. This must include the option of comprehensively federalizing the provisions of the Comprehensive Peace Agreement with southern rebels that ultimately led to independence for South Sudan from the rest of the country. Acting boldly in convening the groups in the Darfur conflict together in its headquarters or other viable and accessible location will establish the AU at the forefront of the responsibility to protect protocol provisions of the UN as well as AU protocol. It will also ensure that the

AU is at the forefront of any final peace talks as well as confirming to all the dedication of African governments to the guidelines of the AU Charter and its commitment to avoiding the failures of the OAU.

Given that the Sudanese government is reported to be "… inviting Arab tribesmen from Niger and Chad to occupy the lands vacated by the refugees" (*The Economist* 2007: 1) in Darfur indicates at least its intent to ethnically cleanse the region and at worst, commit genocide. And, because the Darfur conflict is an African problem with global implications, a basic responsibility for the AU would be to boldly and without equivocation, label the conflict in Darfur as *ethnic cleansing/genocide*. This would include labeling the conflict a grave situation and a crime against humanity—a clear warning to the Khartoum-based Sudanese government and the Janjaweed leadership that failure to stop the large-scale violence will bring them up for charges on crimes against humanity consistent with the International Criminal Court provisions. This would have two immediate results; first, it would activate Article 4(h) of the AU's Constitutive Act requiring the organization to take action; and second, it will avoid the definitional conflict over the term *genocide* and compel African governments to clearly identify their support for the AU's Constitutive Act to which they are signatories. With clear identification of the conflict as genocide/ethnic cleansing, and with the presence of robust military intervention for purposes of establishing a ceasefire in the region, the AU should impose travel restrictions on the top Sudanese and rebel leaders responsible for atrocities, except for travel related to negotiation and resolution of the conflict. The strategy should include freezing the bank accounts of all affected individuals and groups; and impose sanctions on Sudanese companies deemed to be complicit in any atrocity that the AU is attempting to bring to an end, as well as compensate those whose actions help bring an end to large-scale violence against people in Sudan and elsewhere in Africa.

In addition, recognition and recognition-withdrawal can be powerful and effective tools available to the AU for carrying out its responsibility to protect vulnerable people in situations where African governments have failed to protect the people within their territory. In this case, and beyond, social primordial identities and therefore group identities are constructed to create space for inclusion and exclusion. This approach ensures that the Fur or Arabs will remain who they are; however, the Sudanese state may or may not survive an identity reconstruction if war erupts across the country. Thus, while states in Africa as well as their membership in the AU may eventually survive or die, it is individual primordial identities (al-Afif Mukhtar 2007) that are sustained over time as the basis for recognition of our individual existence.

Furthermore, artificially or socially constructed identities are political tools that can be used for purposes of ending conflicts like those in Sudan. In the formation of social or group identities, there is always an in-group such as the AU or the United Nations which represents the desired group identity, and the non-group members such as states that have to adjust if admitted in order to remain members of the group. Thus, the AU is the core group for African states who desire membership in the group. It occupies the center stage of the group identity; and states such as Sudan or Nigeria should be part of the core group or non-group depending on their behavior. The privileges of membership should draw the non-group states to seek inclusion. As such, the AU has the power to legitimize or delegitimize the public behavior of states, especially with regard to their policies toward the people in their territories.

The power of recognition and its withdrawal then becomes a tool that enables the AU to shape the conduct of its member states. It can use withdrawal of diplomatic recognition as sanctions against members whose actions are judged repugnant to civilized standards—especially, when such actions include ethnic cleansing and/or genocide. Indeed, the power of recognition or its withdrawal seems to be the most powerful diplomatic tool available to the AU and members of the UN Security Council such as the United Kingdom and France, who desire to do something to end large-scale violence characteristic of ethnic cleansing/genocide without necessarily participating in joint military intervention with the AU forces.

The power of recognition is not new, as evidenced by the capacity of the United States' legislature to include or exclude states on its "list of terrorist supporting states" on which the Sudanese government was placed in the 1990s and from which it sought to be excluded after it pledged support for the war against terrorism following the September 2001 attacks on the United States. Such diplomatic tools should be used by the AU to recognize and/or withdraw recognition of African states and others whose actions support large-scale violence on the continent either through the supplies of arms, the threat of the use of veto to obstruct the passage of UN Security Council resolutions on military interventions, and/or the use of state power in any form to undermine the responsibility to protect obligations of both the UN and the AU within Africa.

Structurally, the current trials by the International War Crimes Tribunal for Rwanda over the 1994 Rwandan genocide offers a precedent setting and an avenue for the forthcoming AU Court of Justice to be the venue and structural platform for any future trials of Africans and their leaders who commit offenses against humanity as codified in the Geneva Convention. Such sanctions and legal actions within the continent are likely to have a large positive impact, albeit symbolically; but they will also signal Africa's strong disapproval of existing policy and behavior in Darfur.

Similar to the grassroots efforts for divestment during the struggle against the apartheid regime in South Africa, the movement for divestment in Sudan, mostly by groups in Western countries is also important but should be complemented by similar movements sponsored by civil society organizations with help from the AU headquarters where appropriate. NGOs receiving funding from companies and/or organizations whose income are derived from investment in the Sudan should refuse such funding in solidarity with the Darfuris whose lives have been trampled upon by the government of Sudan, the Janjaweed and all countries and companies whose investments enrich the purchase of arms and equipment deployed in the business of ethnic cleansing and genocide. Collectively, African nations should not only cease doing business with companies identified as enhancing the capacity of the Sudanese government's unwillingness to negotiate in good faith, but divest from them, going so far as to freeze the accounts of Chinese, Malaysian, Indian and other states' corporations that do not end their business with the government of Sudan. For major states, especially China and Russia that are involved in the sensitive business of oil and mineral explorations, providing arms, weapons and other support indirectly to the Janjaweed through the government of Sudan, recalling African ambassadors from—a form of recognition withdrawal—will signal the seriousness of AU's desire to end large-scale conflicts on the continent. And, specifically a bold, and maybe unacceptable, move against the Sudanese government is the withdrawal of all AU member ambassadors and diplomats from Khartoum. In a sense, the AU's de-legitimization of the Sudanese state is predicted to intensify a crisis of identity for the ruling elites and might hasten an internal change of government for a more progressive one willing to work within the principles of the AU to protect the rights of all citizens within its member states. The AU decision to deny Sudan its bid to serve as the chair of the Union is a positive example of what a unified strategy can achieve in sending a message of disapproval. Similar actions as suggested above would throw Sudan into a shock. The AU must look to approve and encourage any and all possible strategic moves within its power and charter to force the parties back to the negotiating table on the Darfur Peace Agreement (DPA), which was signed May 5, 2006.

Since both the government of Sudan and the Sudanese Liberation Army/Movement that signed the document have broken and violated its provisions several times and the fact that many of the Darfuri rebels have splintered into different factions, it is necessary for the AU to mediate a renegotiation of the agreement. This effort assumes that a ceasefire, as previously argued, is enforced. As several reports as well as the continuing violence indicate, the growing factional divide since the drafting of the DPA shows lack of political will and faith in its implementation. Therefore, the AU should take the lead in negotiations and diplomatic efforts to consolidate the numerous efforts (by Chad, Libya, Eritrea and the UN) into a single plan under the AU umbrella. A Human Rights Watch report reiterated the need for the UN, Arab League, government of Sudan, EU and others in supporting the efforts of the AU to maintain and expand its efforts of achieving peace in Darfur as well as keeping the organization's effective existence afloat (Human Rights Watch 2006: 9–10). Again, the importance of the AU's role in bringing a successful result to any agreement requires maintenance and expansion of its current monitoring role to one of ceasefire enforcement.

The AU will succeed in its efforts at ceasefire enforcement and peaceful negotiation that end the conflict and pave the way for political settlement of the Darfur conflict if practical strategies include confidence-building among members of the various factions and communities within a familiar framework of local traditions. As Murithi (2005: 76) notes, "For peace to be sustainable, there needs to be a process of consultation and involvement of local grassroots populations as part of the process of re-emphasizing the inherent worth of traditions." Indeed, not paying attention to existing traditions and structures is the very problem that has plagued most of the approaches to development, economics and politics on the continent. Ignoring existing structures and traditions that were put in place to deal with diverse situations as was the case in Darfur only intensifies conflicts whose origins and solutions are alien to the people whose lives are supposed to be transformed. By learning from and including traditional methods, the AU can capitalize on the rich history of enduring African cultures and methods of conflict resolution and management and revitalize them as part of a parallel track of the African Union's formal approach to conflict management and enforcement, especially in less developed regions of the continent like Darfur.

Based on reports from the Christian Science Monitor, the AU already has an ally on the ground from which it could effectively begin a robust counter-strategy to the Sudanese government's policies of reneging on the responsibility to protect obligation. Reports indicate that former Janjaweed and Arab rebels, who fought on the side of the government, have been deserting their ranks to join the Darfur cause. After promises of land, cattle, and money proved to be worthless, "dozens of Janjaweed commanders are joining the struggle against the Sudanese government" (Crilly 2007: 1). This is a clear indication that if salient issues for each party, as previously argued, are identified and dealt with, the crisis could be brought under control. These defectors have played a crucial role in helping protect the roads from attacks, allowing convoys of food and humanitarian aid through to rural and formerly dangerous areas.

By tapping into this group of sympathetic Sudanese Arabs, particularly those who have disassociated themselves from the Janjaweed and are working to protect civilians or defending them by joining SLA or JEM, the AU can identify those who still have ties to the Janjaweed and central government and place pressure on them to prepare for meaningful talks. These defectors and many other Sudanese "Arab" ethnic groups exist within the Darfur region and have continuously opposed the government's policy and refused to take part in the Janjaweed (Crilly 2007). Comprehensive talks would require these Arab groups to be involved and represented as a show of Darfuri unity and rejection of the entirely "ethnic" nature of the conflict; as Prunier (2006: 200) aptly notes, ethnic tensions "were the raw materials, not the cause" of the large-scale violence in Darfur.

Clearly, there is a strategic religious dimension to the conflict in Darfur; but this needs to be clarified to make sense of the recommendation below. The North-South conflict in Sudan since 1956 pitted the Arab Muslims (north) against black Christians (south); but the case of Darfur is different because the National Islamic Front (NIF) that controls the government of Sudan is engaged in large-scale violence against Darfuris who are mostly Africans, but also Muslims. Therefore, considering the Islamist roots of the NIF and al-Bashir's regime, the AU should counter its religious basis for power by strategically and diplomatically making the case that another Muslim-versus-Muslim conflict would shadow the sectarian violence like that in Iraq and elsewhere in the Middle East.

Also, the looming civil war among Palestinians is an affront to Islam and the unity of the "*ummah*" or Muslim world. This is important since the NIF balks at claims of rape by Janjaweed members, or at least government support for it, as impossible and "un-Islamic." This requires the inclusion of predominantly Muslim African nations such as Libya, Egypt, Tunisia, Algeria and others who hold membership in both the Arab League and the AU to use their influence in discussions with Sudan to compel the al-Bashir regime to ensure the protection of the Darfuris against rape, torture, murder and ethnic cleansing by other Muslims. The same can be said in situations like Rwanda where the perpetrators were mostly Christians against other Christians.

In the end, the various actors in the Darfur conflict, especially states, are only likely to act when compelled by either positive or negative incentives to change their behavior; and in contemporary international politics, only the US has the capability and credibility of action to effectively engage the various actors to resolve the Darfur conflict. But as was painfully pointed out by a guest on Wolf Blitzer's *Situation Room*, in the realist world of politics, countries, including the US, never choose friends, but rather whatever is in their national interest at the time (Blitzer 2007). The question is: does the responsibility to protect factor into the national interest of the United States, Russia, China and other major powers who are directly or indirectly involved with the government of Sudan? The answer, for now, is "it depends!".

Therefore, the responsibility to protect, especially Africans, falls to the AU and its potential for doing well is boundless. At the least the AU can succeed in establishing optimism and "override the sense of inevitability of crisis which has framed the way Africans and non-Africans have viewed the continent for decades" (Murithi 2005: 106). Its premise of pan-Africanism and unity might be a way for the AU to convince Sudan to take strong steps to end the terror of the Janjaweed and prepare for a viable end to the conflict. In the meantime, "...security, political, and humanitarian assistance efforts must be supported by adequate funding and logistical support" (United Nations Security Council 2007) by African states, especially South Africa, Nigeria and Egypt that have professed a desire to see an end to the violence in Darfur. To be sure, the foregoing recommendations will be sustainable if complemented by effective political and legal institutions designed to end political and economic corruption across Sudan; institutions that ensure political stability, law and order, transparency in public policies, accountability and economic development policies aimed at peace and stability across Sudan.

Conclusion

The AU has the tools it needs to become a solid entity in mediating African issues—strength in the collective desire to uphold the "responsibility to protect" principle enshrined in both the UN and AU pronouncements. For the international community, especially members of the EU, NATO and the UN, and for capable states such as the United States, the AU has shown the desire to uphold the responsibility to protect. This is evidenced by its willingness to supply troops for peace enforcements, but the AU lacks what those groups and nations have—robust and credible logistical equipment like helicopters, weapons and yes, money to pay an over-stretched, underpaid and unprepared African force—to succeed in an action that is clearly the collective responsibility of the international community if the UN Charter is to remain credible. For the AU, success can occur through logistical and financial support for a hybrid UNMIS/AMIS force, as well as the restart of peace talks as specified above. However, for a sustained capacity to influence external entities to help with African problems, or at least to not block action, especially at the Security Council level, the AU should not hesitate to look beyond Africa for pressure and influence on forcing parties back to the table ready to make real decisions, while maintaining its position of leadership. An international community which focuses on African issues should be strategically institutionalized by funding an Africa Advocacy group in various countries—especially in those countries whose citizens and corporations are likely to be spoilers for African issues and policies in the international system. In the end, the assertion that only when Africa is neglected will it look to solve its own problems, may be true here as the large-scale violence in Darfur did not become a major issue in much of the press in Africa until the international media picked up the cause in 2004. However, the issue came to be a major event for Africa, and its resolution requires the collective efforts of Africans, civil society organizations, governments, media, intellectuals and external actors and organizations like the AU to find a sustainable solution to crimes against humanity in the continent; so rather than *yet again* in Africa, we can say, NEVER AGAIN!

References

Adibe, Clement. 2007. *Once Bitten, Twice Shy: The Evolution of U.S. Policy on the Crisis in the Darfur Region of Sudan.* Paper Presented at the Annual Meeting of the International Studies Association, Feb 28–March 3, in Chicago, Illinois.

African Union. 2000. *Constitutive Act of the African Union.* Addis Ababa, Ethiopia: AU Commission.

African Union. 2002. *Protocol Relating to the Establishment of the Peace and Security Council of the African Union.* 1st Ordinary Session of the Assembly of the African Union, 9 July 2002. http://www.peaceau.org/uploads/psc-protocol-en.pdf.

African Union. 2004. *Protocol Relating to the Establishment of the Peace and Security Council of the African Union.* 1st Ordinary Session of the Assembly of the African Union, 9 July 2002. http://www.africa-union.org/root/au/organs/psc/Protocol_peace%20and%20security.pdf. Accessed on 18 May 2016.

Akol, Lam. 1987. "The Present War and Its Solution." In *Search for Peace and Unity in Sudan*, eds. Francis Deng and Prosser Gifford, 15–26. Washington, DC: The Woodrow Wilson Center Press.

Al-Afif Mukhtar, Al Baqir. 2007. *The Crisis of Identity in Northern Sudan: A Dilemma of a Black people With a White Culture.* Paper Presented at the CODESRIA Humanities Institute.

Blitzer, Wolf. 2007. "The Situation Room." *Cable News Network.* June 12.

Crilly, Rob. 2007. "In Darfur, Some Arabs Now Fight Alongside Rebels." *The Christian Science Monitor.* May 22. Accessed via Yahoo! News. http://news.yahoo.com/s/csm/20070522/wl_csm/oswitch_1 Accessed 18 May 2016.

Daley, M.W. 2007. *Darfur's Sorrow: A History of Destruction and Genocide.* New York: Cambridge University Press.

Francis, David J. 2005. *Uniting Africa: Building Regional Peace and Security Systems.* Aldershot, UK: Ashgate Publishing Company.

Human Rights Watch. 2006. "Imperatives for Immediate Change: The African Union Mission in Sudan." *Human Rights Watch* 18 (1) No. 1: 9–10.

Independent Commission on Kosovo. 2000. *The Kosovo Report: Conflict, International Response, Lessons Learned.* Oxford: Oxford University Press.

Jentleson, Bruce. 2007. *American Foreign Policy: Dynamics of Choice in the 21st Century*, 3rd ed. New York: W.W. Norton and Company.

Kasfir, Nelson. 2005. "Sudan's Darfur: Is It Genocide?" *Current History* 104 (682): 195–202.

Levitt, Jeremy. 2005. "The Peace and Security Council of the African Union, the Use of Force and the United Nations Security Council: The Case of Sudan." In *The Security Council and the Use of Force: Theory and Reality-A Need for*

Change?, ed. Niels Blokker and Nico Schrijver, 213–251. Leiden: Martinus Nijhof Publishers.

Murithi, Timothy. 2005. *The African Union: Pan-Africanism, Peacebuilding and Development*. Burlington: Ashgate Publishing Company.

Murray, Rachel. 2004. *Human Rights in Africa: From the OAU to the African Union*. Cambridge: Cambridge University Press.

Prunier, Gerard. 2006. "The Politics of Death in Darfur." *Current History* 105 (691): 195–202.

Republic of Sudan, Ministry of Social Affairs, Population Census Office. 1958. *First Population Census in Sudan 1955/56, Last (9th) Interim Report*. Khartoum.

Straus, Scott. 2005. "Darfur and the Genocide Debate." *Foreign Affairs* 84 (1): 123–133.

The Economist. 2007. "Pity the People of Darfur, Pity the Peacemakers Too." http://www.economist.com. Accessed 18 May 2016.

United Nations Security Council. 2007. *Report of the Secretary-General on the Sudan. (S/2007/213)*. April 17.

Zweifel, Thomas D. 2006. *International Organizations and Democracy: Accountability, Politics, and Power*. Boulder, CO: Lynne Rienner Publishers Inc.

CHAPTER 7

Conflict Resolution in Africa

George Klay Kieh, Jr.

Introduction

The euphoria that greeted the dawn of independence in Africa was quickly turned into a nightmare in various states, as the contradictions and crises generated by the neocolonial state plunged these states into civil wars. As the post-independence era unfolded, more African states became engulfed in civil wars. By the end of the twentieth century, the continent had experienced 27 civil wars and their associated negative effects, including the death of thousands of innocent civilians, mass displacements (both in terms of the refugee crisis and the internal displacement conundrum), the breakdown of political governance, and serious social and economic costs (Nyanduga 2004; Bariagaber 2006; Arnold 2007).

Although most of the civil wars that engulfed various states across the continent have ended, the one in Somalia, which began in 1988, continues to rage. Also, the high hopes for peace that greeted the Nairobi Peace Accord that ended the Sudanese civil war, the longest in Africa, in 2005, were dampened by the eruption of a genocidal civil war in the country's Darfur region (de Waal 2006; Natsios 2008). In the

G.K. Kieh, Jr. (✉)
University of West Georgia, Carrollton, GA, USA

G.K. Kieh, Jr. (ed.), *Contemporary Issues in African Society*,
African Histories and Modernities,
https://doi.org/10.1007/978-3-319-49772-3_7

Democratic Republic of the Congo, despite the end of the country's third civil war since independence in 1960, post-conflict peace-building efforts are experiencing serious stress as, for example, the eastern portion of the country remains under the control of various warlordist militias (Thom 1999; Padden 2010).

What methods have, and are being used to help resolve Africa's civil wars, and what have been the attendant outcomes? What steps have, and are being pursued to resolve the underlying conflicts and to build durable peace in post-conflict states? And how can durable peace be established in Africa? This chapter seeks to address these three interrelated questions.

Conceptual Framework

The chapter employs two major terms—"conflict resolution" and its attendant derivative "peace"—as the centerpieces of its conceptual framework. By conflict resolution, I am referring to the use of a broad array of "problem-solving" approaches that seeks to identify the causal factors behind a conflict, and the search for ways of dealing with them. It entails addressing such issues as the institutional structure of society; and the making of significant socioeconomic, political and other changes that would restructure society in a more just and inclusive way (Spangler 2005: 1).

Drawing from the works of Cortright (2008: 6–7) and Howard (1971: 225), peace is conceptualized as

> the desirable end product of the conflict resolution process that attempts to establish and maintain an orderly and just society protective against violence and the exploitation of less powerful groups by more powerful ones, and seeks to transcend the conditions that limit human potential.

In essence, "peace is more than the absence of war" (Cortright 2008: 6).

Resolving Africa's Civil Wars

Background

Conflict resolution involves two major stages: war termination (Licklider 1993; Hegre 2004) and peace-building (Call and Cook 2003; Francis 2010). The former is designed to end violent conflict, while the latter is intended to address the causes of the underlying conflict that gave rise to the armed violence (Ghali 1995). As twin processes, each is dependent upon the other. For example, peace cannot be established without the cessation of war; and the establishment of durable peace is the ***sine qua non*** for preventing the recurrence of war or armed violence.

Against this background, this section of the chapter will examine the general modalities that have been used to terminate civil wars on the continent, assess their efficacy, and decipher the efforts that have, and are being made to build durable peace in the continent's post-conflict states. Clearly, the quality of the war termination efforts is a critical determinant of the texture of the post-conflict environment in which the construction of peace takes place. That is, if the post-conflict environment that is created by the termination of the war is not conducive, then it would in turn adversely affect the peace-building project.

The Methods

Generally, the template for the termination of civil wars in Africa has consisted of three interlocking elements: peacemaking, peacekeeping (in the majority of the cases), and peace settlement.

Peacemaking consists of a broad array of methods that are designed to end a war (Assefa 1996; Darby and Mac Ginty 2008). The two most widely used in Africa's civil wars have been mediation and negotiation. In mediation, a third party "guides the [conflicting parties] through a non-adversarial discussion process that has as its goal the settling of the [war]" (Isenhart and Spangle 2000: 72). Operationally, the mediation process in the various civil wars in Africa has entailed the intervention of the Organization of African Unity/African Union (AU), a subregional organization such as the Economic Community of West African States (ECOWAS, and the United Nations. In some cases, these international organizations have acted either singularly or in concert. For example, during the first Chadian civil war (1979–1982), the Organization of African Unity (OAU) was the primary mediator (Kieh 1993; May and Massey 1998). During the initial stages of the first Liberian civil war (1989–1997), ECOWAS was the sole mediator (Sessay 1996; Adebajo 2002). However, since the emergent post-Cold War global order, the practice has pointed toward a collaborative mediatory role involving a regional organization, the AU and the United Nations. For instance, ECOWAS, the AU and the United Nations served as joint mediators in the Ivorian civil war (2002–2008). In other cases, the ambit of mediation has been extended to include some of the major global powers such as the United States, Britain and France. During the second Liberian civil war (1999–2003), ECOWAS, the AU, the UN and the United States served as joint mediators, although ECOWAS played the leading role.

As a practical matter, mediation has always been coupled with negotiation. This is because no peacemaking effort can succeed without the willingness of the belligerents to end the conflict. Thus, negotiation provides the conflicting parties the opportunity to interact directly, especially to articulate their respective positions. Depending on the circumstances, as various civil wars in Africa have demonstrated, negotiation may "create and fuel collaboration" (Isenhart and Spangle 2000: 45). However, such an outcome has been, and is dependent upon what Keltner (1987: 68) calls the "good faith and flexibility" of the conflicting parties.

Peacekeeping has been used as an instrument for helping to create a conducive environment for peacemaking in the majority of the civil wars in Africa. Two major genres of peacekeeping operations have been used: peace observation (Kieh 2009) and the military interposition force (Malan 1998; Bellamy et al. 2004). Peace observation has involved either a regional organization, for example, the Organization of African Unity/African Union, or the United Nations intervening in a civil war with a team of military and civilian personnel. The intervention has been premised on the existence of a ceasefire agreement between or among the warring factions. The peace observers' major task has been to monitor compliance by all of the conflicting parties with the terms of the ceasefire and the observers were prohibited from using military force. This model was used by the United Nations during the first Liberian civil war, and during the initial stage of the Sierra Leonean civil war.

Two major models of the military interposition force have been employed in some of the civil wars in Africa: the traditional model (Mays 2002; Bellamy et al. 2010; Guildimann 2010; Weiss et al. 2016). and the "new or robust model (Curran and Woodhouse 2007; Lipson 2007; Nsia-Pepra 2009; Ramsbotham et al. 2011)." The traditional model has been anchored on several elements: (1) either a regional organization or the OAU intervened in various civil wars with a military force. The intervention required the consent of one or more of the parties involved in the conflict; (2) the existence of a ceasefire between or among the warring parties was a major precondition for the intervention; (3) the interventionist force served as a buffer between the belligerents; (4) the interventionist force created a security corridor for the transport and distribution of humanitarian assistance; (5) the force was required to be neutral by not aligning with any of the conflicting parties; and (6) the force was prohibited from using military force offensively. Instead, it could only use force in self-defense.

Since the emergence of the post-Cold War era, a "new or robust" model has been developed. This was occasioned by the changing dynamics of civil wars on the continent, including the limitations of the traditional model. The "new or robust model" is based on several tenets. First, the intervention is undertaken by either a regional organization, the African Union or the United Nations or jointly—a regional organization and the African Union; a regional organization and the UN; and the AU and the UN. Second, the consent of either one or all of the belligerents is not required for the intervention to take place. Third, a ceasefire does not need to exist prior to the intervention. If one exists, it is then enforced by the military force. Alternatively, if there is no ceasefire, then the force imposes and enforces one. For example, during the first Liberian civil war, ECOMOG, the ECOWAS peacekeeping force, established and enforced a ceasefire. Given the nature of the civil war, the National Patriotic Front of Liberia (NPFL), the major warlordist militia led by Charles Taylor, rejected the ceasefire and proceeded to attack the peacekeeping force. Fourth, the peacekeeping force serves as a buffer between the warring factions, and creates a security zone for the delivery of humanitarian assistance to civilians. Fifth, the peacekeeping force can use military force offensively in peace enforcement operations. ECOMOG's peace enforcement operations during the first Liberian civil war and the Sierra Leonean civil war are good examples. However, the danger is that peace enforcement can undermine the peacekeeping force's neutrality by drawing it into the conflict. Sixth, the peacekeeping force may participate in what is generically referred to as "nation-building activities." These include a range of activities from helping to restructure and retrain the police to the primary assumption of security functions for the affected country during the transitional period.

When the belligerents agree to terminate the war, a peace settlement is then crafted (Walter 2001; Stedman et al. 2002). Its terms are embodied in a peace accord or agreement, which the belligerents sign. Drawing from the lessons of the various civil wars in Africa, peace agreements usually have three major components: the procedural, the substantive and the organizational. The procedural component generally consists of the processes for the establishment and maintenance of peace, such as the establishment and monitoring of the ceasefire. On the other hand, the substantive component embodies what Yawanajah and Quellet (2003: 1) characterize as the "political, economic, and social structural changes that are needed to remedy past grievances and provide for a more fair and equitable future." The organizational dimension encompasses the institutions and mechanisms that are required to implement the terms of the settlement. The Comprehensive Agreement that ended the Sudanese civil war in 2005 is a good example of a peace settlement.

It is important to note that a peace settlement may not end a civil war. This is because since it is a process that spans an appreciable period of time, a peace settlement is vulnerable to being violated either at the onset or at some point in the process. Characteristically, either scenario usually causes a reversion to war. Two common trajectories from some of Africa's civil wars are instructive. Even after the terms of the settlement are formulated and enveloped in a peace agreement or accord, and signed by the warring factions, one or more parties may decide to violate a term or terms of the settlement at the onset without the "ink even having dried on the agreement." In turn, this then reignites the war. For example, during the first Chadian civil war, the various peace settlements collapsed moments after they were signed. Similarly, during the first Liberian civil war, the Taylor-led NPFL recurrently violated a stipulation or stipulations of the various peace accords immediately after the signing ceremonies. The NPFL did this recurrently with sixteen peace accords.

Another trajectory is that one or more of the belligerents uncommitted to ending the war may initially agree to the peace settlement as a strategic move designed to "buy time"—the acquisition of weapons and materials, the repositioning of forces, etc. Once the strategic objective is achieved, the "spoiler" (Newman and Richmond 2006; Stedman 2000) may then decide to violate a term or terms of the peace settlement at a juncture in the settlement process.

What have been the outcomes of the various efforts that have been designed to terminate civil wars in Africa both in the past and present? Generally, there have been three outcomes: successful war termination (Walter 2001; Lyons 2002; Hegre 2004), failed war termination (Walter 1999; Stedman et al 2002; Benningsbo and Dupuy 2009), and mixed

(Hartzell and Hoddie 2003; Kreutz 2010). Successful war termination has been characterized by the full compliance of the warring factions with the terms of the peace settlement. The most important aspect is that there is no re-eruption of war. This then has created the environment for setting into motion the "Herculean" task of post-conflict peace-building (the building of durable peace). Several cases are instructive: The Mozambican peace settlement of 1992; the Angolan peace settlement of 2002; the Sierra Leonean peace settlement of 2002; and the Liberian peace settlement of 2003.

In contradistinction, failed war termination has been evidenced by the collapse of the peace settlement either at the onset or at some point in the settlement process. The resultant effects have been the reversion to war; and the impossibility of transitioning from war termination to peace-building. Several cases provide instructive lessons. As has been mentioned, the first Chadian civil war was the prototype of failed war termination on the continent. Another case was the Rwandan civil war. After the successful conclusion of a peace settlement embodied in the Arusha Peace Accord of 1993, the Rwandan military played the role of the "spoiler" by violating the terms of the accord. The consequence was renewed violence, and significantly, the commission of genocide by the military and its paramilitary collaborators.

Mixed success in war termination is captured by the "tugs and pulls" associated with the implementation of a peace settlement. That is, the war termination efforts tend to oscillate between failure and success—the eruption of a cycle of successful war termination / failed war termination. In short, a peace settlement may either collapse at the onset or at some point in the process; then a new peace settlement is formulated; again, it either collapses at the onset or succeeds for some time, and then collapses again. The first Liberian civil war is the archetype of this genre of war termination efforts in Africa. Beginning with the Banjul Peace Accord, the Taylor-led NPFL violated every subsequent peace agreement from the onset over a six-year period. Interestingly, each violation was followed by the formulation of a new peace settlement ostensibly designed to placate Taylor and his militia. Like failed war termination, the mixed variety can lead to the prolongation of a civil war, and therefore make the prospects for peace-building quite remote. This is because, as I have suggested, successful war termination is the essential precondition for setting into motion the process of building durable peace.

Building Peace in Africa's Post-conflict Societies: A General Assessment

The Peace-building Efforts

With the end of civil wars in several African states, these countries have undertaken the long and arduous task of building durable peace. The vortex of the effort revolves around the trilogy of capacity-building, reconciliation and societal transformation (Ghali 1995). The liberal peace-building model has become the hegemonic framework for reconstituting Africa's post-conflict societies. The model was imposed on these post-conflict states by the United Nations and the dominant metropolitan powers led by the United States.

The model is hoisted on three pivotal pillars: the establishment of political democratization, the re-establishment of peripheral capitalism under neoliberal orthodoxy, and reconciliation (Barnett 2006; Kurtenbach 2007; Sriram 2007). The political democratization dimension consists of the promotion of individual civil liberties and political rights, such as the freedoms of assembly, association and speech and the right to vote; the establishment of the tradition of holding regular elections within a multiparty framework; the establishment of a system of "checks and balances" within the government; the establishment of the sanctity of the rule of law and the independence of the judiciary; the promotion of accountability and transparency in the conduct of public affairs; and the establishment of a vibrant civil society that can serve as an autonomous sphere for checking on the powers of the government. The advocates of the model posit that the success of its principles is contingent upon the undertaking of comprehensive institutional reforms within the public sector of these post-conflict African states. The generic reforms include: judicial reforms, political reforms and security sector reforms. In other words, the contours of the liberal model are powered by an institutional tapestry.

On the economic front, post-conflict African states are instructed by the dominant metropolitan powers to either abandon their socialist economic system (Angola and Mozambique) or adopt the peripheral capitalist mode of production, or reform their existing peripheral capitalist political economies under the ideological guidance of neoliberalism. The basic neoliberal prescriptions include: the removal of all trade barriers; the removal of all obstacles to foreign investment; the dismantling of existing "social safety nets;" the devaluation of currencies; the reduction of the labor force in the public sector; the freezing of employment and salaries in the public sector; and the increase of interest rates. The neo-liberal rationale is that the implementation of these policies would spur private investment, increase exports and save money for the state.

Reconciliation in post-conflict societies in Africa has been based on two major pathways: the restorative and the retributive. The former is based on the efforts to establish interrelationships between and among the offenders, the victims and the extant communities by restoring the harm that has been caused; the rights of the victims and the communities; and the responsibilities of the offenders. Bishop Desmond Tutu, who chaired the South African Truth and Reconciliation Commission, provides an excellent summation of the restorative justice model thus:

> The central concern is not retribution or punishment but, in the spirit of Ubuntu, the healing of breaches, the redressing of imbalances, the restoration of broken relationships. This kind of justice seeks to rehabilitate both the victim and the perpetrator, who should be given the opportunity to be reintegrated into the community he or she injured by his or her offense. (Bell 2002: 90)

In short, the centerpiece of the restorative pathway is the search for "truth and reconciliation." One way in which this is done is through the establishment of a truth and reconciliation commission. Generally, the major functions of the truth and reconciliation commission are to recreate memory about the war; and to encourage those with knowledge about the war, including warlords and their militia men and women, to provide narratives about the war, especially their roles. In keeping with the overarching framework, the commission's terms of reference do not include the issuance of indictments, the holding of trials and the bringing to justice of those who have committed war crimes and crimes against societies. Instead, the focus is on restorative justice. Since the establishment of the truth and reconciliation commission after the end of the South African civil war in 1994, the example has been followed in other African states, including the Democratic Republic of the Congo, Sierra Leone, Sudan and Liberia.

On the other hand, the retributive model's central premise is that "justice requires punishment" (Fisher 2007: 16). That is, more often than not, however, for victims and bystanders alike to feel that justice has been achieved, some form of punishment has to befall the offender (Fisher 2007: 16). Significantly, punishment is necessary because it serves as retribution, deterrence, some form of moral education, incapacitation and society's expression of condemnation (Fisher 2007: 16).

In some of Africa's post-conflict societies, three major retributive mechanisms have been used: war crime tribunal, special court, and the International Criminal Court (ICC). In the case of the war crime tribunal, one was established for Rwanda in 1994 (United Nations Security Council Resolution 955 1994: 1). Under the resolution, the International Criminal Court for Rwanda (ICTR) is to "contribute to the process of national reconciliation in Rwanda and to the maintenance of peace in the region." (United Nations Security Council Resolution 955 1994: 1). During its 21 years of existence, the tribunal handed down 62 convictions (International Criminal Tribunal for Rwanda 2008: 1; United Nations Mechanism for International Criminal Tribunals 2016). In Sierra Leone, a special court was established through an agreement between the Government of Sierra Leone and the United Nations in 2002. The court was mandated to try those who bore the greatest responsibility for the commission of serious violations of international humanitarian law and Sierra Leonean law (The Special Court for Sierra Leone 2008: 1). During the court's 10 years of existence, it convicted 9 persons, including Charles Taylor, the President of Liberia (Special Court for Sierra Leone 2008: 1; Dana 2014).

Also, the ICC is playing a pivotal role in bringing to justice those accused of violating various aspects of international humanitarian law in some of Africa's civil wars. In the case of the Democratic Republic of the Congo, for example, by late 2016, the ICC had tried and convicted three of the major warlords in the country's seemingly unending civil war, including the country's former Vice President Jean Pierre Bemba (AFP 2016; Bowcott 2016). As for the Ugandan civil war, the ICC has indicted and subsequently issued arrest warrants against Joseph Kony, the leader of the rebel Lord's Resistance Army (LRA), and four of his commanders for the commission of sundry crimes in contravention of international humanitarian law (McGreal 2008: 1). Interestingly, however, Ugandan President Yoweri Museveni, who requested the ICC's intervention, has refused to effect the court's arrest warrants. This is because President Museveni used the court as leverage in dragooning the LRA leader into signing a peace agreement to end the country's 22 year-old civil war (McGreal 2008: 1).

A "Balance Sheet" on Peace-building Efforts

Are Africa's post-conflict states on the path to building durable peace? On the positive side, the termination of most of the continent's civil wars is a major step forward in creating a conducive environment for ultimately addressing and resolving the underlying conflict that is at the root of these various wars. Based on this, some progress has been made in liberalizing the political space in these various states, including improvements in the areas of political rights and civil liberties and the establishment of political institutions, rules and processes.

Despite the progress that has been made in the political sector, the various peace-building projects on the continent are generally plagued by several major problems. First, the liberal model, which provides the compass for navigating the terrain of peace-building, is not the best framework for addressing the taproots of civil conflicts in Africa for several reasons. The framework's democratization plank is quite limited to the political domain. That is, it is exclusively concerned with the promotion of individual political rights and civil liberties and overall political procedures. While these are important, they only address one aspect of the puzzle; hence, they are not sufficient to address the undercurrents of civil conflicts on the continent. In other words, they lack the expansiveness that is exigent to address the multidimensional crises, the bedrocks of civil conflicts, which have been generated by the neocolonial African state. This is the case because liberal democratization is not comprehensive. Neither does liberal democratization seek to fundamentally alter the portrait of the neocolonial African state—nature, character, mission, values and policies—and its resultant political economy. Hence, for example, pivotal issues such as socioeconomic inequities and disparities in power relations between and among classes and social justice are not addressed. In short, the democratization dimension of the liberal peace-building model is primarily concerned with the establishment of political procedures, and accords virtually no attention to the material well-being of the continent's subaltern classes.

Similarly capitalism, whether developed or peripheral, is intrinsically an undemocratic economic system. This is because it is anchored on inequality and exploitation. Thus, it privileges the ruling class at the expense of the subaltern ones. Such an economic system cannot address the serious human needs deficit that is confronting the continent's post-conflict societies. Instead, capitalism in its peripheral form in Africa's post-conflict states is exacerbating the socioeconomic problems that contributed to the various civil conflicts in the first place. For example, the privatization project is simply transferring wealth from the state to private capitalists principally from various metropolitan states such as the United States, without improving the material conditions of the subalterns.

As for the reconciliation efforts, they are driven by Western approaches that fail to accord the requisite attention to the specific cultural context of the various post-conflict societies on the continent. As Kotzo (2002: 73) appropriately warns, "Conflict resolution efforts must take cognizance of the cultural context."

Second and related, although traditional African methods are now being used in some cases, much still needs to be done. One helpful step could be to take cognizance of the historical and contemporary realities in a conflict-affected African state, prior to making the determination about the appropriate method or methods that could be helpful in resolving the conflict. Accordingly, in those cases in which the use of traditional African methods is still deeply rooted in the society, it would then be useful to use those methods. However, this should not preclude the use of Western or other methods as supplements, if they have utility under the circumstances.

Third, the peace-building projects on the continent are driven and dominated by external actors, some of whom contributed to planting the seeds of civil conflict in the continent's various post-conflict societies. For example, the United States played a pivotal role in the germination of the civil conflict in Liberia that occasioned two civil wars. Specifically, the United States was a major participant in the creation of the peripheral capitalist Liberian state, and provided the economic, political and military support that Liberia's ruling class used to suppress, repress and exploit the subaltern classes. Similarly, Britain was the chief architect of the neocolonial Sierra Leonean state, and thus contributed to the multidimensional crises that were germinated over time. Clearly, based on the history of the involvement of these external actors in these post-conflict societies in Africa and their broader imperialist agendas, there is no doubt that these metropolitan powers are not interested in peace-building projects that would fundamentally alter these societies, including the transformation of power relationships. Accordingly, as Gounden (2002: 3) observes, "[The imperialist powers'] cardinal goal is to attempt to influence the process of resolution to their interests sidelining and or worse ignoring local ideals." This is done through withholding support for initiatives that may result in undesired outcomes but that are supported by a majority of the polity in question (Gounden 2002: 3).

Fourth, the various peace-building projects in progress on the continent have generally ignored the role of the Bretton Woods institutions—International Monetary Fund and World Bank—and the totality of the global capitalist system in planting and nurturing the seeds of civil conflict on the continent. For example, the Bretton Woods institutions' "structural adjustment programs" have played pivotal roles in the facilitation of the continual plundering and pillaging of the resources of these post-conflict states by metropolitan-based multinational corporations, and the decimation of the "social safety nets" that have provided a modicum of the basic human needs of the members of the various subaltern classes. Broadly, the required attention has not been paid to the characteristic inequities inherent in the nature and dynamics of the global capitalist system. For example, the "international division of labor" still requires that these post-conflict states remain producers of raw materials and the consumers of comparatively expensive manufactured goods from the metropolitan states. The "system of unequal exchange" remains intact. Under this arrangement, the post-conflict states will continue to be paid less for their raw materials, while being required to pay more for the manufactured goods from the United States, Europe and Japan. The point is that the global capitalist system will continue to remain hostile to development of these post-conflict states; hence, these societies will not be able to generate the resources that are required for them to address the problems of inequities in wealth and income, mass and abject poverty, social malaise and the strangulating effects of the overall precariously low standards of living.

Rethinking Conflict Resolution in Africa: Some Suggestions

There is the need to rethink conflict resolution in Africa. This is because as has been argued the various conflict resolution projects on the continent are fraught with major problems that undermine the abilities of Africa's post-conflict states to build durable peace. One of the major lacunas of the war termination efforts is the pervasive practice of rewarding "warlordism". This is especially done by allotting various positions in the transitional administration to the various warlordist factions. A major resultant effect is that such a practice has encouraged rather than deterred warlordism. This is because warlords are cognizant of the fact that if their respective militias do not win outright military victories, they will be rewarded with various positions in an interim administration. In turn, these positions are used to foster the process of the practice of accumulation of capital by the warlords and their coteries of top advisors. Alternatively, while it is important for the various warlordist militias to be involved in the peace process, they should not be rewarded with positions in the interim regime. Instead, the office holders in the interim regime should be people with the requisite skills, who are not affiliated with the warlordist militias. This approach would help to deter warlordism, because potential war-makers would be aware that they would not be rewarded with positions in the state bureaucracy simply because they establish militias and participate in raining violence and mayhem on innocent civilians.

Another problem is that the larger society is often marginalized in the war termination efforts. Instead, the focus is on the various warlordist militias and the government. Thus, the larger society, which represents the majority of the citizens, does not participate in the fashioning of the peace settlement, but is required to live and abide by the terms. Moreover, since it is usually a spectator in the peace process, the larger society has no basis for holding the interim regime—including the various office holders from the warlordist militias—accountable. Consequently, as has been demonstrated in post-conflict societies like Liberia, Sierra Leone and the DRC, the larger society is forced to suffer the consequences of the incompetence and poor policies of the interim administration without recourse. Clearly, this approach needs to be changed and replaced with one that emphasizes the inclusion of various citizen-based organizations representing various segments of the affected countries in the war termination efforts. Moreover, it should be clearly stipulated in the peace accord that the transitional regime would be accountable to the people. In order to practicalize such a provision, the major citizen groups should have representation in the transitional legislature. The transitional legislature should have oversight responsibilities over the transitional regime, including the power to remove the officers in the transitional executive branch.

In the area of peace-building, Lederach's (1995: 65) "elicitive approach" would be a useful pathway for several reasons. It places a premium on the cultural context and the associated knowledge and views of the citizens of the society in conflict as the foundation of peace-building. Also, it values the indigenous participants in the peace-building process as resources rather than recipients of conflict resolution knowledge, especially from "external experts." In this regard, the methods for the establishment of a peaceful society based on "constructive change"—the flow of human interaction in social conflict from cycles of destructive relational violence toward cycles of relational dignity and respectful engagement (Lederach 2005: 243)—are collectively established through the critical reflection.

Building on the aforementioned approach, the liberal peace-building model that has been imposed by the powerful forces in the international system as the template for post-conflict African societies needs to be transcended. The alternative model should be framed around changing the portrait of the neocolonial African state, and addressing the deeper issues of class inequities and the associated asymmetries in power in various relationships, human well-being and social justice. In terms of the transformation of the African state, this is the paramount task, because the neocolonial African state is the generator of the contradictions and crises that lead to civil conflict and war. Specifically, the nature of the African state needs to reflect the historical-cultural realities of each African state rather than external ones (the nature of the neocolonial African state is a continuation from the colonial era). This would enable the citizens to take ownership of the state.

The character of the state needs to be changed from being criminalized, exploitative, negligent, prebendal, and repressive to productive, protective, meritorious, supportive and responsive to the needs and aspirations of its citizens. This would have profound positive ramifications for improving state-society relations. Ultimately, the citizens would accept the state as their own, rather than as a construct that visits hardship on them.

Another important element of the state that requires transformation is the mission. In its current formulation, the central mission of the neocolonial African state is to create propitious conditions for the owners of metropolitan-based multinational corporations and other businesses, and the members of the local ruling classes and their relations to accumulate wealth, to the detriment of the majority of the citizens. Alternatively, the new primary mission of the state should be attending to the welfare of the citizens—employment, education, healthcare, housing, food security, etc.

Moreover, the perennial problem of class inequities needs to be addressed. Two steps are instructive. Measures need to be taken to prevent the members of the local ruling class and their relations from illegally acquiring wealth through various corrupt means. This could be done through the establishment of an effective anti-corruption regime. The transformed state would then formulate and implement various policies that are designed to address the issue of inequities in income and wealth.

Addressing the vexing problem of asymmetries in power in various relationships is another major dimension of deep peace-building. This would cover the cultural, economic, gender, political and social spheres. For example, steps would need to be taken to curtail the expansion of presidential powers and its resultant "hegemonic presidency." Such a step would be important for ensuring a "balance of power" between and among the various branches of government.

Central to the establishment of a new "culture of social justice" is the imperative of empowering people at the grassroots level, especially economically and politically. The rationale is that empowered citizens can serve as effective bulwarks against injustice. This is because the citizens would be able to hold public officials and others accountable for their actions. Ultimately, this would serve as an effective deterrent against actions such as the abuse of power, a major source of injustice on the African continent.

Importantly, the success of this alternative peace-building trajectory would be dependent upon the participation of a conscious and engaged citizenry and a visionary national leadership in a post-conflict African state. An important initial step would be to hold national conferences as an integral part of the peace-building process. That is, the peace-building in a post-conflict African society should be preceded by the holding of a national conference involving the representatives of all of the major stakeholders in the society. The major purpose would be to redesign the state and society through the peace-building process.

Within the framework of a democratically reconstituted state, traditional African approaches to conflict resolution should be valued. This is because as Zartman (1999: 3) suggests, "Traditional societies in Africa…are reputed to hold secrets of peacemaking locked in their ways, formed from centuries of custom before the disruption of colonization." For example, lessons can be drawn from the various traditional African approaches to conflict resolution such as the Mato Oput

Justice clan-based model (Bangura 2008: 2). In turn, these lessons can be appropriately applied to various conflicts across the continent. On the other hand, lessons from the conflict resolution approaches of other societies and cultures, including Western ones, can be applied to conflicts in various African states when the determination is made that they are relevant. This would represent a fundamental change from the current practice under which Western approaches are superimposed on African civil conflicts, without taking into consideration their cultural relevance and suitability to helping to resolve these conflicts.

Yet, another major consideration in rethinking conflict resolution in Africa's post-conflict states needs to be the formulation of strategies for addressing the conflict-inducing dynamics of the global capitalist system. That is, post-conflict states, other African states and Third World states would need to organize a united front and work collaboratively in struggling to make changes in the international capitalist system. For example, the "international division of labor" that requires African and other Third World states to be the producers of cheap raw materials needs to be changed so that these developing countries can develop industrial and technological bases. In addition, the "system of unequal exchange" under which the dominant powers have determined that the raw materials from Africa and the rest of the Third World are sold at prices cheaper than the manufactured goods mainly from the industrialized capitalist states needs to be changed. This is because by accruing less for their primary products and paying more for manufactured goods, African states do not generate enough foreign exchange earnings to be able to address the multitude of domestic economic and social challenges such as education, healthcare, housing and transportation. The resultant adverse impact on the well-being of the members of the subaltern classes has been a major contributor to planting the seeds of civil conflict in Africa.

Conclusion

The chapter has attempted to address three major interrelated issues relating to the resolution of civil conflicts in Africa. First, the chapter tackled the war termination conundrum by examining the various methods—peacemaking, peacekeeping and peace settlement—that have been used to terminate civil wars in Africa. The results indicate that these efforts have produced three general outcomes: success, failure and mixed. Successful war termination is characterized by the complete cessation of armed violence. On the other hand, failed war termination is distinguishable by the reversion to war either at the onset of the peace settlement process or at a subsequent juncture. The mixed war termination genre is hoisted on a series of cycles of successes and failures.

Second, the issue of war termination was then linked to peace-building. Against this background, the article deciphered the nature and dynamics of the liberal peace-building model, the hegemonic pathway for reconstituting Africa's post-conflict states, and ultimately "building durable peace" in them. Specifically, the central tenets—political democratization, capitalist economy and national reconciliation—and their dynamics were examined within the context of the continent's post-civil conflict states. The central finding is that liberal peace-building with its focus on political rights and freedoms is inadequate for addressing the general undercurrents of civil conflict in the continent's various post-conflict societies.

Finally, the *sine qua non* for the building and maintenance of permanent peace in Africa's post-conflict states and its other polities is the establishment of substantive or deep democracy on the continent beyond the limits of political liberalization and its pathological fixation with procedures. In other words, Africa—both its post-conflict states and others—needs a new kind of state that is anchored on holistic democracy and its tenets of, among others, mass empowerment, equality and social justice—what Ake (1996: 124) correctly refers to as "real democracy." Correspondingly, the new democratic African states would need to establish a united front among themselves, as well as with other democratic polities in the Third World to struggle for the fundamental restructuring of the structure and dynamics of the global capitalist system. One of the major outcomes of the restructuring must be what Muiu (2007: 55) calls "Africa's control over its own economic resources." That is, African and Third World states, both post-conflict and otherwise, must control their resources if they are to build and maintain peaceful societies.

References

AFP. 2016. Africa in the Dock at the ICC. *New Vision*. October 21.

Adebajo, Adekeye. 2002. *Liberia's Civil War: Nigeria, ECOMOG, and Regional Security in West Africa*. Boulder: Lynne Rienner Publishers.

Ake, Claude. 1996. *Democracy and Development in Africa*. Washington, D.C: The Brookings Institution Press.

Arnold, Guy. 2007. *Historical Dictionary of Civil Wars in Africa*. Lanham, MD: Scarecrow Press.

Assefa, Hizkias. 1996. *Peacemaking and Democratization in Africa*. Nairobi: East African Educational Publishers.

Bangura, Abdul Karim. 2008. *Africa Peace Paradigms*. Dubuque, IA: Kendall/ Hunt Publishing Co.

Bariagaber, Assefaw. 2006. *Conflict and the Refugee Experience*. Aldershot, UK: Ashgate Publishing.

Barnett, Michael. 2006. Building a Republican Peace: Stabilizing States After War. *International Security* 30 (4): 87–112.

Bell, R.H. 2002. *Understanding African Philosophy: A Cross Cultural Approach to Classical and Contemporary Issues*. New York: Routledge.

Bellamy, Alex, Paul Williams, and Staurt Griffin. 2004. *Understanding Peacekeeping*. 1st ed. London: Polity.

Binningsbo, Helga Malmin, and Kendra Dupuy. 2009. *Power Sharing and the Civil War in Sierra Leone*. Paper presented at the Aegis Conference, October 1–2, in Hamburg, Germany.

Bowcott, Owen. 2016. Congo Politician Guilty in First ICC Trial to Focus on Rape as War Crime. *The Guardian*. London. March 21.

Call, Charles, and Susan Cook. 2003. Post-Conflict Peacebuilding. *Global Governance* 9: 135–140.

Cortright, David. 2008. *Peace: A History of Movements and Ideas*. Cambridge, UK: Cambridge University Press.

Curran, David, and Tom Woodhouse. 2007. Cosmopolitan Peacekeeping and Peacebuilding in Sierra Leone: What can Africa Contribute?. *International Affairs* 83 (6): 1055–1070.

Dana, Shahram. 2014. The Sentencing Legacy of the Special Court for Sierra Leone. *Georgia Journal of International and Comparative Law* 42 (3): 617–686.

Darby, John, and Roger Mac Ginty (eds.). 2008. *Contemporary Peacemaking*, 2nd ed. New York: Palgrave Macmillan.

De Waal, Alex. 2006. *Darfur: A Short History of a Long War*. London: Zed Books.

Fisher, Kirsten. 2007. *Demanding Accountability: Judgment and Punishment in Uganda's Restorative Mechanisms*. Paper presented at the 2nd Annual Graduate Student Symposium, March 16, in Dalhousie University, Canada.

Francis, Diana. 2010. *From Pacification to Peacebuilding*. London: Pluto Press.

Ghali, Butros-Butros. 1995. *An Agenda for Peace*. New York: United Nations Publications.

Gounden, Vasu. 2002. *Managing and Resolving African Conflicts: A Critical Review Paper*. Ethiopia: Addis Ababa.

Guldimann, Tim. 2010. Peacekeeping Under Stain: Coping With Evolving Contradictions?. *Peace and Conflict Review* 4 (2): 68–79.

Hartzell, Caroline, and Matthew Hoddie. 2003. Institutionalizing Peace: Power Sharing and Post-Cold War Conflict. *American Journal of Political Science* 47 (2): 318–332.

Hegre, Havard. 2004. The Duration and Termination of Civil Wars. *Journal of Peace Research* 41 (3): 243–252.

Howard, Michael. 1971. *Studies in War and Peace.* New York: Viking Press.

International Criminal Tribunal for Rwanda. 2008. *Fact Sheet No. 1.* Arusha, Tanzania: ICTR.

Isenhart, Myra Warren, and Michael Spangle. 2000. *Collaborative Approaches to Resolving Conflicts.* Thousand Oaks, CA: Sage Publications.

Keltner, John. 1987. *Mediation: Toward a Civilized System of Dispute Resolution.* Annandale, VA: Speech Communication Association.

Kieh, George Klay. 1993. Resolving Africa's Conflicts. *Peace Review* 5 (4): 447–454.

Kieh, George Klay. 2009. The United Nation's Peace Observation Mission and the First Liberian Civil War. *Peace Studies Journal* 2 (1): 45–62.

Kotzo, Dirk. 2002. Issues in Conflict Resolution. *African Journal on Conflict Resolution* 2 (2): 77–100.

Kreutz, Joakim. 2010. How and When Armed Conflicts End: Introducing the UCDP Conflict Termination Dataset. *Journal of Peace Research* 47 (2): 243–250.

Kurtenbach, Sabine. 2007. Why is Liberal Peacebuilding So Difficult? Some Lessons from Central America. GIGA Working Papers No. 59, German Institute of Global and Area Studies at Hamburg, Germany.

Lederach, John Paul. 1995. *Preparing for Peace: Conflict Transformation Across Cultures.* Syracuse: Syracuse University Press.

Lederach, John Paul. 2005. *The Moral Imagination: The Art and Soul of Building Peace.* New York: Oxford University Press.

Licklider, Roy (ed.). 1993. *Stopping the Killings: How Civil War Ends.* New York: New York University Press.

Lipson, Michael. 2007. A 'Garbage Can Model' of UN Peacekeeping. *Global Governance* 13 (1): 79–97.

Lyons, Terrence. 2002. *Postconflict Elections: War Termination, Democratization, and Demilitarizing Politics.* Working Paper No. 20, Institute for Conflict Analysis and Resolution, George Mason University at Fairfax, VA.

Malan, Mark. 1998. *Peacekeeping in Africa: Trends and Responses.* ISS Occasional Paper No. 31, Institute for Security Studies at Pretoria.

May, Roy, and Simon Massey. 1998. The OAU's Interventions in Chad: Mission Impossible or Mission Evaded?. *International Peacekeeping* 5 (1): 46–65.

Mays, Terry. 2002. *Africa's First Peacekeeping Operation: The OAU in Chad, 1981–1982.* Westport, CT: Praeger Publisher.

McGreal, Chris. 2008. Uganda Defies War Crimes Court Over Indictments. *Guardian* (United Kingdom). March 12, p. 1.

Muiu, Mueni. 2007. "Peace-building and Conflict Resolution". In *Stakes in Africa-U.S. Relations: Proposals for an Equitable Partnership*, eds. Abdul Karim Bangura et al., 41–60. Lincoln, NE: iUniverse.

Natsios, Andrew. 2008. Beyond Darfur: Sudan's Slide Toward Civil War. *Foreign Affairs* 87 (3): 77–93.

Newman, Edward, and Oliver Richmond. 2006. Peace building and Spoilers. *Conflict, Security and Development* 6 (1): 101–110.

Nsia-Pepra, Kofi. 2009. *Robust Peacekeeping? Confronting the Failures of Traditional Peacekeeping in Preventing Human Rights Violations.* Paper presented at the 50th Annual Convention of the International Studies Association, February 15, in New York City, New York.

Nyanduga, Bohame Tom. 2004. The Challenge of Internal Displacement in Africa. *Forced Migration Review* 21: 58–59.

Padden, Emily. 2010. Beyond Creed, Greed and Booty: Conflict in the Democratic Republic of the Congo. *Africa: The Journal of the International African Institute* 80 (2): 322–331.

Ramsbotham, Oliver, Tom Woodhouse, and Hugh Miall. 2011. *Contemporary Conflict Resolution: The Prevention, Management and Transformation of Deadly Conflicts.* Cambridge: Polity Press.

Sessay, Max. 1996. Civil War and Collective Intervention in Liberia. *Review of African Political Economy* 23 (67): 35–52.

Spangler, Brand. 2005. Settlement, Resolution, Management, and Transformation: An Explanation of Terms. In *Beyond Intractability*, eds. Guy Burgess and Heidi Burgess. Boulder, CO: Conflict Research Consortium, University of Colorado at Boulder. www.beyondintractability.org/essay/development_conflict_theory. Accessed on 24 May 2016.

Special Court for Sierra Leone. 2008. *Documents and Cases.* Freetown, Sierra Leone: Special Court for Sierra Leone.

Sriram, Chandra Lekha. 2007. Liberal Peacebuilding and Strategies of Transitional Justice. *Global Society* 21 (4): 579–591.

Stedman, Stephen John. 2000. Spoiler Problems in Peace Process. In *International Conflict Resolution after the Cold War*, eds. Paul Stern, and Daniel Druckman, 178–218. Washington, D.C.: National Academic Press.

Stedman, Stephen John, Donald Rottchild, and Elizabeth Cousens (eds.). 2002. *Ending Civil Wars: The Implementation of Peace Agreements.* Boulder: Lynne Rienner Publishers.

Thom, William. 1999. Congo-Zaire's 1996–1997 Civil War in the Context of Evolving Patterns of Military Conflict in Africa in the Era of Independence. *Journal of Conflict Studies* 19 (2). www.lib.unb.ca. Accessed on 25 May 2016.

United Nations Security Council. 1994. *Resolution 955 on the Establishment of An International Criminal Tribunal for Rwanda and Its Statute.* New York: United Nations.

Walter, Barbara. 1999. Designing Transitions from Civil War. In *Civil Wars, Insecurity and Intervention*, ed. Barbara Walter, and Jack Synder, 38–72. New York: Columbia University Press.

Walter, Barbara. 2001. *Committing to Peace: The Successful Settlement of Civil Wars*. Princeton: Princeton University Press.

Weiss, Thomas George, David Forsythe, Roger Coates, and Kelly-Kate Pease. 2016. *The United Nations and Changing World Politics*. 8th ed. Boulder: Westview Press.

Yawanajah, Nita, and Julian Ouellet. 2003. Peace Agreements. In *Beyond Intractability*, eds. Guy Burgess, and Heidi Burgess. Boulder, CO: Conflict Research Consortium, University of Colorado at Boulder. www.beyondintractability.org/essay/developmentconflicttheory. Accessed 25 May 2016.

Zartman, I William.1999. Introduction: African Traditional Conflict Medicines. In *Traditional Cures for Modern Conflicts: African Conflict "Medicine"*, ed. I William Zartman, 1–14. Boulder, CO: Lynne Rienner Publishers.

CHAPTER 8

Africa and the European Union

Jack Mangala

Introduction

EU-Africa relations represent, in many ways, a unique experiment in international relations. Over the past fifty years, the two regions have intensely engaged each other and developed a dense and complex web of institutional, economic, political, social and cultural ties. This unique experiment in interregionalism has however, for the most part, not been studied in its totality. Most scholarly endeavors tend to approach the relationship from the perspective of a single issue (trade, development cooperation, human rights). Deeply rooted in history, the relationship between the two regions has gradually evolved from fragmented and "often painful colonial arrangements" into a comprehensive, multilayered and multifunctional "strategic partnership" that seeks not only to address issues of interest to the two regions but also to allow them to "face with confidence the demands of our globalizing world" (Lisbon Declaration 2007). The adoption of a Joint Africa-EU Strategy by the second EU-Africa Summit in Lisbon in December 2007 attests to this

J. Mangala (✉)
Grand Valley State University, Allendale, MI, USA

G.K. Kieh, Jr. (ed.), *Contemporary Issues in African Society*,
African Histories and Modernities,
https://doi.org/10.1007/978-3-319-49772-3_8

changing partnership and its centrality in the relationship between the two regions.

The EU has emerged as Africa's most important economic partner with exportation of merchandise amounting to €91.1 billion, and importation reaching €125.6 billion in 2005. EU's official development assistance (ODA) accounts for 60% of the total ODA going to Africa, reaching €48 billion in 2006. Against this background, the EU has unequivocally stressed that "African economic prosperity is essential for European prosperity" (European Commission, 2007a: 2). The two regions have also, in recent years, strengthened their political cooperation in areas such as peace and security, governance and human rights, and migration and mobility. For example, in response to a 2003 request from the AU Summit in Maputo, the EU has established the African Peace Facility (APF), a €300 million development instrument in support of African peace support operations (PSO) and capacity-building in the area of peace and security.

While recent developments seem to indicate a significant shift—at least conceptually—of EU-Africa relations, they also raise some pressing questions: What are the forces driving these changing EU-Africa relations? Would this proclaimed new "strategic" partnership be fundamentally different from the unequal, fragmented, sometimes incoherent and donor-recipient type relationship of the past? How can we, theoretically, explain the two partners' past and current pattern of behaviors? What are the guiding principles and policy priorities of EU-Africa relations and how have they been translated into concrete areas of cooperation? These are the central questions that the present chapter seeks to address. The chapter is structured into three sections. The first section offers a broad historical perspective that captures the evolution of Africa-EU relations over the past fifty years while discussing its major conceptual, institutional, strategic and policy frameworks. The second section reviews the major theoretical explanations of the relationship with a particular emphasis on the contribution of interregionalism—which needs to be related both to globalization and the restructuring of the nation-state—to the general theory of international relations. The third section discusses the implementation of policies in four major areas of cooperation (trade and regional integration, peace and security, governance and human rights and key development issues). It assesses the implementation of the vision, principles, strategies and policies outlined in the first section.

Historical Perspective and Frameworks for EU-Africa Relations

In the negotiations preceding the creation of the European Economic Community (EC) in 1957, France made a *sine qua non* for signing the Treaty of Rome that its overseas dependencies would be accommodated in the new common market. France's position was backed by Belgium and Italy, two other founding members that had colonies in Africa. Thus, the "Association of Overseas Countries and Territories" is listed in an annex to the Treaty of Rome. This association marked the beginning of "privileged" relations between the EC and Africa. Over the past fifty years, these relations have evolved from a mere "unilateral associationism" to a multifaceted strategic partnership embedded in the Joint Africa-EU Strategy adopted at the second EU-Africa Summit in Lisbon in 2007, which heads of states and governments would like to "be remembered as a moment of recognition of maturity and transformation in our continent-to-continent dialog, opening new paths and opportunities for collective action for our common future" (Lisbon Declaration 2007).

This section will analyze the multiple frameworks for Africa-EU relations, as well as the vision and guiding principles that define the relationship. It will also discuss the objectives, approaches and strategies pursued by the two partners, as well as the institutional architecture in charge of this complex relationship.

Multiple Frameworks for EU-Africa Relations

Over the last decades, the EU and African states have adopted various arrangements of different nature that reflect the intricacies of their common history as well as evolving geo-strategic considerations and policy priorities and needs.[1] These fundamental dynamics have led to a fragmented framework of relationship within which coexist four bodies of agreements and political processes that speak to the complexity and density of Africa-EU relations: the Cotonou Agreement, the Barcelona process, the Trade and Development Cooperation Agreement with South Africa and the Cairo process. This network of agreements and political processes has often raised issues of consistency that the 2007 Joint Africa-EU Strategy seeks to address (Farrell 2005; Koulaimah-Gabriel 1997).

The Cotonou Agreement: Formally known as the ACP-EU Partnership agreement, the Cotonou Agreement was signed in 2000 to regulate various aspects of the relationship between African, Caribbean and Pacific countries (ACP) and the EU. It combines a political dimension with trade and development issues in a single comprehensive instrument. All sub-Saharan African countries are parties to this agreement.[2] The Cotonou Agreement is the latest in a succession of trade agreements and arrangements between the EC and former European colonies in Africa, the Caribbean and the Pacific that can be traced back to the negotiations leading up to the creation of the European Economic Community (EEC) in March 1957.

On France's insistence, backed by other founding members who had an interest in maintaining trade flows with their overseas dependencies and keeping their economic presence in these countries, the Treaty of Rome (Part IV) provided for the "Association of Overseas Countries and Territories", listed in an annex. The core elements of the association centered on free trade, the right of establishment of firms, and development assistance. The association stressed the "privileged" nature of the relationship between the ECC and its overseas associates and called for "solidarity", which was materialized with the establishment of the European Development Fund (EDF) in 1958. While African colonies' accession to national sovereignty compelled their progressive exclusion from the provisions of Part IV of the Treaty of Rome, the two sides expressed the desire to maintained "privileged links" that had existed. Hence the conclusion, in 1963, of the first Yaoundé Convention, which shifted the relationship from "unilateral associationism" to a contractual and negotiated agreement based, on the part of the EC, on Article 238 of the Treaty of Rome. Trade preferences and aid constituted the main conventional benefits.[3]

In the 1970s, Euro-African relations reached a turning point under Yaoundé II, due to a number of changes affecting the international system, and the EC's integration process. The deepening of European integration and the UK's accession to the Common Market in 1972, led to a redefinition of the geographical scope of the EC's foreign aid and trade relations aimed at accommodating British dependencies and former colonies in Africa and in the Caribbean and Pacific. Some of the EC's members, mainly Germany and the Netherlands, were advocating for an overall EC development policy and its de-linkage from the colonial past of certain member states. These EC internal debates were taking place against the background of an international system where the call for a change in North-South relations was gaining momentum. It suffices to mention the work of the United Nations Conference on Trade and Development (UNCTAD) and discussions at the UN General Assembly calling for a New International Economic Order. It was within this international environment, considered by many as "favorable to Southern countries" that the EC and ACP countries adopted the first Lomé Convention in 1975—a new and broad framework of relationship intended to replace the Yaoundé Convention. The adoption of the Lomé Convention was accompanied by the globalization of EC's development policy. The EC engaged in a balancing act of promoting a world-scale development policy while preserving "privileged relations" with former ACP countries (Koulaimah-Gabriel 1997; Brown 2000).

The Lomé Convention was primarily intended to promote the development of the signatory ACP states via trade, economic assistance and technical assistance. The "privileged" status of relations between the EC and Africa was reflected in the non-reciprocal duty-free arrangement,[4] the provision of economic assistance to ACP countries via the European Development Fund[5] and the provision of industrial and technical cooperation that would enable the utilization of the EU's know-how for the industrial development of ACP countries.[6] This "generous" outcome was indicative of sub-Saharan Africa's relative bargaining power and the EU's geo-strategic interests in the region based, as the European Commission (1996: 9) put it, on the "concern to defend ... economic and geopolitical interests in the age of the Cold War ... the international situation ... European anxiety at the first oil crisis, i.e. a fear of raw material shortages and a desire to hold on to valued overseas markets, united with geostrategic interests."

Between Lomé's inception in 1975 and its expiration in 2000, successive conventions were agreed upon with increasing conditionalities on human rights, democracy and the rule of law—and little development success in Africa.[7] The Lomé Convention, often described as a model for North-South cooperation, did not live up to its expectations. It has been convincingly argued that "all it did was to perpetuate dependency links toward former colonial powers" (Koulainah-Gabriel: 16). In the 1990s, the accumulation of a number of forces compelled the two sides to seek profound changes to the Lomé Convention. Chief among them were the push toward international trade liberalization,[8] the evolving position of the EU in the world economy,[9] the end of the Cold War, and the widening and deepening of the EU.[10] At the turn of the century, a fundamental overhaul of the Lomé Convention had become virtually unavoidable.

Signed in 2000, the Cotonou Agreement differs from the Lomé Convention in many fundamental ways. First, while the latter were self-contained rule systems, the former is a framework agreement consisting of objectives, principles and options for instruments. Second, by stressing the reduction and eventual eradication of poverty as its central goal, the Cotonou Agreement is consistent with the objectives of the EU's development cooperation policy as formulated in Article 177 of the EC Treaty. Third, the principles of cooperation have been refined in order to account for the new political dimension of the EU-ACP relationship, which calls for the respect for human rights, democratic principles and the rule of law in advancing the objectives of the Agreement.[11] Cotonou also insists on participation of other sections of society (civil society and private sector organizations), dialog and fulfillment of mutual obligations and differentiation and regionalization in the implementation of the cooperation. Fourth, unlike the non-reciprocal preferences granted to ACP countries under Lomé, the Cotonou Agreement introduced the prospect of reciprocal trade preferences to be negotiated between the EU and African subregional entities, leading to the establishment of Economic Partnership Agreements (EPAs) by 2008. The least developed ACP countries can opt for the continuation of non-reciprocal preferences under EU's preferences for least developed countries. These trade regime options are intended to make EU-ACP trade relations compatible with WTO rules, especially the non-discrimination principle. Fifth, the distribution of resources under the EDF will be based on more explicit criteria than in Lomé, chiefly need and performance. We will discuss more in-depth various dimensions of the Cotonou Agreement when we analyze EU-Africa sectoral trade cooperation in the third section of the chapter. The intent here was to present an overview of the evolution of this first framework of EU-Africa relations.

The Barcelona process: The EU's relations with Northern African countries are partly organized under this second framework, which was launched in Barcelona in 1995 as a platform for political dialog and partnership between the EU and countries around its southern Mediterranean borders. The Barcelona Declaration identified three main objectives to the Euro-Mediterranean Partnership: (1) establishing a common area of peace and stability through the reinforcement of political and security dialog; (2) creating an area of shared prosperity through an economic partnership and the gradual establishment of a free-trade area; and (3) bringing peoples together through a social, cultural and human partnership aimed at promoting understanding between cultures and exchanges between civil societies. The Partnership is implemented through bilateral Association Agreements between the EU and each of the partner countries.[12]

The challenges posed by the EU's enlargement in 2004 and the subsequent redefinition of EU's external borders led to the development of a new instrument, the European Neighborhood Policy (ENP), which offers a general framework that applies to all of the EU's immediate neighbors by land or sea. The ENP is predicated on the premise that

> The EU has a vital interest in seeing greater economic development, stability and better governance in its neighborhood. Spreading peace and prosperity across the borders of the EU prevents artificial divisions and creates benefits for the ENP partners and the EU alike. The ENP is a partnership for reform that offers "more for more": the more deeply a partner engages with the Union, the more fully the Union can respond, politically, economically and through financial and technical cooperation. (European Commission 2007c: 2)

The ENP offers EU's immediate neighbors a "privileged" relationship, built upon "mutual commitment to common values" that should result in a deeper political relationship and economic integration.[13] The central instrument of the ENP is the bilateral ENP Action Plans agreed between the EU and each individual partner. ENP Action Plans outline an agenda of political and economic reforms with short and medium-term priorities.[14]

The Trade, Development and Cooperation Agreement with South Africa: Although a signatory of the Cotonou Agreement,[15] South Africa concluded a separate, parallel and ambitious Trade, Development and Cooperation Agreement (TDCA) with the EU in 1999. The TDCA represents the legal basis for the overall relations between South Africa and the EU. It covers political dialog, trade, development cooperation and economic cooperation as well as cooperation in a whole range of other areas. The EU is South Africa's most important economic trade partner, accounting for over 40% of its imports and exports, as well as 70% of foreign direct investment. European exports to South Africa have risen by 9.5% per year on average since the TDCA came into force in 2004. Taking into account these deepening links and South Africa's particular position on the regional and global stage, the two sides agreed, in a 2005 "Joint Report", that "new steps need to be taken to ensure that South Africa-EU relations develop into a truly strategic partnership that … would do justice to the role of South Africa as an anchor on the continent and key player on the international scene" (European Commission, 2006: 6).[16]

The proposed Strategic Partnership, which is seen as an "important further building block in the overall EU-Africa partnership", is intended to upgrade EU-South Africa relations

> By bringing the member states, the Community and South Africa together in a single and coherent framework, with clearly and jointly defined objectives, covering all areas of cooperation and associating all stakeholders; by moving from political dialog to strategic political cooperation and shared objectives on regional, African and global issues; by enhancing existing cooperation, developing stronger and sustainable economic cooperation, fully implementing the TDCA provisions on trade-related areas and extending cooperation to the social, cultural and environmental fields (European Commission 2006: 6).

South Africa has clearly emerged as a pivotal actor, whose status and role have been recognized by the signing of additional and specific instruments of cooperation that add to the complexity of the framework for EU-Africa relationship.

The Cairo process: Held in Cairo in 2000, the historic first EU-Africa Summit set in motion a more structured continent-to-continent political dialog, which culminated in the adoption of a new strategic partnership and a Joint Africa-EU Strategy at the second summit in Lisbon in 2007.[17] The Cairo Summit launched a comprehensive framework for political dialog between the EU and African states along four priority areas: (1) regional integration in Africa; (2) integration of Africa into the world economy (trade, private sector development, investment, development resources, industrial infrastructure, research and technology, debt, cooperation international fora); (3) human rights, democratic principles and institutions, good governance and rule of law (including the role of civil society, migration and refugees); (4) peace-building, conflict prevention, management and resolution; and (5) development issues (sustainable development challenges and poverty eradication, health, environment, food security, drug consumption and trafficking and culture—including the export and removal of African cultural goods).

While Cairo's ambitious agenda was translated into an increasing convergence of interests in the years following the summit, its practical implementation, however, has run into difficulties due to differences between the EU and African states with regard to the primacy given to the identified priorities. As noted by the European Center for Development Policy Management (ECDPM 2006: 2)

> Europeans by and large [were] putting the accent particularly on peace and security issues, and Africans more and more on the trade and economic aspects of the partnership, including the need to address the debt problem. On the African side, many still consider that some of the issues set out in the Cairo agenda have not been really addressed or at least not had the attention they deserved (e.g. debt issue and the return of African cultural goods), and these are, to some extent, still a source of frustration.

In response to the aforementioned situation as well as a number of other changes affecting both the EU (the deepening of the European integration, the development of a Common Foreign and Security Policy and the subsequent push for a European Security and Defense Policy) and Africa (the launching of NEPAD in 2001 and the transformation of the OAU into the African Union in 2002 and the subsequent reinforcement of trends toward greater regional integration and pan-African cooperation), the EU developed its own strategy for Africa in 2005. In presenting the strategy, the European Commission (2005: 2) stressed that

> ...For too long the EU's relations with Africa have been too fragmented, both in policy formulation and implementation between the different policies and actions of the EU member states and the European Commission; between trade cooperation and economic development cooperation; between more traditional socio-economic development efforts and strategic political policies. Neither Europe nor Africa can afford to sustain this situation. The purpose of this strategy for Africa is, therefore, to give the EU a comprehensive, integrated and long-term framework for its relations with the African continent.

The formulation of the EU Strategy for Africa was predicated on three central assumptions outlined as follows by the European Commission (2007: 4):

> (1) without good governance, rule of law, security and peace, no lasting development progress is possible; (2) regional integration, trade and interconnectivity are necessary factors to promote economic growth; and (3) if Africa is to achieve the MDGs, more support is needed on issues with a direct impact on living standards, such as health, education and food security.

The dual concept of "One Africa and One Europe" was the centerpiece of this strategy in that, for the first time, the EU wanted to "address Africa as one entity" and act toward it in a more unified manner than before.[18] But the EU also made it clear that the principal objective of its strategy toward Africa was to promote the achievement of the UN Millennium Development Goals (MDGs).[19]

Unilaterally formulated by the EU, the strategy for Africa was, from its inception, received with skepticism and a great deal of criticism by key African players. Criticisms centered on the fact that the "Africa Strategy" had been developed without sufficient consultations, and retained elements of a traditional, unilateral donor-client approach. It was also pointed out that the strategy reflected a "too biased European priority agenda, which would not be conducive to creating African ownership" (ECDPM 2006: 4).

In response to these criticisms, the two sides agreed, during the 5th EU-Africa Ministerial meeting in December 2005 in Bamako, "to take their partnership to a new, strategic level and develop a Joint EU-Africa Strategy—a partnership *with* Africa, rather than a strategy *for* Africa" (European Commission 2007: 5). The EU and Africa were determined to make a quantum leap in their relationship by gradually transforming it into a more political, more global and more equal partnership. They also agreed on the need to seek the input of a wide range of stakeholders and key actors (members of civil society, trade unions, entrepreneurs and simple citizens) on both sides in the formulation of the Joint Strategy,[20] which was adopted by the second EU-Africa Summit in December 2007 in Lisbon. The Joint Strategy epitomizes EU-Africa's newly declared "strategic partnership". It is intended to bring a measure of coherence to a largely fragmented system of interactions. The remainder of the section will address the vision, guiding principles, objectives, approaches and strategies, as well as the institutional architecture that support the Joint Strategy, which seeks to provide "an overarching long-term framework for EU-Africa relations".

Vision and Guiding Principles

The vision of the EU-Africa Strategic Partnership—projected in the Joint Strategy—stems from a changing regional and international context that has been captured as follows by the European Commission (2007: 3):

> Africa is now at the heart of international politics, but what is genuinely new is that Africa—and the African Union in particular—is emerging, not as a development issue, but as a political actor in its own right. It is becoming increasingly clear that *Africa matters*—as a political voice, as an economic force and as a huge source of human, cultural, natural and scientific potential... Meanwhile, the EU too has changed – its membership has expanded to 27 States, its role in the world has developed and it has adopted ambitious common policies on security, energy, climate change and innovation. Europeans have recognized that African economic prosperity is essential for European prosperity... The world has changed with the forces of global capital and financial markets, climate change, global media and information and communications technology, trans-national terrorism and organized crime, and global pandemics all making the world smaller by the day. The need for common global responses is therefore more vital than ever before. The EU and Africa are old partners, but in a world transformed".

This transformed world is also one in which the traditional European dominance in Africa is being fiercely challenged by newcomers.[21] Taking into account this highly competitive environment, the European Commission (2007: 3) has candidly admitted that if it "wants to remain a privileged partner and make the most of its relations with Africa, it must be willing to reinforce, and in some areas reinvent, the current relationship—institutionally, economically and culturally".

The shared vision formulated in the Joint Strategy is to strengthen the EU-Africa political partnership and enhance cooperation at all levels. The new strategic partnership is based on a "Euro-African consensus on values and common interests," and should strive to bridge the development gap between the two continents. It is worth investigating those common values and interests before venturing further. In its opening paragraph, the Joint Strategy lists the following as forming the "community of values" between the EU and Africa: the respect for human rights, freedom, equality, solidarity, justice, the rule of law and democracy. Without dismissing Africa's progress in several of these elements over the past decade, it is only fair to mention that this community of values is still far from being a tangible reality in Africa. These values are more present on the European side than they are on the African side. Their affirmation seems more to correspond to a declaration of intent—a value agenda—than any political reality on the ground. As for the "common interests", they are not as clearly stated as the common values. They must therefore be inferred from selected priority areas and objectives pursued by the two partners in their political dialog.

The EU-Africa Strategic Partnership is to be guided by a number of fundamental principles: unity of Africa, interdependence between Africa and Europe, ownership and joint responsibility, respect for human rights, democratic principles and the rule of law, coherence and effectiveness of existing agreements (Joint Strategy, § 6). In addition to these basic principles, a strong emphasis is also placed on the working principles of political dialog, co-management and co-responsibility, burden-sharing and mutual accountability, solidarity and mutual confidence, equality and justice, common and human security, respect for international law and agreements, gender equality and non-discrimination and long-term approach. Some of these principles are new (e.g., long-term approach, mutual confidence and coherence and effectiveness of existing agreements), while others (e.g., ownership, equality and partnership) have been restated, over time, through multiple frameworks that govern specific aspects of EU-Africa relations. Ten years after the adoption of the Joint Strategy, the former need still to be tested while the latter are more settled and deserve further comments to assess whether "their sense, significance and implications have changed with developments in the external political and economic context" (European Commission 2005: 18).

Equality: The principle of equality of partners has been consistently reaffirmed in all important instruments governing EU-Africa relations. The establishment of the AU and regional economic communities (RECs) as well as the consolidation of European integration have given new impetus to the principle of equality. Both developments have created a new and more symmetrical institutional framework for relations between Europe and Africa, between the EU and the regional and continental institutions. Within this new environment, it has been stated that "equality implies mutual recognition, mutual respect and the definition of mutual collective interests" (European Commission 2005: 18).

While the two partners have been keen to stress the centrality of the principle of equality, their relationship is dominated by such extreme asymmetrical distribution of power that equality has only been confined to the rhetorical realm, a situation that has been referred to as "the myth of equal partners" which underscores "the credibility gap associated with presenting this as a partnership of equals when the reality showed the African countries to have institutional weaknesses and a dependence on aid, and an inability to withstand the conditionality demands now being imposed by the European Union" (Farrell 2005: 271).

Recent positive economic and political developments in Africa have not been able to alter the fundamental dynamics of the relationship. The principle of equality still retains its mythical status and doesn't reflect the reality of EU-Africa relations. An unequal client-donor relation is more reflective of the current state of affairs.

Partnership: Partnership appears to be the most praised principle and working method of EU-Africa relations. Mentioned 52 times in only 100 articles in the Cotonou Agreement, "partnership" is the defining concept of the recently agreed Africa-EU Strategic Partnership. However, it is difficult to find much reference to the concept of partnership in any of the main theoretical approaches, much less to find a useful definition of the term in any of the explanations of international cooperation on offer in the contemporary literature.

Although the European Union has been the architect of the "partnership model", an examination of various policy papers from the EU doesn't provide that much definitional clarity. The European Commission (2005: 19) has stressed that, in the context of EU-Africa relations, the concept of partnership has implications at two levels. First, between the two partners, the relationship must not encompass only development or commercial issues but also include broad, concrete and constructive political dialog. The relationship is expected to "go beyond the donor-recipient relationship of the past and reflect a political partnership of equals" (Commission, 2007a: 3). Second, the EU and Africa must be strategic partners in dealing with the rest of the world in that "EU-Africa dialogue should not exclusively be a forum for discussions on African matters." The pursuit of a more multilateral world order, fairer global development and the promotion of diversity constitute, among other things, the basic values and objectives that the two partners must seek when engaging the world. In short, partnership means going beyond development cooperation and going beyond Africa. But, as Farrell (2005: 244) asks

> How does the EU model of partnership work out in practice? To what extent does this institutionalized form of interregional cooperation reflect the core values that the EU claims to espouse and, equally important, are these values shared by the other partner?

As a test of the success of any political partnership, Farrell (2005: 265) suggests that we consider "the extent to which substantive outcomes can be measured against the aspirations of each party." While the partnership concept brings an added dimension, for it suggests free will, equal weight in terms of influence and ability to shape negotiations and outcomes, and the expectation of favorable results for each partner, a close examination of the power structures—especially aid conditionality—and implementation of the Cotonou Agreement for example, seems to suggest quite "an Orwellian relation where one partner has no rights at all, the other perfect arbitrariness" (Raffer 2001: 19). The concept of equal partnership seems more conjectural than fundamental. The New Strategic Partnership feeds into, rather than challenges, the existing patterns of economic and trade relations—relations of dependency—which characterize the relationship between two sides. It has rightly been observed that "partnership cannot be assumed just because a contract has been signed; it needs to be achieved rather than declared" (ECDPM 1996: 33).

Ownership: The principle of ownership has emerged as a fundamental tenet of the international consensus on development cooperation.[22] In the context of EU-Africa relations, the principle of ownership permeates all sectoral areas of cooperation and is based on the belief that "development policies and strategies cannot be imposed from the outside" (European Commission 2005: 19). The African partner has particularly insisted on the need for African-based and African-owned solutions and strategies to the continent's problems. While there seems to be a consensus on this premise, the two partners tend to emphasize different corollaries of the principle when it comes to its practical implementation.

The EU, on the one hand, tends to underscore responsibility and participation. It (European Commission, 2006) has stressed that

> Developing countries have the primary responsibilities for creating and enabling domestic environment for mobilizing their own resources, including coherent and effective policies ... The EU acknowledges the essential oversight role of democratically elected citizens' representatives. Therefore it encourages an increased involvement of national assemblies, parliaments and local authorities ... The EU supports the broad participation of all stakeholders in countries' development and encourages all parts of the society to take part. Civil society, including economic and social partners such as trade unions, employers' organizations and private sector, NGOs and other non-state actors of partner countries in particular play a vital role as promoters of democracy, social justice and human rights.

The African partner, on the other hand, tends to insist on modalities of aid delivery and assistance that support and strengthen Africa and country-owned policies, programs and priorities. It has been agreed that (European Commission 2005: 19):

> In order to turn the principle of ownership into policy, *budget support* (aid directly contributing to a partner government's budget for sectoral policies or general programs) should increasingly become the main aid delivery mechanism. This approach not only improves the ownership, efficiency and predictability of the support, but it will also enhance a more mature policy dialog leading partner countries to take their responsibilities in terms of objectives, means and governance mechanisms.

Although not always easy in practice (ECDPM 2006: 7), finding a sound balance between the imperatives of responsibility, participation and adequate aid delivery mechanisms represents a crucial test when it comes to the implementation of the ownership principle.

Objectives, Approaches and Strategies

Goals and Modalities

The Joint Africa- EU Strategy identifies four main objectives of the long-term strategic partnership:

> (1) to reinforce and elevate the Africa-EU political partnership to address issues of common concern (peace and security, migration and development, and a clean environment); (2) to strengthen and promote peace, security, democratic governance and human rights, fundamental freedoms, gender equality, sustainable economic development, including industrialization, and regional and continental development in Africa, and to ensure that all MDGs are met in all African countries by the year 2015; (3) to jointly promote and sustain a system of effective multilateralism, with strong, representative institutions, and the reform of the UN system and other key international institutions, and to address global challenges and common concerns; and (4) to facilitate and promote a broad-based and wide-ranging people-centered partnership (Joint Africa-EU Strategy, Objectives, par. 8).

The formulation of these central objectives underscores the desire to transform the EU-Africa relationship into a political partnership that goes beyond the issues that have traditionally dominated their relations (trade and development cooperation) and embraces a broad range of problems of interest to the international community. Deepening the relationship and jointly engaging the world community are the two fundamental dynamics that drive the current phase of EU-Africa relations. To that end, the two partners have identified ten key political challenges that need to be addressed to achieve the success of the new partnership:

> (1) to move away from a traditional relationship and forge a real partnership characterized by equality and the pursuit of common objectives; (2) to build on positive experiences and lessons learned from our past; (3) to promote more accurate images of each other; (4) to encourage mutual understanding between the peoples and cultures of the two continents; (5) to recognize and fully support Africa's efforts and leadership to create conducive conditions for sustainable social and economic development and the effective implementation of partner-supported development programs; (6) to work together towards gradually adapting relevant policies and legal and financial frameworks; (7) to ensure that bilateral relations, dialog and cooperation between one or more European and African countries contribute to the achievement of the objectives set out in this Joint Strategy; (8) to integrate in our agenda common responses to global challenges and strengthen our dialog and cooperation in multilateral context; (9) to encourage the full integration of members of migrant communities/diasporas in their countries of residence; and (10) to bear in mind that we can only achieve our objectives if this strategic partnership is owned by all stakeholders (Joint Africa-EU Strategy, New approaches, par. 9).

This new approach should guide EU-Africa relations in four defined "strategic inter-related priority areas": peace and security; governance and human rights; trade and regional integration and key development issues. These areas of sectoral cooperation will be discussed in more detail in the third section of the chapter. For now, it suffices to mention the importance that the two partners attach to the principle of coherence for development, whose goal is to promote "interactions and positive complementarities between sectoral policies and strategies" and to ensure that "measures taken in one policy area do not undermine results in other areas" (Joint Africa-EU Strategy, 2007). The affirmation of this principle is aimed at addressing one of the criticisms of EU-Africa relations, which seem to sometimes indicate a low level of coherence between the overall objectives of the partnership and the formulation and implementation of specific policies.

Institutional Architecture

Relations between the EU and Africa are conducted through a complex institutional setup that reflects different levels (continental, subregional and national) and frameworks (the Cotonou Agreement, the European Neighborhood Policy, the Trade and Cooperation Agreement with South Africa) of interaction between the two partners. This institutional framework has long been characterized as lacking coherence (ECDPM 2007: 2). The new EU-Africa strategic partnership is to be implemented through "an institutional architecture, which allows and promotes intensive exchange and dialog on all issues of common concern" (Joint Strategy, § 92). While recognizing the involvement of a large number of institutional and non-institutional actors in the partnership, the Joint Strategy stresses the central role of the AU and EU—as continental organizations—in advancing its objectives.[23] The overarching partnership formalized in the Joint Strategy is structured around the following mechanisms of political dialog:

> To reflect the importance of their partnership, the Joint Strategy calls for EU-Africa Summit of Heads of States and Governments to be organized every three years alternatively in Africa and the EU. These Summits should take stock of the progress made in the implementation of commitments made and provide political guidance for further work. In the period between the Heads of States and Governments' Summits, it is

recommended that leaders of major EU and AU institutions—Council, Commission and Parliament—meet on a regular basis to review progress and provide political guidance to the partnership (Joint Strategy, § 96).

Africa-EU Troikas: Regular meetings of senior EU and African officials and ministers are also recommended to maintain the political dialog in the period between the Summits. The troika format, which brings together a small number of representatives (3), who are mandated to speak on behalf of the EU and Africa, is preferred "in order to ensure an effective and balanced representation of both Unions." EU-Africa troika meetings of Foreign Ministers—and if possible other sectoral Ministerial meetings—will take place biannually to review and monitor the implementation of the Joint Strategy (Joint Africa-EU Strategy, Africa-Eu Troikas, par. 100–102).

Commission-to-Commission Dialog and Joint EU-Africa Task Force: The EU and AU Commissions represent the central institutional actors of the partnership. To that end, the two commissions are expected to enhance their cooperation. The Joint EU-AU Task Force serves as an instrument of permanent working level dialog in support of the work of the commissions whose meeting is scheduled on an annual basis.

Parliaments and other Representative Institutions: The institutional architecture adopted by the Joint Strategy seeks to foster collaboration and political dialog between "institutions that represent the peoples of the two continents", mainly the European Parliament, the Pan-African Parliament (PAP), the EU Economic and Social Committee (EESC) and the AU Economic, Social and Cultural Council (ECOSOC). Dialog between these different representative institutions is intended to "complement and/or feed into the institutional EU-AU troika dialogue … to achieve maximum coordination, coherence and consistency of policies and approaches" (Joint Strategy, § 105).

Civil Society: In accordance with the principle of ownership, the Joint Strategy reserves a special place to various segments of the civil society in advancing the objectives of the partnership. It calls for "the development of a vibrant and independent civil society and of a systematic dialog between it and public authorities at all levels." While civil society is encouraged to get involved in the partnership and take an active role in the implementation and monitoring of the Joint Strategy and Action Plans, the concrete modalities of its participation in the political dialogue are yet to be defined (Joint Africa-EU Strategy, Civil Society, par. 106).

The EU-Africa partnership represents the most complex and dense continent-to-continent relations in modern international relations. As we have seen, the two partners have developed a multilayered and multifaceted cooperation that has been carried out through an evolving complex web of institutional and legal frameworks. What are the theoretical approaches through which we can explain EU-Africa relations and the actors' behavioral patterns? This question will be answered in the next section.

Theoretical Approaches to EU-Africa Relations

Many theoretical approaches have been offered to explain EU-Africa relations. The vast bulk of these theoretical efforts fall under the realist, liberal and international political economy approaches to international relations. While each individual theoretical framework cannot adequately explain the totality of EU-Africa relations, they do however offer insight into the fundamental dynamics driving the relationship and help to make sense of it beyond sporadic events and specific actions that have marked its evolution. This section will bring the conversation between contending theoretical approaches up to date by discussing their relevance in explaining EU-Africa relations under conditions of increasing globalization. Although the underlying arguments within each approach remain constant, there have been discernible shifts in the political purposes for which those arguments have been utilized.

The Realist Approach

In considering general approaches to explaining European motivations regarding international commercial policy in general and interregionalism in particular, some have advanced a standard realist approach to international relations, which holds that the EU as a unit responds to the structure of the international system in formulating its international economic policies, pushing those policies that promote the EU's collective economic security as well as its global structural power (via the use of relational power) in ties with individual countries and regions. This view contends that continuities are more important than changes in EU-Africa relations and that the patterns of intercourse between the world's poorest continent and one of the leading economic powers have remained constant over the past fifty years. They point out that, beneath the rhetoric of universalistic sentiments and equal partnership, the past fifty years seem to show patterns of political and economic control and domination aimed at maintaining Europe's sphere of influence in Africa. The interplay of national interests is thus the best guide in understanding the evolution of EU-Africa relations. Farrell (2005: 265–266) writes:

> EU-Africa relations have, from the beginning, been characterized by the realist tendencies of individual European states … The earlier phase of EU-Africa relations was initiated because certain member states wished to retain formal links with former colonial dependencies in order to ensure continued access to raw materials and natural resources, and to protect economic investment already made or being contemplated in what were now newly independent states.

Contemporary EU-Africa relations seem to indicate continuity in the pursuit of national interests by the EU and its member states, a situation which has been perpetuated due to the asymmetric bargaining strengths of both partners. Reflecting on the ongoing negotiations, under the Cotonou Agreement, of EPAs, Farrell (2005: 266) stresses that

> The EU is promoting a model of regional integration that is far removed from the model of regional integration that has evolved within the EU itself. In fact, what the EU is promoting is a model of economic liberalization across the African continent and, in the process, attempting to secure for itself continued market access and privileged economic status in the continent's emerging markets. However, the European policy is much less active in addressing the real problems of poverty and instability that are likely to place severe limitations on either achieving economic liberalization or securing broad-based societal benefits in the long term.

Even the normative agenda (promotion of democracy, good governance and the rule of law—all of which are conditions for EU development assistance) embedded in the political dialog under both the Cotonou Agreement and the Joint Strategy is seen as "one effective way by which the EU can seek to impose its values" upon African countries and promote "the objectives of economic liberalization more than any fundamental support for democratization". In that regard, the realist approach doesn't see the EU-Africa partnership as a genuine alliance that would seek fundamental changes in the international system because "the current neo-liberal hegemony of ideas sits broadly compatible with the self-interest of political elites and the outward-oriented fraction of capitalist class in the EU member states" (Hurt 2003). Beyond the rhetoric on equal partnership and common values, it is argued, EU policy toward Africa is strongly realist in tone.

The Liberal Approach

Contrary to the realist approach, a liberal paradigm of EU-Africa relations underlines the fact that cooperation is necessary and desirable not merely in pursuit of self-interest but as part of a wider agenda for peace, justice and equality, where power and politics are supplanted by an institutionalized framework to support dialog and enhance the achievement of core values, including democracy and the rule of law. The liberal ideological underpinning of EU-Africa relations is believed to reflect the liberal nature of the European integration project itself which emerged after WWII. The European project struck a compromise between the principles of integration and autonomy and emphasized interdependence and transnational cooperation in order to resolve common problems, as well as "consciously devised machinery" to serve the imperatives of peace and prosperity. It has been argued that the same liberal institutional ideas and assumptions that served as a catalyst for integration theory in Europe continue to define EU's actorness in world politics and guide its interaction with other world regions. The nature of the EU as "political animal" is presented in the following terms by Rifkin (2004):

> Recent events on the world stage have thrown into sharp relief the apparent differences between the US approach to international cooperation, and its reliance upon military power and the creation of ad hoc coalitions of the willing to support international policy. By contrast, the European Union represents itself as the supporter of a world based upon the rule of law, where multilateralism rather than unilateralism is the driving force behind collective actions to solve common problems and resolve disputes. In contrast to the hard power which is the basis of US influence, the European Union favors the use of soft power in order to exert influence on the international stage, with an agenda that is considered much more normative in tone.

Important aspects of EU-Africa relations have thus been analyzed through the lenses of core liberal and neoliberal concepts. For example, the neoliberal institutional concept of "democratic peace" has been used to justify the increased centrality of conditionality— which has expanded from the requirement to liberalize and privatize the economic sector to include targets on good governance and compliance to human rights—in EU-Africa relations. Conditionality policies are thus seen as needed institutional leverage aimed at widening the zone of peace by embedding formerly nonliberal states into the liberal world, as a guarantee of peace and security. This globalization of liberalism is being pursued on the liberal internationalist assumption that liberal values are universally shared. A more critical view, however, sees this expansion of liberal values, underneath that of conditionality, as no more than a convenient fiction for promoting the commercial interests of European firms.

The same liberal approach has also been applied to explain the increasing importance reserved for civil society and non-institutional actors in advancing the objectives of the EU-Africa partnership. This trend is seen as a direct response to the neo-idealist contention that encouraging or even coercing nonliberal states to become more democratic is only part of what is required in order to bring about a truly liberal order. A more radical approach should seek democratization at the "grass roots" by bringing civil society and other social movements into the decision-making structures since they are closer to the ordinary people than their own governments. The embedment of the EU parliament and the Pan-African Parliament into the institutional framework of EU-Africa relations is also regarded as an illustration of the "cosmopolitan" model of democracy advocated by neo-idealists.

The liberal theory of complex interdependence has also been used to explain EU-Africa growing sectoral cooperation on a number of issues (migration, environment and peace and security) that have compelled the two sides to find commonly agreed upon solutions which don't necessarily correspond to the realist logic of immediate self-interest. Koulaimah-Gabriel (1997: 19) writes:

> The end of the Cold War clearly deprived the African continent of its strategic position in international politics and of its bargaining power in relation to the Northern donors. There is, however, another entry point for Africa in the international arena as it is an important stakeholder in the so-called "new interdependencies". There has been a growing awareness that certain problems have a global reach and that they cannot be solved at a country or regional level… The geographical proximity between Africa and

> Europe makes the common management of these interdependencies all the more desirable.

The liberal approach echoes the notion that Europe is a "Grand experiment," which, as Rifkin (2004: 282) says, "is articulating a bold new vision for the future of humanity", a vision that attempts "an accommodation between the new forces of individuation and integration that are stretching human consciousness inward to the multiple identities of the post-modern persona and outward to the globalizing forces of the economy", and emphasizes "cooperation and consensus over got-it-alone approaches to foreign policy." EU's relations with Africa are ultimately seen as a reflection of this vision, which projects a path that departs from traditional power politics in international relations.

International Political Economy Approach

A number of interesting explanations of EU-Africa relations have been advanced from the International Political Economy (IPE) perspective. Some are rooted in the radical tradition, while others represent new approaches to IPE. Brown (2000) contends that to truly understand the nature and character of the EU-Africa relationship and its development, one needs to investigate the interplay between economies and politics at the global stage and adopt a historical perspective which places the relationship within a much broader context of the origins and evolution of North-South relations more generally. This politico-economic context shows wider patterns that are reflected in the particular EU-Africa relations as it has responded and adjusted to global forces and trends. Against this background, Brown (2000: 368) argues that development cooperation must be seen and approached "as encapsulating particular political and economic relationships rather than constituting some kind of 'apolitical' or 'technical' endeavor." The EU-Africa relationship mirrors the shapes and contours of North–South relations as it has evolved and can be observed through four periods.

First, the origins of AU-Africa relations must be situated in the context of decolonization which saw the accession of African states to independence under conditions of negative sovereignty that set the stage for the development of a dependent relationship and the multilateralization of postcolonial ties under the Yaoundé Conventions of 1963 and 1969.[24] By granting particular and favorable treatment to ACP products, the Yaoundé Conventions also represented, in some respects, a departure from the liberal and multilateral order that emerged after WWII.

Second, while the signing of the first Lomé Convention in 1973—in replacement of the Yaoundé Convention—seemed to have given some limited accommodation to southern countries' attempts to redefine North-South relations through the demands for a New International Economic Order (NIEO)[25], it also retained the same dependent nature that had been characteristic of North –South relations in that, as Brown (2000: 373) puts it,

> The more "political" aspects of the agreement reflected the "negative sovereignty" pattern of post-colonial relations in the explicit, formal recognition of equality between the parties, recognition of 'sovereign rights' of the ACP states, in particular over their development strategies, and in the formality of the agreement as one conducted between equal, independent states. That all these formal declarations of equality were included in an agreement that was based on one side granting financial and trade support to the other is a perfect illustration of the Convention as an example of this wider pattern of North-South relations.

Third, the limited advances made in the Yaoundé Convention toward an NIEO would be progressively eroded in the 1980s and 1990s through successive renegotiations of the Lomé Convention. These decades were a time of restructuring North-South relations through a reassertion of political and economic liberal principles (Brown 2002). This restructuring is reflected in the place that these instruments reserved for the political dialog and the principle of conditionality; elements that were deepened and consolidated in the 2000 Cotonou Agreement, which replaced the Lomé Convention and represented a "wholesale reform" aimed at adapting EU-Africa relations to the imperatives of the global economy as mandated in particular by the WTO.

Fourth, the 2007 Africa-EU Joint Strategy can be seen as an attempt to solidify the neoliberal changes made to the relationship since the 1990s, while reasserting the centrality of EU-Africa relations at a time when the dialectic interactions between the two partners are being transformed due to a number of internal and external factors, chiefly the increased international competition for Africa's resources and political and economic reforms on the continent, all of which have—although in a limited way—increased Africa's actorness and bargaining power in a relation that still functions, very much, on a client-donor mode that perpetuates dependency.

In contrast to the aforementioned traditional IPE approach, a new approach highlights social constructivist concepts of ideas and identity. From this vantage point, EU external commercial policies are believed to be determined by the overarching need to construct 'Europe' by defining its internal and external identity through relations with non-Europeans. Identity-building has been identified as one of the systemic functions of interregionalism as exemplified in the case of the EU-Africa partnership (Aggarwal and Fogarty 2004). Against this background, it is argued that the ideas, norms and values embedded in various legal and institutional frameworks of EU-Africa relations don't necessarily respond to the 'rational' calculations of long-term economic advantage and benefits from cooperation. They contribute to foster regionalism through interregionalism by sharpening differences between self and other, and thus help galvanize regional solidarity on the basis of shared norms. From this perspective, Europe and Africa are said to build their respective collective identity by interacting with each other at different levels of their extensive sectoral cooperation.

Sectoral Cooperation

After offering a broad historical overview of EU-Africa relations and discussing the main theoretical approaches through which to understand these complex relations, we turn now to sectoral cooperation, which has been organized into four main "interrelated" areas by the parties themselves: trade and regional integration, peace and security, governance and human rights and key development issues. The intent here is not to cover in detail each of these clusters of policy priorities. Rather, this third section will highlight the general conceptual framework and discuss major challenges as well as key operational initiatives that give substance to each area of cooperation. This exercise will be conducted with a particular reference to the Joint Africa-EU Strategy and its first action plan.

Peace and Security

Over the past years, EU-Africa relations have seen a multiplication of policy and operational initiatives in the area of peace and security as part of the political dialog between the two partners. The 2003 EU Security Strategy, the 2005 EU Strategy for Africa, and the 2007 Joint Africa-EU Strategy all contain major policy initiatives in this area. Conceptually, a number of core ideas and principles have been formulated in or can be inferred from these instruments. It's fair to say that the EU partner has played the leading role in shaping the discussion of what is slowly emerging as the EU-Africa peace and security doctrine.

First is the understanding and recognition of "the importance of peace and security as preconditions for political, economic and social development" (Joint Strategy, 2007 § 13). Peace and security are considered "the first essential prerequisites for sustainable development" (EU Strategy for Africa, 2005). Second, the two partners are promoting a holistic approach to security, which encompasses conflict prevention and long-term peace-building, conflict resolution and post-conflict reconstruction, with a view to addressing both structural and root causes of conflicts, "including poverty, degradation, exploitation and unequal distribution and access to land and natural resources, weak governance, human rights abuses and gender inequality." (Joint Africa-EU Strategy, para. 13). Third is the reiteration of the principle of African ownership in that cooperation in the peace and security area should support "African-led peace operations." (Joint Africa-EU Strategy, para 20). To that end, the goal is to help build an effective and functioning African Peace and Security Architecture (APSA) with the African Union and its Peace and Security Council at the center. Fourth, an EU-Africa peace and security partnership is expected not only to address common security threats (terrorism, non-proliferation of weapons of mass destruction, illegal export of arms) but also to serve as the hub for jointly identified responses and strategies to new global, human and security challenges (climate change, environmental degradation, water management, toxic waste deposits and pandemics). Over the past years, the two partners have taken some concrete steps toward the implementation of their comprehensive and holistic approach to peace and security.

In 2004, in response to a request from the 2003 AU Summit in Maputo, the EU established a €250 million development instrument in support of African PSO and peace-building in the area of peace and security. Funded from the resources of the 9th European Development Fund, the APF is now a key instrument that has been instrumental in financing some of the costs incurred by African peacekeeping forces used to support, among others, the African Union Mission in Sudan (AMIS), and the *Force Multinationale en Centrafrique* (FOMUC) of the *Communauté économique et monétaire de l'Afrique Centrale* (CEMAC).[26] The APF has also been used to fund a smaller short-term AU-led mission in Comoros and to provide capacity-building support for the AU.[27] In April 2006, the EU agreed to provide an additional amount of €300 million under the 10th EDF that continued the APF for another three-year period (2008–2010).[28] The first action plan for the implementation of the Africa-EU Strategic Partnership identified three priority actions for the 2008–2010 period: to enhance dialog on challenges to peace and security, to achieve full operationalization of APSA and to secure predictable funding for African-led peace support operations.

Others

Governance and Human Rights: Promotion of good governance and human rights has become a central feature of EU-Africa relations. Good governance and respect for human rights figure prominently in all the major frameworks of the partnership concluded since the mid-1990s—the Lomé Convention, which was replaced by the Cotonou Agreement; the European Neighborhood Policy; the Trade, Development and Cooperation Agreement with South Africa; and the EU-Africa Partnership. What is the general conceptual and operational approach to governance and human rights promotion that emerges from these various frameworks of cooperation?

In line with the international consensus on development, the parties have recognized that "democratic governance and human rights are key for sustainable development and for cooperation between the partners, and are an integral part of both the EU and AU's core values" (Africa-EU Partnership on Democratic Governance and Human Rights). The parties have also adopted a broad approach to governance which calls for

> an open, intensive and comprehensive dialogue on all aspects and concepts of governance, including human rights, children rights, gender equality, democratic principles, the rule of law, local governance, the management of natural resources, the transparent and accountable management of public funds, institutional development and reform, human security, security sector reform, the fight against corruption, corporate social responsibility, and institution building and development (Joint Strategy, § 27).

The EU and Africa have also stressed the principle of ownership, which recognizes that the "primary responsibility for building democracy lies in the hands of Africa's peoples and of its ruling classes … democracy cannot be created or imposed by domestic elites or external actors … the appropriate role of external actors is therefore instead to support and encourage domestic efforts to build, strengthen and sustain democratic norms, procedures and institutions" (EU Strategy for Africa, 2007: 24). Consequently, the partnership is aimed at supporting Africa-owned governance reform programs and democracy-building efforts, such as the African Peer Review Mechanism (APRM) and the African Charter on Democracy, Elections and Governance. In particular, the EU Commission (2006: 6) has emphasized that "respecting ownership also means respecting the pace and schedule of reform processes, which are intrinsically complex and long-term, as they go to the very heart of the organization of a state and a society."

At the operational level, EU-Africa sectoral cooperation in the area of governance and human rights is expected to follow an 'incentive-based approach' by which the EU will grant additional financial support to "countries adopting or ready to commit themselves to a plan that contains ambitious, credible measures and reforms."[29] How are these principles and approaches being implemented?

The political dialog, enhanced in the Cotonou Agreement and consolidated in the Africa-EU Strategic Partnership, distinguishes between "essential" and "fundamental" elements of cooperation. According to Article 9 of the Cotonou Agreement, "respect for human rights, democratic principles and the rule of law are essential elements of the partnership", while good governance is considered to be a "fundamental element." Article 96, which gives teeth to the political dialog, allows for the suspension of cooperation in the event of serious violations of the essential elements by the state parties. The suspension of cooperation is, however, a last resort measure. In the event of serious breaches of human rights and democratic principles in ACP countries, political dialog—consultation—is the first step that should be taken to avoid sanctions. Article 96 of the Cotonou Agreement has been regularly activated over the past years. For example, in 1998, consultations were initiated with Togo and, in the following year, with Niger, Guinea-Bissau and Comoros for breaches of the democratic process and violation of the essential elements clause.[30] In 2000, consultations were conducted in the aftermath of the military coup in Ivory Coast. In 2001, measures were taken against

Zimbabwe under Article 96 of the Cotonou Agreement and aid was suspended to all areas except social assistance.

EU-Africa relations in the area of governance and human rights have attracted a mixed response ranging from skepticism to cautious optimism. Olsen (1998: 345) questions European motives in promoting democracy and human rights in Africa. He writes, "When implementing the policy, the 'non-declared' interests of the donor countries themselves were decisive and not the official ones found in treaties and public statements, irrespective of the fundamental changes of the international system which followed the ending of the Cold War." In the same vein, Farrell (2005) argues that the neoliberal agenda being promoted under the cover of the normative agenda—particularly the model of a weak state—doesn't correspond to what most African states need at this stage of their development. The focus of a genuine democracy promotion agenda should be on consolidating the foundations of any democracy, building the deliberative, legislative and executive capacity of state institutions. For Farrell (2005), the inclusion of a normative agenda in the political dialog may appear to support the objectives of economic liberalization more than any fundamental support for democratization.

Trade and Regional Integration: The EU and Africa have had special trade relations since 1975. EU's trade relations with sub-Saharan Africa (SSA) are organized under the Cotonou Agreement, while relations with North Africa countries are covered by specific instruments. Europe is Africa's biggest trading partner. For example, in 2013, the EU's exportation of merchandise amounted to €153.3 billion and importation reached €168.2 billion. The volume of trade between the partners has been steadily increasing over the past years. This increase in the volume of trade has taken place within an interregional environment characterized, on the one hand, by renewed calls by African leaders for continental regional integration and, on the other hand, by profound changes to EU-Africa trade regimes mandated by the WTO's liberalization imperatives. Overall, the two sides seem to express slightly different views on the dual issue of trade and regional integration. While African leaders tend to consider trade liberalization and regional integration as necessary yet far from sufficient conditions to fostering development and alleviating poverty, the EU argues that regional integration is a key requirement for Africa's development (ECDPM 2006).

The Africa-EU Strategic Partnership takes stock of these changes and tensions by restating the fundamental principle of ownership, which calls for the respect and support of Africa's integration processes on the basis of the Abuja Treaty (1991) establishing African RECs as the building blocks of the African Economic Community (AEC). But the Strategic Partnership (§ 39) also identifies the key goals which will be pursued by Africa-EU cooperation on trade and regional integration as follows:

> (1) private sector development, supported by foreign investments, to strengthen the supply side of African economies; (2) the development and strengthening of physical infrastructure networks and related services, which are needed for the movement of persons, goods, information; and (3) trade integration, which is essential to increase both South-South and North-South trade flows.

The aforementioned principles, approaches and goals must be assessed against the background of the fundamental changes introduced to EU-Africa trade relations by the Cotonou Agreement. One such change is the regional economic integration agreements—also known as Economic Partnership Agreements (EPAs)—to be negotiated between the EU and groups of countries within the ACP bloc. The EPAs must be WTO compatible, which requires the signatory states to ensure liberalization of trade (remove tariffs) affecting substantially all products and services, and covering all sectors. The second important departure from the previous policy is the shift away from treating the ACP as a unified bloc, and instead resorting to negotiations with groups of countries with a view to creating regional economic agreements.[31]

Farrell (2005) argues that the new policy (EPA) represents a direct threat to existing subregional organizations in Africa, thus contradicting the stated principle of supporting and respecting the autonomous regional integration agenda of Africa. She goes on to assert that "From the perspective of the European Union, the Cotonou Agreement and the policy activities that arose out of the agreement allow the European Union to protect European interests, while also facilitating a mini 'regime change' in the African countries, in accordance with EU values and standards" (Farrell 2005: 270). Other comments have focused on the economic effects of EPAs and the EU's use of leverage to bring the ACP countries to agree to the new policy (Aid 2005; Keek and Piermartini 2005). On the latter, the Commission for Africa

(2005), while welcoming liberalization, has cautioned that it "must not be forced on Africa through trade or aid conditions" because, pursues the Commission, "forced liberalization will not work." Analyzing the potential impact of EPA policy on existing RECs, Stevens (2006) has concluded that EPAs being negotiated under Cotonou will weaken African regionalism by encouraging countries "to reinforce rather than eliminate barriers to free circulation of goods between them because of the choices they make in the details of their trade regimes with Europe." These are legitimate concerns that underline the tensions between trade and regional integration and unveil the disjunction between stated goals and principles and the actual impact of policy implementation.

Key Development Issues: This last cluster of EU-Africa cooperation includes a broad range of issues organized into four general themes: financing and external debt, migration, investing in people (including poverty and hunger, health, education, labor markets and decent work, gender equality and empowerment of women, agriculture, environment and climate change, and information and communication technology), and infrastructure. Cooperation in these matters is directly linked to the overall goal of "supporting Africa's efforts to achieve the MDGs." (Joint Africa-EU Strategy, para 49). The First Action Plan (2008–2010) for the implementation of the Africa-EU Strategic Partnership adopted a set of specific partnerships and priority actions aimed at advancing the objectives of cooperation in all the aforementioned areas. The concrete implementation of this ambitious action plan is yet to be seen. Within the limited framework of this section, we would like to elaborate on two areas which have been at the forefront of the cooperation agenda and attracted some interesting policy initiatives over the recent years: official development assistance (ODA) and migration.

EU's ODA to Africa accounts for 60% of the total ODA going to the continent in 2005, making the EU by far the biggest donor with €15 billion. This is up from €5 billion in 1985. The increase of EU's ODA to Africa must be understood and situated in the context of the global dialog on MDGs, which has seen a consensus among the world's leading donors to increase their ODA to poor countries.[32] But it also reflects the particular character of EU-Africa relations. In 2005, the European Council agreed to double EU's ODA between 2004 and 2010 but, more importantly, to allocate half of it to Africa. This was supposed to put the EU on track to achieve the UN target of allocating 0.7% of its GNI to development aid by 2015.

With these additional ODA funds, there has been considerable debate on aid effectiveness. The European Commission (2007: 10) recognized that "in the past, lack of coordination and complementarity between donors has often prevented sound development policies from being converted into tangible development achievements ... Overall, it will be important to demonstrate that the substantial increases in aid flows have served their purpose in helping recipient countries in their attainment of the MDGs." As part of this debate, the EU and Africa have agreed to strengthen their cooperation in the implementation of the Paris Declaration on aid effectiveness, which calls for, among other things, the alignment and harmonization of development aid instruments along with the use of general and sector budget support.[33] The predictability of development aid and the limitation of conditionalities have also recently been stressed by the parties in their political dialog (Joint Africa-EU Strategy, § 52).

Besides ODA, migration is another hot topic that has dominated EU-Africa political dialog over recent years. The amount of agenda space given to the migration question reflects the growing common understanding of its strategic, economic, security, social, political and humanitarian importance in the relationship between the two continents. About 4.6 million African migrants live in Europe. But the Migration Policy Institute believes there are between 7 to 8 million irregular African immigrants living in the EU.[34] Some highly publicized tragic events in which dozens of illegal migrants from Africa died on their journey to Europe have also helped to put the issue of migration on top of the political agenda within the various frameworks of EU-Africa relations.

Under a joint initiative by Morocco, Spain and France, the Euro-Africa Ministerial Conference on Migration and Development was organized in Rabat on July 10–11, 2006. This conference brought together West, Central and North African states with EU member states to discuss common responses to migratory flows along the West African migration route to Europe. The Rabat Conference was followed by an EU-Africa Ministerial Conference on Migration and Development held in Tripoli from November 22–23 of the same year. This conference was particularly significant in that, for the first time, the EU and the whole of Africa came together to make a political commitment to work together on migration. It was, in many respects, a recognition of the interdependent nature of the issue and the limitations of unilateral solutions and approaches to the problem. The final Declaration of the conference rightly emphasized "the need to work together in a spirit of mutual respect and partnership for better management of migration for our two continents in a comprehensive, integrated and holistic manner." (Final Declaration, Tripoli Conference on Migration and Develpment, 2006).

On a bilateral level, political dialog on migration has been pursued between the EU and key states of origin of migrants in Africa (Mauritania, Senegal and Mali) on the basis of Article 13 of the Cotonou Agreement, which covers a wide range of topics in the area of migration and development. Where relevant, every Country Strategic Paper for ACP countries now contains a migration profile that identifies priorities, activities and projects. It's worth noting that EU-Africa political dialog on migration has been developing within an international context marked by a renewed interest in the issue as shown by the ongoing UN General Assembly High Level Dialog on Migration and Development.[35]

What are the core principles, approaches, goals and policy priorities that emerge from these different EU-Africa processes on migration? First is the affirmation of the conceptual link between migration and development. The overall goal is to better "manage legal migration" so as to support "the socio-economic development of both countries of origin and countries of destination" (Joint Strategy, § 68). To that end, the parties have adopted a balanced and holistic approach that seeks, on the one hand, to combine restrictive and controlling measures with actions supporting legal mobility and the integration of migrants; and, on other hand, to comprehend the migration phenomenon in all its complexity as it relates to issues of development, peace and security, human resources and brain drain, human rights and refugee protection (Tripoli Declaration on Migration and Development, 2006). The central principles of ownership, solidarity and adherence have been reaffirmed as well as the belief "that the management of migratory flows cannot be achieved through control measures only, but also requires a concerted action on the root causes of migration" (Preamble, Rabat Declaration on Migration and Development, 2006).

The Africa-EU Partnership on Migration, Mobility and Employment agreed upon during the 2007 EU-Africa Summit in Lisbon identified three priority actions for the 2008–2010 period: the implementation of the 2006 Tripoli Declaration on Migration and

Development, the implementation of the EU-Africa Plan of Action on Trafficking of Human Beings, and the implementation of the 2004 Ouagadougou Declaration and Action Plan on Employment and Poverty Alleviation in Africa. Along these lines, a number of concrete activities have been proposed or are already being implemented, such as the creation of a network of migratory observatories to collect, analyze and disseminate data on migratory flows; the establishment of a €25 million intra-ACP migration facility to focus in particular on the management of south-south migration; the facilitation of safer, faster, and cheaper remittances from Africans living in Europe (First Action Plan for the implementation of the Africa-EU Strategic Partnership).

It is worth noting that EU-Africa political dialog and partnership on migration has evolved against the background of profound changes in the EU's own migration policies and approaches. In fact, many of the concepts and ideas that have been incorporated into the EU-Africa dialog had originally been formulated within the EU's own internal debate. The strategic decision to abolish systematic controls on movements of people (and goods) across internal borders of the common space, operated under the Schengen Treaty and later, by way of the Treaty of Amsterdam in 1997, has in fact brought about a radical rethinking of the forms of traditional security controls (and of migration controls in particular). One important aspect of this policy change has been the "outsourcing" of migrant controls to Africa and the reinforcement of controls on EU external borders. Over the past years, the EU has been developing its operational capabilities in the area of border controls with, among others, the establishment of the European Agency for the Management of Operational Cooperation at the External Borders of the member states of the European Union (FRONTEX) in 2002, the proposed Mediterranean Coastal Patrols Network (MEDSEA) and European Surveillance System of Borders (EUROSUR). All these initiatives will be implemented through the new External Borders Fund (European Commission 2006).[36] The development of these operational capabilities is a clear indication that the EU is determined to seal its borders while engaging in a "frank and constructive" dialogue on migration with Africa. It remains to be seen how the pursuit of these two objectives would impact each other.

Conclusion

The EU and Africa have developed a rich and complex relationship which is deeply rooted in their common history, and reflects the density of cultural, geographic, economic and human bonds between the two continents. This relationship has evolved from fragmented arrangements in the 1960s into a multilayered, multifunctional, comprehensive and strategic partnership conducted through a web of legal, institutional and policy frameworks that give the measure of the parties' level of engagement.

In surveying the historical and institutional development of EU-Africa relations, the first section of the chapter has demonstrated how different changes in the relationship could be linked to major forces and dynamics impacting either EU's own integration process or broader North-South relations, such as the developing countries' demands for an NIEO in the 1970s and the current political and economic neoliberal agenda under the forces of globalization.

The second section has attempted to put the relationship into some coherent theoretical framework by resorting to both traditional theoretical canons of international relations and other innovative approaches. From the perspective of the dominant partner, EU-Africa relations can be seen either as expressing classical realist tendencies of member states that seek to secure and preserve their interests; or as a reflection of the EU's liberal integration project which emphasizes interdependencies, cooperation and shared values in the pursuit of the common good. In substance, a liberal lecture of EU-Africa relations contends that the EU represents a "Grand experiment," whose core liberal values are being translated into its relationship with other regions. To this theoretical view, an approach grounded in IPE has responded by stressing the dependent nature which has only been amplified by economic globalization processes. The growing importance of the normative agenda in EU-Africa relations is seen as lacking substance and serving to perpetuate dependency in the relationship. We have shown that, while each of these theoretical perspectives provides insight into the relationship, they all carry limitations and cannot, taken separately, adequately explain the EU-Africa relationship in all its complexities and manifestations.

This theoretical approach has been complemented by a more pragmatic approach in the final section of the chapter, which has analyzed and discussed six areas of cooperation: peace and security, governance and human rights, trade and regional integration and development cooperation and migration. In each of these sectoral areas of cooperation, it has been demonstrated that the parties appear to have adopted a more pragmatic and functional approach. They have identified and are implementing a host of concrete and incremental measures, and appear to be committed to developing a "strategic partnership" that addresses "common contemporary challenges" of the two continents.

Notes

1. The only African country that is not party to any contractual agreement with the EU is Libya.
2. Although a signatory of the Cotonou Agreement, South Africa has concluded a separate parallel ambitious Trade, Development and Cooperation Agreement with the EU.
3. Article 238 provides that "the Community may conclude with one or more States or international organizations agreements establishing an association involving reciprocal rights and obligations, common action and special procedures". 18 Associated African and Malagasy States (AAMS) were party to the agreement. EDF remained the financial source of assistance under the Yaoundé Convention.
4. More than 90% of ACP exports, predominantly primary commodities, qualified to enter the EU duty free.
5. The EDF also financed two commodity insurance schemes, STABEX and SYSNIN, respectively for countries that were dependent on agricultural exports and on the exports of mineral products. These insurance schemes responded to a demand from the south in the context of the NIEO.
6. Other major concessions of the Lomé conventions included special protocols for bananas, sugar and rum.
7. Despite two-and-a-half decades of EU privileges, 40 of 63 countries in the World Bank's unenviable category of least-developed countries (LDCs) in 2000 were ACP member states.
8. A compelling argument for not renewing the Lomé Convention was the recognition that any new ACP-EU arrangement had to be fully compatible with GATT/WTO rules.
9. Since the 1990s, trade between the EU and "preferred" partners in Africa and the Middle East had become rather marginalized.
10. The end of the Cold War broadened the horizon and scope of the external economic relations of EU with countries in Central and Eastern Europe. This resulted in an increase of economic assistance toward these countries and a drop in total EU assistance to ACP countries.

11. The European Commission, for a long time, had argued that EU-ACP cooperation was non-political, stating boldly that "the ideological neutrality of Lomé rules out the possibility of the Community living by doctrines" (CED-DG VIII, 1992, p. 16).
12. In North Africa, Association Agreements exist with Morocco, Algeria, Tunisia and Egypt; Libya has observer status in the Partnership.
13. Democracy and human rights, rule of law, good governance, market economy principles and sustainable development have been identified as common values. It must be noted that the ENP remains distinct from the process of enlargement although it does not prejudice, for European neighbors, how their relationship with the EU may develop in the future, in accordance with Treaty provisions.
14. Three Northern African countries (Morocco, Tunisia and Egypt) have concluded ENP Action Plans with the EU, while two (Algeria and Libya) have not.
15. South Africa doesn't have access to Cotonou's financial instruments or preferential trade regime.
16. South Africa is the political, economic, financial, human resources and trade hub of the Southern African Development Community (SADC) region, representing close to 75% of its total GNP. At the continental level, South African has been one of the driving forces behind the African Union and the New Partnership for Africa's Development (NEPAD). At the international level, South Africa has consolidated its standing by speaking on many occasions on behalf of the emerging and the developed world in international fora.
17. Originally scheduled for 2003, the second summit had to be postponed, on the EU's request, due to opposition to the political and human rights situation in Zimbabwe.
18. For the EU, acting in a more unified way became crucial given the challenges posed by the enlargement process which saw a sharp increase of EU members from 10 to 25.
19. The centrality of MDGs in the EU's objectives toward Africa is reflective of a larger effort of redefinition of EU development policy which led to the adoption of the European Consensus on Development by the European Community and the member states in 2006. See European Parliament, Council and Commission, The European Consensus on Development, 2006/C 46/01.
20. A large-scale consultation was carried out (including via a special website http://europafrica.org which was managed on behalf of the EU and the AU by an independent foundation, the European Center for Development Policy Management) to collect input for the drafting of the Joint Strategy from a broad range of non-institutional stakeholders in

Europe, Africa and beyond. Regular consultations have also taken place with representatives from the European Parliament and the Pan-African Parliament.

21. China, for example, has emerged as Africa's most important trade partner, with total trade amounting to about €120 billion in 2016.
22. See, for example, the Paris Declaration on Aid Effectiveness adopted in 2005 by over one hundred Ministers, Heads of Agencies and other Senior Officials who have committed their countries and organizations to continue to increase efforts in harmonization, alignment and managing aid for results with a set of monitorable actions and indicators. The Declaration is available at http://www.oecd.org/document/18.
23. To facilitate this continent-to-continent dialog, the EU has decided to open a Delegation to the AU in Addis Ababa. For its part, the AU has been strengthening its representation in Brussels.
24. Multilateralization of postcolonial ties refers to the idea that postcolonial agreements were concluded with the whole EU rather than simply the former colonial power.
25. Elements of the managed trade projects of the NIEO campaign were incorporated into Lomé particularly the STABEX scheme for the stabilization of export earnings.
26. Under no circumstances can AFP money be used to cover direct military and arms expenditure.
27. In the 9th EDF, an amount of €35 million was earmarked for capacity-building purposes.
28. This decision followed an evaluation of the APF—carried out by independent consultants in the fall of 2005—which assessed that, overall, the instrument had proved to be very relevant and generally effective, and that the core APF principles of African ownership, African-European partnership and African solidarity had contributed to its success.
29. Part of the financing (€2.7 billion) allocated to ACP countries under the 10th EDF (2008–2010) has been set aside to support this incentive-based policy.
30. The legal basis for these consultations was Article 366a of Lomé IV.
31. The RECs and other organizations involved in the EPA negotiations are: ECOWAS, UEMOA, ECCAS, CEMAC, COMESA, SADC, SACU, EAS, EAC and IOC.
32. See, for example, the Monterrey Consensus adopted in 2002 by over fifty Heads of State and two hundred Ministers of finance, Foreign Affairs, Development and Trade who committed their countries to mobilizing domestic and international financial resources for development. The Declaration was the outcome of the UN International Conference on Financing for Development.

33. Direct budget support, whereby EU contributions are paid directly into a partner country's national budget, is one solution being promoted and gradually used but with some level of skepticism among EU member states.
34. Data available at <http://www.bbc.co.uk/2/hi/europe
35. More information about the dialog can be found at http://www.un.org/migration
36. The External Borders Fund has received a total of €1.82 billion for the period 2007–2013.

References

Aid, Christian. 2005. *For Richer or Poorer: Transforming Economic Partnerships between Europe and Africa*. London: Christian Aid.

Aggarwal, V.K., and E. Fogarty. 2004. Explaining Trends in EU Interregionalism. In *European Union Trade Strategies: Between Globalism and Regionalism*, ed. V. Aggarwal, and E. Forgarty. London: Palgrave.

Babarinde, O., and G. Faber (eds.). 2005. *The European Union and the Developing Countries: The Cotonou Agreement*. Leiden and Boston: Martinus Nijhoff.

Bossuyt, J. 1996. The Future of EU-Africa Development Co-operation: With or Without the Lomé Convention? *ECDPM Working Paper* No. 95–2.

Bretherton, C., and J. Vogler. 1999. *Europe as a Global Actor*. London: Routledge.

Brown, W. 2000. Restructuring North-South Relations: ACP-EU Development Co-operation in a Liberal International Order. *Review of African Political Economy* 27 (85): 367–383.

Brown, W. 2002. *The European Union and Africa: The Restructuring of North-South Relations*. London: I.B. Tauris.

Chabal, P. 2002. The Quest for Good Governance in Africa: Is NEPAD the Answer? *International Affairs* 78 (3): 447–462.

Dannreuther, R. (ed.). 2004. *European Foreign and Security Policy. Towards a Neighborhood Strategy*. London: Routledge.

Euro-African Partnership for Migration and Development, Rabat Declaration. 2006. July 11.

Euro-African Partnership for Migration and Development, Action Plan. 2006. July 11.

European Center for Development Policy Management. 2006a. *The EU-Africa Partnership in Historical Perspective*. Issue Paper I.

European Center for Development Policy Management. 2006b. *How to Deliver on the EU-Africa Partnership's Ambitions? Adapting the Institutional Framework for EU-Africa Relations*. Issue Paper II.

European Center for Development Policy Management.2006c. *Towards a Joint Africa-Europe Partnership: Setting the Agenda*. Issue Paper III.

European Commission. 1996. *Green Paper on Relations between the European Union and the ACP Countries on the Eve of the 21st Century.*

European Commission. 2005. *Communication to the Council and the European Parliament and the European Economic and Social Committee, EU-Strategy for Africa: Towards a Euro-African Pact to Accelerate Africa's Development.* COM (2005) 489 final.

European Commission. 2006a. *Communication to the Council, Reinforcing the Management of the European Union's Southern Maritime Borders.* COM (2006) 733 final.

European Commission. 2006b. *Communication to the Council and the European Parliament, The Global Approach to Migration One Year One: Towards a Comprehensive European Migration Policy.* COM (2006) 735 final.

European Commission. 2006c. *Communication to the Council and the European Parliament, the European Economic and Social Committee and the Committee of the Regions, Governance in the European Consensus on Development: Towards a harmonized approach within the European Union.* COM (2006) 421 final.

European Commission. 2006d. *Communication to the Council and the European Parliament, Towards an EU-South Africa Strategic Partnership.* COM (2006) 347 final.

European Commission. 2006c. *Communication, European Neighborhood Policy.* COM (2004) 373 final.

European Commission. 2007a. *Communication to the European Parliament and the Council, from Cairo to Lisbon-The EU-Africa Strategic Partnership.* COM (2007) 357 final.

European Commission and Council Secretariat. 2007b. *Beyond Lisbon Making the EU-Africa Strategic Partnership Work.* SEC (2007) 856.

European Commission. 2007c. *Communication, A Strong European Neighborhood Policy.* COM (2007) 774 final.

European Parliament, Council and Commission. 2006. The European Consensus on Development. *Official Journal of the European Union*, 2006/ C 46/ 01.

Faria, E. 2004. Crisis Management in Sub-Saharan Africa: The Role of the European Union. Institute for Security Studies Occasional Paper No. 51. Paris.

Farrell, M. 2005. A Triumph of Realism over Idealism? Cooperation Between the European Union and Africa. *European Integration* 27 (3): 263–283.

First Action Plan (2008–2010) for the Implementation of the Africa-EU Strategic Partnership. 2007. Lisbon. December 9.

Forje, G. 2001. The Road to Cotonou: Negotiating a Successor to Lomé. *Journal of Common Market Studies* 39 (3): 423–442.

Gibb, R. 2000. Post-Lomé: The European Union and the South. *Third World Quarterly* 21 (3): 457–481.

Ginsberg, R.H. 1999. Conceptualizing the European Union as an International Actor: Narrowing the Theoretical Capability-Expectations Gap. *Journal of Common Market Studies* 37 (3): 429–454.

Gomez, R. 2003. *Negotiating the Euro-Mediterranean Partnership: Strategic Action in EU Foreign Policy?* Hampshire: Ashgate.

Grilli, E. 1993. *The European Community and the Developing Countries.* Cambridge: Cambridge University Press.

Grimm, S. n.d. EU Policy Towards Africa, at http://www.odi.org.uk/rapid/projects. Accessed 3, June 2016.

Holland, M. 2002. *The European Union and the Third World.* Basingstoke: Palgrave.

Hurt, S.R. 2003. Co-operation and Coercion? The Cotonou Agreement between the European Union and ACP States and the End of the Lomé Convention. *Third World Quarterly* 24 (1): 161–176.

Joint Africa-EU Declaration on Migration and Development. 2006. July 22–23, Tripoli, Libya.

Keek, A., and R. Piermartini. 2005. The Economic Impact of EPAs in SADC Countries. *Staff Working Paper* ERSD -2005–04. Geneva: World Trade Organization.

Koulaimah-Gabriel, A. 1997. Beyond Lomé IV: Future Challenges to EU-Africa Relations. *Rectel* 6: 14–22.

Krause, A. 2003. The European Union' Africa Policy: The Commission as Policy Entrepreneur in the CFSP. *European Foreign Affairs Review* 8: 221–237.

Kronenberger, V., and J. Wouters. 2004. *The European Union and Conflict Prevention: Policy and Legal Aspects.* Cambridge: Cambridge University Press.

Lisbon Declaration, EU-Africa Summit. 2007. December 9. Lisbon.

Lister, M. 1998. *The European Union and the South: Relations with Developing Countries.* New York: Routledge.

Maipafia, O. 2007. *Europe and Economic Reform in Africa: Structural Adjustment and Economic Diplomacy.* London: Routledge.

Ojo, O. 1996. *Africa and Europe: The Changing Economic Relationship.* London: Zed Books.

Orbie, J. 2003. EU Development Policy Integration and the Monterrey Process, A Leading and Benevolent Identity? *European Foreign Affairs Review* 8 (3): 395–415.

Olsen, G.R. 1997. Western Europe's Relations with Africa Since the End of the Cold War. *Journal of Modern African Studies* 35 (2): 314–327.

Olsen, G.R. 1998. Europe and the Promotion of Democracy in Post Cold War: How Serious Is Europe and for What Reason? *African Affairs* 97 (388): 343–367.

Ouagadougou Action Plan to Combat Trafficking in Human Beings, especially Women and Children. 2006. November 22–23. Tripoli.

Raffer, Kunibert. 2001. Slowly Undoing Lomé's Concept of Partnership. European Development Policy Study Group Discussion Paper No. 10. Manchester, UK: EDPSG.

Ravenhill, J. 2004. Back to the Nest? Europe's Relations with the African, Caribbean, and Pacific Group of Countries. In *European Union Trade Strategies: Between Globalism and Regionalism*, ed. V. Aggarwal, and E. Forgarty, 118–147. London: Palgrave.

Rifkin, J. 2004. *The European Dream*. New York: Tarcher / Penguin.

Scheipers, S. and D. Sicurelli. 2007. *Empowering Africa: Normative Power in EU-Africa Relations* at http://www.Unc.edu/euce/eusa2007/papers/sicurelli. Accessed 3, June 2016.

Sheehy, O. 2003. *The Positive Application of Human Rights within EU-ACP Development Co-operation Policy,* at http://www.uwc.ac.za/ecsa-sa/docs/sheehy.

Söderbaum, F., and L. Van Langenhove. 2005. Introduction: The EU as a Global Actor and the Role of Interregionalism. *European Integration* 27 (3): 249–262.

Stevens, C. 2006. The EU, Africa and Economic Partnership Agreements: Unintended Consequences of Policy Leverage. *Journal of African Studies* 44 (3): 441–458.

Stokke, O. (ed.). 1995. *Aid and Political Conditionality*. London: Frank Cass.

Taylor, R. 2004. *Africa in International Politics: External Involvement on the Continent*. London: Routledge.

The Africa-EU Strategic Partnership, A Joint Africa-EU Strategy. 2007. December 9. Lisbon.

Walz, K. 1979. *Theory of International Relations*. New York: Random House.

CHAPTER 9

Toward Addressing the African Condition: The Lessons

George Klay Kieh, Jr.

Introduction

Irrespective of whether one is a so-called "Afro-optimist" or "Afro-pessimist," the empirical evidence lays bare the fact that the African condition needs to be improved for the betterment of the majority of the people. In other words, there is no denying that Africa is enveloped in a labyrinth of major challenges that span the broad gamut—from cultural to security issues. Clearly, there is no doubt that the continent has made some progress in these various areas. However, it would be quite premature to raise any banner as a sign of exuberance. Alternatively, the best approach is to build on the successes that have been made by consolidating them, and tackling the issues where little or no progress has been made. This would mean that the continent needs to undergo a major paradigmatic shift: there is the imperative for African states to abandon the failed practice of uncritically accepting packaged formulas and their accompanying imported solutions from the "Global North"

G.K. Kieh, Jr. (✉)
University of West Georgia, Carrollton, Georgia

G.K. Kieh, Jr. (ed.), *Contemporary Issues in African Society*,
African Histories and Modernities,
https://doi.org/10.1007/978-3-319-49772-3_9

as the panacea to the continent's condition. Alternatively, while assistance from the "Global North" has some utility, ultimately, the success or failure of addressing the African condition would require, among other things, committed and patriotic citizens and visionary servant-leaders. In other words, Africans must find the best solutions to their region's and the constituent states' condition.

Against this background, drawing from the various chapters in this book, the purpose of this chapter is to suggest some solutions to the dimensions of the African condition that have been examined in this volume. Hopefully, this will contribute to the building of a human-centered democratic, prosperous and stable Africa with "social citizenship" as the anchor (Marshall 1950).

The Proposed Solutions

The Epicenter: The Democratic Reconstitution of the State

The state in Africa is of the wrong type (Samatar and Samatar 2002: 5). Hence, it is incapable of serving as an enabling environment in which the various dimensions of the African condition can be addressed and improved. In other words, the peripheral postcolonial state that has visited mass deprivation, poverty, malaise and repression on the majority of the African peoples cannot serve as the engine for human-centered democracy and development.

Against this backdrop, it is imperative for the state in Africa to be democratically reconstituted (Kieh 2009a, b). The process would consist of several interrelated parts. One major aspect is the transformation of the nature of the state. In its current formulation, the postcolonial state is an alien construct that does not represent the cultural and historical experiences of the peoples of Africa (Agbese 2007; Kieh 2009a, b; Ihonvbere 2014). Instead, it was designed by European imperialists and colonialists at the notorious Berlin Conference of 1884–1885 and imposed on Africa (Kieh 2007). Regrettably, with very few exceptions, the first and subsequent generations of African leaders have failed to provide the requisite leadership in democratically reconstituting the state. Alternatively, the nature of the reconstituted democratic state would be reflective of the historical and cultural experiences of the various ethnic groups that constitute the various states in Africa without privileging any particular one.

Another major aspect would be the fundamental changing of the mission of the state. Since the post-independence era, the mission of the state in Africa has been twofold. First, it is to provide an enabling environment in which multinational corporations and other businesses from the "Global North" can engage in predatory investment and reap huge profits by exploiting the natural resources and labor of African states (Kieh 2008, 2009a, b, 2015). The other aspect is that the state enables the members of the faction of the local ruling class that is running the government and their relations to use their respective political positions in the state's bureaucracy and their stations in the class structure to engage in the primitive accumulation of wealth (getting rich through the use of various corrupt means such as extortion, bribery and embezzlement of public funds). Clearly, the mission of the reconstituted state would be to promote and protect the cultural, economic, environmental, gender, political, religious and social rights of all citizens. Specifically, for example, this would include the empowerment of the people, so that they can meaningfully participate in the affairs of the state. Also, the new mission would focus on creating public investments in basic human needs such as job creation, education, healthcare, public housing, public transportation, food security, access to clean drinking water and acceptable sanitation (Ake 1996). In short, the state's mission would be to use public resources to improve the material conditions of the people.

Also, the character of the state would need to be transformed. This is because the current multidimensional character of the state, which has been described variously as "criminalized," "corrupt," "exploitative," "negligent," and "predatory," among others, (Agbese 2007; Kieh 2007, 2008, 2009a, b, 2012) cannot shepherd the African "renaissance." Accordingly, the reconstituted state would have a new enabling, inclusive, productive, protective and service-oriented character, among others. In short, this means that the democratically reconstituted state would create propitious conditions for all Africans to live fulfilled lives (United Nations Development Program 1990).

The transformation of the political economy of the state would be another major step in addressing the African condition. This would entail specifically, for example, the restructuring of class relations, so that there can be equity in the distribution of income and wealth. Moreover, power relations both within the broader society and between and among the various institutions of the state would be changed as well. In the case of the former, there would be no privileging of ethnic, religious and other communal groups at the expense of others, as well as the termination of patriarchy. In the latter case, the hegemony of the presidency would be ended, so that "horizontal accountability" (public institutions and public officials being able to hold each other accountable) can be effective.

Furthermore, the formulation, and the resulting contents and implementation of public policies covering the broad gamut of issues would be human-centered. That is, the general interests of the people would shape and condition the creation and implementation of the policies that affect their lives. For example, the formulation of policies on natural resource management would be based on deriving financial resources that can be used to invest in basic human needs such as education and healthcare.

Ethnicity

Clearly, ethnic diversity in Africa is not inherently conflictual. That is, simply because Africans belong to various ethnic groups does not make inter-ethnic conflicts inevitable. Instead, ethnic conflicts on the continent are the by-products of fissures in the political economy, and their resulting impact on various ethnic groups. Hence, these pathologies would need to be addressed as the precondition for promoting ethnic harmony and stability. A major issue is the crisis of legitimacy that has enveloped various African states since the post-independence era. Several African states have lost the support of the majority of their citizens as the result of the horrendous performances of their respective governments. So, bereft of mass support, various regimes in Africa have resorted to the instrumental use of ethnicity as a strategy for clinging onto power. Therefore, the underlying crisis of the legitimacy of the state that underlies ethnic conflicts should be addressed by ensuring that regimes are compelled to perform well.

Another step is the imperative of ending ethnic privileging. This is the perennial practice of an illegitimate regime giving preferential treatment to a particular ethnic group in terms of the access to and share of state resources, at the expense of the other ethnic groups. Clearly, excellent regime performance is the foundation of legitimacy. And a legitimate regime would not need to privilege a particular ethnic group as a survival strategy, because it would have broad-based support. In short, the ending of ethnic privileging would require a synergy of regime performance and the garnering of mass support.

The related measure would be the promotion of ethnic pluralism. This would entail all ethnic groups learning about each other's culture, and being mutually sensitive and respectful. In other words, the demonization of particular ethnic groups would be discouraged and not tolerated. Ultimately, this will lead to the peaceful co-existence of ethnic groups, the development of harmony and the building of durable peace and stability.

The building of what Osaghae (2006: 16) refers to as "positive ethnicity" would be another major element of the ethnic dimension of the African condition in a democratically reconstituted state. Specifically, this would entail various ethnic groups mobilizing their members for the ostensible purpose of undertaking various development projects, such as the construction of health centers and schools for the betterment of their various communities. In so doing, ethnic groups and the state will develop a harmonious and productive partnership. The resulting benefits would include the promotion of socioeconomic development, and the minimization of violent conflicts between ethnic groups and the state, and between and among ethnic groups over the vexing issue of the distribution of public resources.

Importantly, the process of nation-building would be greatly enhanced by convincing the various ethnic groups through demonstrable state policies that they are partners and stakeholders. In this way, the members of the various ethnic groups would feel confident to transfer their loyalties to the state. In other words, by its actions, the state would demonstrate that its various ethnic groups or nations can be woven together into a nation-state based on equal citizenship.

Religion

As has been discussed, there is no doubt that the charismatic Christian churches have experienced a meteoric rise in Africa, as evidenced by the tremendous influence they have come to wield in the economic, educational and political spheres of various African states. For example, some of these churches have amassed tremendous wealth, as have some of the leaders of these churches who live in opulence, some of whom even have private jets. In the political sphere, as has been discussed some of the leaders of these churches are venerated by politicians.

However, one of the major emergent criticisms of these charismatic Christian churches as was raised in the chapter in this volume on religion is their lack of internal democracy. That is, the leaders of these churches have absolute control over every facet of their respective churches. For example, the leaders control the finances, including expending money without being accountable to the members. Similarly, economic ventures that are established with these churches' money are personalized by their leaders: the leaders convert them to their personal "cash cows." Furthermore, while most of the members of these churches are experiencing economic challenges, their pastors, apostles and bishops are living in opulence. Interestingly, the leaders of these charismatic churches rationalize their ostentatious life styles by claiming that since the God they serve is rich, they too have to become rich. But, this is a bastardization of the Bible as this outlandish claim does not have any Biblical grounding. On the contrary, the Bible stresses the recurrent theme of the imperative of religious leaders being modest, and making the betterment of the lives of the "least of these" their primary focus (Matthew 25: 40). In other words, these churches have become bastions of authoritarianism similar to the majority of the states on the African Continent (Freedom House 2015).

So, how can internal democracy be constructed within these charismatic Christian churches? The answer lies with the members of these churches. That is, it is only the members of these churches who can mobilize and press for the establishment of internal democracy. The reason is that religion is a private matter that is fully within the domain of the individual. Hence, in exercising their religious freedoms the progressive members of these congregations can wage democratic struggles within their respective churches. The focus would be on, for example, the democratization of decision-making, the establishment and implementation of the norms of accountability and transparency in the conduct and management of the church, and the use of the churches' economic resources to help improve the material conditions of the members and the "least of these" within the broader society.

Democratization

Similarly, as discussed in Chap. 1 of this volume, although the "third wave of democratization" has achieved some modest success on the continent, it has failed to make human-centered democracy a way of life on the continent. Even most of the continent's democratic states have not transcended the realm of political democracy—political rights and civil liberties—to establish socioeconomic democracy. In other words, very little progress has been made in the areas of basic human needs such as jobs, education and healthcare. This has led to the situation in which, for example, the holding of elections, an important element of political or liberal democracy, has not led to an improvement in the material conditions of the majority of Africans.

Alternatively, in order for democracy to be meaningful to the majority of Africans, several major challenges must be addressed. At the heart of this transformative process must be a democratic trajectory that transcends political rights and civil liberties. That is, although these rights are important and essential for democracy, they are not sufficient. Thus, democracy within the context of the reconstituted state in Africa would embody the confluence of cultural, economic, environmental, gender, political, religious, security and social rights, based on the premise of empowering and serving the people.

Several domestic obstacles also serve as major barriers to the establishment of human-centered democracy on the continent. In the political realm, three of the major challenges are the "hegemonic presidency" (Prempeh 2008; Kieh 2008, 2012, 2013, 2015), weak public institutions, and the lack of political will and commitment on the part of the local ruling classes. The "hegemonic presidency" has been an enduring mainstay of the African political landscape, since the post-independence era. Functionally, it has undermined the development of democracy by, among other things, concentrating state powers in the hands of the president. In turns, this has made accountability and transparency very difficult. Linked to the problem of the "hegemonic presidency" is the existence of weak public institutions. That is, the parliament and judiciary, despite their constitutional powers, are operationally subordinated to the presidency. Hence, they cannot serve as checks on the presidency. One of the negative consequences is that the presidency has a virtual blank check to do anything without being held accountable. Another major political challenge is that the majority of the members of the local African ruling classes are not really committed to the establishment of people-centered democracy. Instead, they give lip service to democracy, because it is fashionable to do so, and it placates international patrons, donors and lenders. Hence, the powers of the presidency need to be reduced, so as to help cage its hegemony. Also, the legislative and judicial bodies need to be strengthened in terms of personnel and other operational resources. Moreover, African states need visionary leadership that is committed to the pursuance of people-centered democracy.

Economically, class inequities and inequalities would have to be addressed. Two major pathways are the redistribution of income and wealth. Specifically, the income gap needs to be narrowed by improving the salaries of those in the middle and lower tiers. Similarly, societal resources need to be distributed in ways that ensure that the upper stratum does not receive a disproportionate share. Inextricably tied to the issue of class inequality and inequities is the centrality of poverty reduction. In addition, the state needs to play a pivotal role in ensuring job creation, as well as insisting that workers earn decent wages which will enable them to meet their basic human needs. In essence, overall, the state would need to ensure that the national resources are not disproportionately cornered by the members of the ruling classes and their relations, while the vast majority comprising the subordinate classes are dispossessed and live precariously at the margins of the society.

In the social domain, African states must make substantial public investments in healthcare, education, housing and public transportation. As for healthcare, the thrust should be on the quality and quantity of health professionals, and the physical infrastructure such as hospitals and other medical facilities, equipment, supplies and drugs for medication. Similarly, educational investment should focus on the quality and quantity of personnel, school buildings, instructional materials, equipment and supplies. Further, quality public housing should be constructed to help provide shelter for the millions of people who are presently living in uninhabitable houses throughout the continent. In addition, substantial public investment needs to be made in the development of a comprehensive public transportation system involving land, air and rail, among others. This approach would help address the growing transportation problem that is plaguing virtually every African state.

Furthermore, the state should accord importance to food production, so that the populations of the various African states have enough food to eat. Specifically, this would involve investment in agricultural research and development, equipment, supplies and related materials, as well as the development of a collaborative relationship between the state and farmers. Major public investments are also required for the provision of clean and safe drinking water to the people in every African state. Similarly, the provision of acceptable sanitation needs to be made a national priority as well.

Importantly, the promotion of human-centered democracy in Africa would also require addressing the various external obstacles. A major one is the support of non-democratic regimes by various external powers, including the United States and France. The rationale is that these regimes serve as handmaids in serving the interests of these external powers, often to the detriment of the peoples of these African states. In this vein, the peoples of Africa would need to be actively involved in working to ensure that major external powers do not impose and/or maintain non-democratic regimes in their respective countries. In short, Africans would need to oppose leaders who are not fundamentally committed to the promotion of their political rights and civil liberties, as well as the advancement of their material conditions.

Another major external obstacle is the imposition of the neoliberal development strategy by the United States and other developed capitalist states, and the Bretton Woods Institutions—the World Bank and the International Monetary Fund. As empirical evidence clearly shows, the neoliberal development strategy has exacerbated class inequities and inequalities, poverty, unemployment and social malaise. Hence, the people of Africa need to become fully engaged in the affairs of their respective states, and lead the charge in rejecting this development model. Alternatively, African states need to design and implement development strategies that have as their focus the improvement of the material conditions of all Africans.

Non-Governmental Organizations

Undoubtedly, some non-governmental organizations have made invaluable contributions to the development of the African Continent. However, much work needs to be done in helping to improve the relationship between the state and NGOs, so that these two actors can work together in addressing the plethora of development challenges on the African Continent. One of the major issues is the need to address the contestation for power between the state, on the one hand, and local and international NGOs, on the other—the phenomenon Clapham (1996): 3 aptly refers to as "the destating of Africa." Idahosa (2008): 70 poignantly summarizes the problem thus: "[There] is a shift away from state-centered forms of governance to the dual process of more decentralized, but also transitional forms of authority, all of which locate resources and authority in places other than the state." In other words, some local and international NGOs have tried to displace the state by wrestling authority from it in critical areas of development governance. This is made worse by the practice of the United States and other countries using local NGOs as handmaids to oppose adversarial governments in the interest of the former. This then creates needless tension between the government and the NGO to the detriment of the development needs of the people in the particular African state. Alternatively, ways need to be found to develop a partnership between the government of an African state and local and international NGOs that is designed to promote development in the interest of the people. This partnership however, must be anchored on the premise that the promotion of development is primarily the responsibility of an African state; and the NGO, whether local or international, is a secondary and complementary actor.

Another major change that is required is the accentuation of the positive roles that NGOs play in the development of African states. For example, NGOs should be encouraged by the state and the citizens to continue promoting democracy through, for example, the provision of civic education and training, the monitoring of compliance with political human rights, and election observation, for the ostensible purpose of ensuring fairness. Similarly, NGOs should be encouraged to continue their work in the various sectors of human development, including education, food production and healthcare. Simultaneously, NGOs should encourage the development of a culture of self-reliance. That is, the ultimate end product of the various projects that NGOs undertake should be helping to empower Africans so that they can take responsibility and control of their own affairs.

On the other hand, local NGOs need to address some of their major shortcomings, so that they can play meaningful roles in the promotion of human-centered development on the continent. A major issue is that local NGOs need to explicitly state their mission. In other words, what is the NGO's reason for existence? What are the resulting purposes? And how will these be implemented? Answers to these will help address the problem of the ambiguity in mission that is prevalent among local NGOs throughout the continent. Linked to the lack of clarity in the mission is the pervasive problem of donor-driven NGOs. That is, it is commonplace for NGOs to be organized in various African states at the urging of external donors or because of the availability of donor funding for particular missions and their associated purposes. The alternative would be for local NGOs to be organized by local persons in an African state on the basis of a need that requires to be addressed either locally or nationally. Central to the formation of such an NGO should be the involvement of the people, so that they can provide it with legitimacy and support, among others. These are indispensable to the viability and durability of the NGO. Also, local NGOs need to extend the scope of their operations beyond the capital city region to include other sections of an African state. This is important because virtually all of the local NGOs usually claim to have national ambit. Another challenge is the issue of funding. Local NGOs need to have sustainable funding sources in both local and international domains. In other words, local NGOs need to transcend the common practice of relying exclusively on short-term funding from international donors. This is because such a practice has negatively affected the legitimacy, viability and survival of the NGO.

Civil Conflicts

The diagnoses of the causes of the various civil conflicts in Africa need to transcend the realm of predetermined often stereotypical causal factors, and focus on the objective conditions or specificities of the particular case. For example, in examining the causes of civil wars on the continent, there is the need to transcend the pathological fixation with ethnicity and other communal factors as the causal variables. Some cases are illustrative: the Rwandan civil war and genocide, for example, were attributed to ethnic animosities between the Hutu and the Tutsi ethnic groups. Hence, little consideration was given to the portrait of the peripheral capitalist Rwandan state—nature, mission, character, political economy and public policies—and the way it sowed, nurtured and shaped the conditions that led to the civil war and genocide.

Thus, in order to resolve the underlying civil conflict that underpins civil wars, there is the need to give attention to the travails of the postcolonial state in Africa. This is because it sets the parameters within which all interactions and transactions take place, irrespective of their specificities. For example, one major issue concerning the postcolonial state that is a critical contributor to civil conflicts and wars is the exclusionary dimension of its character. On this basis, in countries like Rwanda that have experienced genocidal civil wars, for instance, a binary is created between "us" and "them." The former category refers to the privileged group, while the latter concerns the marginalized group. So, while it is true that the "us" versus "them" binary may assume various complexions, including ethnic ones, it is the character of the state that is responsible for the creation of such a division. Hence, in order to address the underlying division, the character of the state must be transformed, so that the construct can become inclusive. In short, it is important to focus on the root cause rather than the manifestation.

Similarly, the cause of terrorism is laid at the doorsteps of so-called Islamic fundamentalism. Again, very little attention is given to the domestic political economies of African states, especially, cleavages and power relations and public policies. For example, with few exceptions, African states have been saddled with various types of undemocratic regimes since the post-independence period. And these regimes have, among others, engaged in the violation of political human rights such as the freedoms of association, assembly, press and speech. In addition, the basic human needs of the vast majority of the African peoples have been neglected by even liberal democratizing regimes. To make matters worse, non-democratic regimes have either closed or limited the "political space" so that aggrieved Africans do not have legal recourse for addressing their complaints. In turn, these conditions of repression, neglect and marginality provide a propitious environment for the resort to the use of terror as a tactic for waging struggles. Likewise, little consideration has been given to the policies of external actors like the United States and France that help create the conditions that give rise to the use of terrorism as a form of struggle by various aggrieved groups. For example, the United States and France, among others, have and continue to support various non-democratic regimes on the African Continent that suppress the political rights of their citizens. In addition, these two global powers also support regimes that refuse to invest in improving the material conditions of their citizens. By supporting such regimes, both the United States and France are viewed by various aggrieved Africans as major accomplices in creating the conditions that negatively affect their livelihoods and well-being.

Clearly, terrorism and its associated maiming and killing of innocent people is irreprehensible. But, it is very important that serious attention be given to both the internal and external factors that create the conditions for terrorism. This is because such an approach would provide the basis for the formulation and implementation of policies that are designed to address the conditions that give rise to the use of terror. In addition, the approach would contribute to the development and implementation of viable counter-terrorism strategies that go beyond the primacy of the use of military force.

Conflict Resolution

The Foundational Pillars

Conflict resolution in Africa needs to take cognizance of three major interrelated sets of issues. The core set consists of the foundational pillars. A major pillar is the imperative of examining the specifics of each type of civil conflict. In other words, while the experiences of other conflict-afflicted states are an important consideration, their realities cannot simply be transferred and imposed without giving primacy to the specifics of a civil conflict within the context of a particular African state. In sum, the puzzle that needs to be addressed revolves around an examination of the domestic and external causes of a civil conflict in an African state, and the conflict dynamics. Such an approach would then facilitate the formulation of conflict resolution modalities that are calibrated to the specifics of the civil conflict.

A related contour is that the perennial practice of imposing conflict resolution templates should be avoided. That is, in the efforts to resolve various civil conflicts in Africa, the tendency, especially on the part of global actors such as the United Nations, is to transfer conflict resolution methods that were used in non-African countries such as the Balkans region of Europe to civil conflicts in Africa. Again, while there is nothing wrong with learning from the experiences of other countries and regions that have experienced civil conflicts, it is problematic to assume that conflict resolution methods that were employed in one or two or more cases would work in Africa. This is because a civil conflict takes place within a specific state construct. Hence, as has been pointed out, it is the particular state construct that provides the context in which the seeds for a civil conflict are planted and nurtured. Accordingly, the conflict resolution mechanism should be tailored to the portrait of the particular state construct if it is to succeed in addressing the underlying civil conflict. Therefore, transferring conflict resolution models without taking into consideration the historical, cultural, economic, political and social conditions within a conflict-afflicted state would not be a useful way of resolving the underlying civil conflict.

Another pillar is the importance of fairness in conflict resolution. By this, it is meant that every facet of the conflict resolution effort should be fair to all parties. For example, the peacemaker must be neutral, that is, the peacemaker should not support and/or privilege one party at the expense of the others. Another major requirement is that the evidence concerning the conflict should be collected in a comprehensive manner, by, among others, focusing on the actions of all of the conflicting parties pertaining to the civil conflict. Further, the findings should be based on the evidence collected. In other words, the peacemaker should not seek to manipulate the evidence so that predetermined conclusions that favor a particular party can be reached.

Conflict Termination

Two major aspects of conflict termination would require particular attention: the role of subregional and regional organizations, and dealing with the conflicting parties. In the case of the former, the various subregional organizations on the African Continent such as the Economic Community of West African States (ECOWAS), Southern African Development Community (SADC), and the Intergovernmental Authority on Development (IGAD) need to be given the primary role as peacemakers in the various civil conflicts that affect their respective areas. The overarching rationale is twofold: these subregional organizations have the greatest degree of familiarity with their respective areas, and it is the constituent member states of the subregion that would bear the greatest share of the adverse consequences of civil conflicts. In addition, the AU should play its role as the supervisory continental body in these civil conflicts, while the United Nations and other external actors should play complementary roles.

The other major aspect is that extreme caution should be used in the design of the conflict termination agreement so that the perpetrators are not rewarded. For example, in some of the civil wars in Africa, various warlordist militias that were responsible for the commission of war crimes and crimes against humanity were rewarded with positions in the transitional government as a central feature of the war termination agreement. For example, in countries like Liberia and Sierra Leone, warlordist militias were assigned state agencies in some of the most important areas of the economy. During the second Liberian civil war (1999–2003), for instance, the Liberians United for Reconciliation and Democracy (LURD) and the Movement for Democracy in Liberia (MODEL) were assigned state institutions such as the Ministry of Finance, National Port Authority and the Liberian Petroleum Refining Corporation. Similarly, during the Sierra Leonean civil war (1991–2002), the Revolutionary

United Front (RUF), the main rebel group, was assigned the agency that controlled the country's diamond resources. The overarching problem with rewarding warlordism is twofold: the key problem is that it strengthens the culture of impunity, that is, instead of being held accountable for their actions pertaining to a civil war, the belligerents are instead rewarded. The related issue is that the leaders and members of these various warlordist militias, who occupied these positions in the transitional arrangement, often use them to engage in the primitive accumulation of wealth through sundry predatory means, including the outright theft of public funds, extortion and the receipt of bribes.

Post-Conflict Peacebuilding

Clearly, the building of peace after a civil conflict is a very critical process in conflict resolution. And this is multidimensional, encompassing the broad gamut of spheres and issues, including cultural, economic, political, religious, security, social, national reconciliation, security sector and other sectorial reforms, and power-sharing. The specific dimensions that are used are dependent upon the nature of the civil conflict.

Several major overarching principles should drive the post-conflict peacebuilding process. Two of them are the avoidance of the use of templates, and the critical issue of transitional justice. In the case of the former, as has been discussed, the post-conflict peacebuilding modalities must be tailored to the specificities of a civil conflict. In other words, consideration should be given to the lessons learned from the experiences of other conflict-afflicted states; however, these lessons must be situated within the specifics of the experiences of a particular African state that is recovering from civil conflict, rather than superimposing them. The other major driver, transitional justice, should be based on several major pillars. A major one is the imperative of holding all of the culprits responsible for their actions in the civil conflict, irrespective of the particular method of justice that would be subsequently used. In other words, based on the evidence, all the parties, including individuals, that committed horrendous offenses during a civil conflict, need to be brought to justice. In short, the meting out of justice needs to be depoliticized. A related issue is the critical importance of ending the culture of impunity. The holding of all of the culprits responsible would contribute to the process of terminating the culture of impunity, which often provides the context in which horrendous acts are committed during civil conflicts.

International Cooperation

African states need to consider several major factors, as they seek to strengthen and improve their relations with other countries in the "Global South," and the "Global North." One major issue is the importance of African states repositioning themselves internally. Specifically, this would entail building and consolidating domestic legitimacy by promoting human-centered democracy and development. That is, the citizens of the various African states must become major stakeholders in the affairs of their various countries, in order to provide their support for foreign policy. In addition, African states would need to democratize and strengthen public institutions and the broad gamut of governance, and build a strong economic base.

Then, in their relations with other countries in the "Global South," African states should learn from their counterparts' experiences. For example, what development lessons can be learned from South Korea and Singapore? This would be a more useful approach, because other countries in the "Global South" have shared similarities with African states in terms of the legacy of colonialism, and culture, among others. Also, in their bilateral and multilateral relations with other countries in the "Global South," African states should focus on helping to ensure that these cooperative frameworks yield concrete mutual benefits. In other words, less consideration needs to be given to symbolism that consumes time and much-needed resources without yielding concrete benefits that can help improve the material conditions of ordinary Africans.

In terms of their relations with the "Global North," two major issues would require consideration. The key one is what I refer to as the "vulnerability syndrome." The bilateral and multilateral relations between African states and the countries of the "Global North" are based on asymmetries in national power, and the resulting dependence on perpetual begging for assistance—economic and otherwise. One major way to address the vulnerability syndrome is for African states to use their economic and financial resources prudently. Specifically, this would involve, for example, the minimization of corruption and mismanagement, and the reaping of substantial benefits from metropolitan-based multinational corporations and other businesses that exploit the oil, mineral and agricultural resources of various African states. In this vein, African states would be able to develop a strong economic base that would in turn militate against the continuation of the vulnerability syndrome. The related issue is that African states would need to ensure that mutual benefits are reaped with these bilateral and multilateral relations that can be used to help improve the material conditions of their respective peoples. But, in order to do this, the thrust of these relations would need to shift from serving the interests of the various countries of the "Global North" to the reaping of mutual benefits. In short, the critical question that African states need to ask is: How would our citizens benefit from a bilateral or multilateral relationship with the countries of the "Global North?"

Conclusion

Undoubtedly, only Africans can address the major challenges that are facing their continent. This is not to suggest autarky. Instead, the point that is being made is that even if external actors only had altruistic and benevolent intentions toward Africa, these outside actors cannot be responsible for the promotion of human-centered development and democracy in the African Continent. In short, at best, these external actors can only play complementary roles. In addition, all of these external actors have their own class and national interests, which they are seeking to serve by their relations with Africa, both at the bilateral and multilateral levels.

So, in contemplating the way forward, four major domestic actors are critical to the establishment of people-centered democratic and developed African states that are well-positioned to interact with the countries of the "Global North" in ways that yield benefits for the peoples of Africa. First, African states need to have committed citizens, who will, among other things, hold their leaders accountable. Second, vibrant and independent civil society organizations are needed that would complement the citizens in ensuring accountability. Third, visionary servant-leaders are needed to provide the requisite leadership for the "African Renaissance." Fourth, nationalistic business people are needed to anchor the private sector of the various African states. Specifically, this genre of entrepreneurs would need to invest in the creation of jobs and wealth so that African states can be productive and their citizens can have a decent standard of living.

References

Agbese, Pita Ogaba. 2007. The Political Economy of the African State. In *Beyond State Failure and Collapse: Making the State Relevant in Africa*, ed. George Klay Kieh, Jr, 33–50. Lanham, MD: Lexington Books.

Ake, Claude. 1996. *Democracy and Development in Africa*. Washington DC: The Brookings Institution Press.

Clapham, Christopher. 1996. *Africa and the International System: The Politics of State Survival*. New York: Cambridge University Press.

House, Freedom. 2015. *Freedom in the World*. Washington, DC: Freedom House.

Idahosa, P.I.E. 2008. The Norms of Displacement: NGOs, Globalization and the State in Africa. In *Africa and the New Globalization*, ed. George Klay Kieh, Jr, 69–95. Aldershot, UK: Ashgate Publishing.

Ihonvbere, Julius. O. 2014. Civil Society, the State and the New Politics. In *The State in Africa: Beyond False Starts*, eds. Pita Ogaba Agbese and George Klay Kieh, Jr, 97–115. Ota, Nigeria: Third World Publishers.

Kieh, George Klay. 2007. Introduction: The Terminally Ill Berlinist State in Africa. In *Beyond State Failure and Collapse: Making the State Relevant in Africa*, ed. George Klay Kieh, Jr, 3–22. Lanham, MD: Lexington Books.

Kieh, George Klay. 2008. *Liberia's First Civil War: The Crises of Underdevelopment*. New York: Peter Lang Publishing.

Kieh, George Klay. 2009a. Reconstituting the Neo-colonial State in Africa. *Journal of Third World Studies* 26 (1): 41–55.

Kieh, George Klay. 2009b. The State and Political Stability in Africa. *Journal of Developing Societies* 25 (1): 1–25.

Kieh, George Klay. 2012. *Liberia's State Failure, Collapse and Reconstitution*. Cherry Hill, NJ: Africana Homestead Legacy Publishers.

Kieh, George Klay. 2013. *The African Peer Review Mechanism, The "Hegemonic Presidency," and Democratic Governance in Africa*. Paper presented at the Tenth Anniversary Colloquium of the African Peer Review Mechanism. Held in Addis Ababa, Ethiopia. May 21–22.

Marshall, T.H. 1950. *Citizenship and Social Class and Other Essays*. Cambridge, UK: Cambridge University Press.

Matthew. Chapter 25. *The King James Version of the Bible*.

Osaghae, Eghosa. 2006. *Ethnicity and the State in Africa*. Working Paper Series No. 7. Afrasian Center for Peace and Development Studies. Kyoto, Japan: Afrasian Center for Peace and Development Studies.

Prempeh, H. Kwasi. 2008. Presidents Untamed. *Journal of Democracy* 19 (2): 109–123.

Samatar, Abdi and Ahmed Samatar. 2002. "Introduction." In *The State in Africa: Reconsiderations*, eds. Abdi Samatar and Ahmed Samatar, Portsmouth, 1–16. NH: Heinemann.

United Nations Development Program. 1990. *Human Development Report*. New York: Oxford University Press.

Index

G.K. Kieh, Jr. (ed.), *Contemporary Issues in African Society*, African Histories and Modernities,
https://doi.org/10.1007/978-3-319-49772-3

T

U

W

Y